Business for Beginners

a simple
step-by-step guide
to starting
a small business

Frances McGuckin

Published by Eastleigh Publications
A division of Eastleigh Management Services
2003

First edition published in 1997 by Productive Publications
Second edition published in 1998 by Eastleigh Publications

Third edition published in January 2003 by
Eastleigh Publications, a division of Eastleigh Management Services
21944 6th Avenue
Langley, British Columbia
Canada V2Z 1R6

Telephone: 604-530-3601
Toll-free: 1-888-771-2771
Fax: 604-530-6447

Web site: www.smallbizpro.com
e-mail: contact@smallbizpro.com

National Library of Canada Cataloguing in Publication

McGuckin, Frances
    Business for beginners: a simple step-by-step guide to starting a
small business / Frances R. McGuckin.—3rd ed., rev. and expanded.

    Includes index.
    ISBN 0-9684011-1-2

    1. New business enterprises—Canada—Planning. 2. Small
business—Canada—Planning. I. Title.

HD62.7.M228 2003   658.1′141′0971   C2002-905045-6

Project Manager: Heidi LeRossignol of Behind the Book Production Services
Editor: Tita Zierer
Cover design: Lee Fodi
Back cover photo: Brian Bury Photography
Text design: Shirley Olson
Proofreading: Naomi Pauls
Indexing: Annette Lorek

Printed and bound in Canada by Transcontinental Printing Ltd.

15 14 13 12 11 10 9 8 7 6 5 4   06 07

More Praise For 'Business for Beginners'

"When we were searching for a well-written financial manual to include with our Business Plan software, the obvious choice was *Business for Beginners*. Frances McGuckin has produced a thorough, easy-to-read guide to personal finances that even beginners, with the most basic understanding of business needs, can use effectively."

DAMIAN CRISTIANI, PRESIDENT, GLOBAL STAR SOFTWARE

"The book is exactly as promised—a simple step-by-step guide for starting your own business! The easy-to-read style makes the information seem like anyone is able to start a business... Congratulations on a job well-done! We feel privileged and proud we are able to feature such a wealth of information in our Career Centre by a local author."

MARY ELLEN KUEHL, TRINITY WESTERN UNIVERSITY, LANGLEY, B.C.

"The easy-to-read formula and 'back to basics' approach is just what we have been looking for in training material. I commend Frances on her excellent book."

SUSANNA LACHANCE-WATSON, SELF-EMPLOYMENT COORDINATOR,
COMMUNITY FUTURES DEVELOPMENT CORP. (CFDC) OF CARIBOO, B.C.

"We have found this book to be a valuable resource in business start-up...very informative and easy to understand. Starting a business has never been the easiest task to accomplish...*Business for Beginners* makes the task achievable."

CAL PURCELL, GOVERNMENT LIAISON, SPROTT-SHAW COMMUNITY COLLEGE

"The book has an excellent format...the language used makes the book very easy to read... it can be read and understood by the various ethnic groups whose first language is not English.... Please accept my congratulations on your efforts to contribute to the development of entrepreneurship in Canada."

KOFI OHENE-ASANTE, EASE SELF EMPLOYMENT PROGRAM

"As an observer of small business, it has long struck me that there was so little information available in easily readable form for the new entrepreneur. Then Fran McGuckin's book came on the scene offering a simple, step-by-step guide and I thought, Hallelujah, at last someone has offered a thorough course in business start-up that's understandable by the neophyte. I congratulate Fran, because *Business for Beginners* fills the niche that no one seemed to want to fill."

TONY WANLESS, MONEY AND SMALL BUSINESS WRITER, *THE PROVINCE*

"*Business for Beginners* is an excellent resource guide for entrepreneurs who are just starting their business.... It is clearly written, concise and filled with valuable information that both my students and I have greatly benefitted from. I recommend this book to anyone wanting to achieve success in their entrepreneurial endeavours."

CRYSTAL FLAMAN, ENTREPRENEUR AND FACILITATOR,
CFDC ENTREPRENEURIAL ASSESSMENT PROGRAM

"The material is thorough and covers all the basics when it comes to small business start-up.... This book provides the perfect introduction to starting a small business. I am going to recommend it to my next self-employment class."

TONYA FURLONG, SE BENEFIT COORDINATOR,
NIPISSING EAST COMMUNITY OPPORTUNITIES, ONTARIO

"With the rapid rise in self-employment, *Business for Beginners* is in the right place at the right time, providing practical, easy-to-read advice and guidance for start-up companies. Well done, Frances!"

PETER THOMSON, DIRECTOR, VENTURE DEVELOPMENT CENTRE,
BRITISH COLUMBIA INSTITUTE OF TECHNOLOGY

"I'm only halfway through your book and I have to honestly say that it is one of the best, if not the best book on small business that I have read—and I've read a lot in my time. I have found that most other small biz books are too institutional, which in most cases creates confusion, not clarity. I think it would be safe for me to say that there is genius in your simplicity."

MIKE PHIPPS, MARKETING MANAGER, DELTA CHAMBER OF COMMERCE

"It's a great book! You are to be congratulated on having written such an informative and interesting book.... It is a valuable contribution for both new business owners and as a small business information resource."

DORIS MIEDZINSKI, OFFICE MANAGER, KIWANIS ENTERPRISE CENTRE

Praise from satisfied readers

"I would like to thank you for *Business for Beginners*.... I have used it extensively and it's a great reference."

"We found your book very informative!"

"I would like to compliment you on this excellent book. I teach entrepreneurship at U.S. public schools and at a university. I would like permission to use part of this text in my classes."

"I just purchased *Business for Beginners*. It is terrific! Now my future business partner is reading it, taking note of everything I underlined."

Dedication

This book is dedicated to all new entrepreneurs.
The road to success is paved with speed bumps and potholes.
Some prefer a smooth ride and turn around to find an easier route,
but those people never experience the satisfaction
of realizing their dream.

There is no easy route when you are self-employed,
but the rewards of hard work, perseverance, focussed goals
and dreams will be yours if you travel this road
equipped with knowledge, drive, a true
entrepreneurial spirit—and a plan.

Follow your dreams.

Table of Contents

   • Follow your entrepreneurial dream • Reap the rewards of success

   • Are you ready to be an entrepreneur? • Why start your own
   business? • Why are *you* starting your business? • Seven skills
   for success • Do you have the management skills? • Why do
   businesses fail?

   • What type of businesses are available? • Which business is
   right for *you*? • Why are businesses sold? • What is a business
   opportunity? • How do you assess a potential business?

   • Why do we need accounting? • Definition of a financial statement
   • What information is in a financial statement? • Accounting terms
   and definitions • How to analyze a financial statement

   • Does your idea have market potential? • What do you research?
   • Perform a market survey • Where do you find research material?

   • What does a lawyer do? • How do you find the right lawyer?
   • What is a buy-sell agreement? • What do those legal terms
   mean? • A simple buy-sell agreement

Acknowledgments

The wonderful feedback and continued success of *Business for Beginners* over the last five years has spurred me on to revise—if not completely rewrite—this third edition. I extend my deepest thanks to the many colleges, institutions, self-employment programs and entrepreneurs across Canada and the U.S. who use the book and who have generously provided testimonials.

Knowing that you have written a book that helps people is the ultimate inner reward. It's like giving birth—a painful and tedious process involving months of research, writing, editing, proofing and sore eyes. But when you give birth, you quickly forget the pain.

Because change is a constant factor, this edition reflects some changes that have occurred over the last four years in small business. It's expanded in areas that came to light during keynotes, consultations and workshops. To all those wonderful people—thanks for your questions, support, enthusiasm and feedback.

All major projects involve a dedicated team working together. A special thank you to Heidi LeRossignol of Behind the Book Production Services, my production consultant, who helped produce the second edition and organize nearly a dozen reprints involving over 100,000 books, plus ensure that this edition is a quality publication.

To Tita Zierer, my e-editor in Toronto who also edited *Big Ideas for Growing Your Small Business,* thank you for working with me again and teaching me that we never stop learning; that one word easily replaces ten. You are top-notch.

Gord Evans of the London Small Business Centre in Ontario has been a continual supporter. Using the book to teach entrepreneurial classes, he has given me invaluable feedback and long-distance friendship. Two of his students' stories are featured in Chapter 13. Thank you Gord; I love our conversations and your unselfish, positive attitude.

Thank you Russell Smart of Equinox Financial Group, who contributed invaluable insurance information in Chapter 6. Zosia Ettenberg did a brilliant job updating the provincial directory; thank you Zosia. Many thanks to Merle Campbell, lawyer, who reviewed Chapter 5 and contributed legal information for the last two editions. To my many friends, clients and associates whom I may have forgotten to thank—thank you for your input and support.

To my very dear and beautiful teenage daughter, Katrina, what can I say? Thank you for understanding his stubborn writing maniac. I love you too. To my wonderful 97-year-old mother Emilie, and son Richard, what would this world be without your love and constant support? You are all my inspiration and reason for keeping on.

Preface

FOLLOW YOUR ENTREPRENEURIAL DREAM

As we hurtle through the new millennium, the number of people who want to start their own business continues to grow. With technology leaping ahead at a dizzy pace, more people have the option of starting a small or home-based business, with wonderful tools at their fingertips.

There is nothing like being your own boss. It gives one a feeling of supreme power and confidence—or does it? For some, the experience is lonely and isolating. Being self-employed requires a myriad of skills, so the more skills you develop, the more successful you will be.

It takes courage, determination, expertise, long hours and commitment, but the rewards of starting and growing your own business are well worth the effort. You gain knowledge, build confidence and expertise, and hopefully, grow your bank balance. Ah, but there is so much to learn, so much to do, and often, so little money to do it with—and an abundance of unanswered questions.

Where do you start? What is the first step? Which business is the right one for you? What will it cost? Where will you get the money from? Do you have a viable idea? How should you market? How much competition is out there? The questions continually spin in your mind. You are probably eating and sleeping the thought of owning your own business—but in which direction do you take the first step?

Love what you do

Not everyone is born an entrepreneur, but you *can* learn to be a truly great one. Most skills can be learned, but one "skill" can't—passion. So start by choosing a business that you love, because without passion for your business, the novelty will soon wear off. Clients can sense when an entrepreneur has passion for what they do, and it is contagious. You must also work hard to develop good organizational, financial, business administration, sales and marketing skills, plus possess a sound emotional state of mind and a practical, level head. A good sense of humour will often be your lifesaver.

When I was writing the sequel to this book, *Big Ideas for Growing Your Small Business,* I wondered how many jobs a sole proprietor was responsible for. I came up with a list of 58, and my editor, Tita Zierer, added two more. Think about it. As a business owner, you will be responsible for 60 different jobs and you will need to have your finger on the pulse of them all. To successfully achieve this, take the time to formulate a practical business plan, be willing to acknowledge your areas of weakness and then work to improve on them.

Many new (and not so new) entrepreneurs make the mistake of becoming "too busy" to network and learn and grow both their business and themselves. This is the worst mistake you could make, so as you plan your business and formulate this exciting new idea, plan to make time for these important tasks. Learn to understand yourself. Are you a decision-maker or a procrastinator? Because now you are the boss, and there is no room in your business for procrastination.

Find a mentor

One of the best things you can do to turbocharge your business is to find a mentor in your community who is willing to help you. Seek out a successful business owner who devotes time to his or her community. There are many people willing to share their knowledge and experiences with you—sometimes, all you have to do is ask. If you are not sure where to look, contact your local chamber of commerce, Community Futures Development Corporation or small business centre. Some of the most successful people in business achieved great heights with the help of a mentor.

If you can't find a mentor, read this book carefully, and refer to it often. The author will be your silent mentor, and is always willing to answer questions by e-mail. I too am here to give back and help those who need it. This book will lead you through each step of start-up, warn you of the tricks, traps and pitfalls that many fledgling entrepreneurs make, offer solutions and directions as well as a formula for success.

REAP THE REWARDS OF SUCCESS

It is indeed a wonderful feeling to be your own boss, but it's also scary. You are alone and master of your own destiny. This book is here to keep you company and answer those hundreds of questions that are keeping you awake at night. Once you have successfully run your own business, you will never want to be an employee again.

It *is* a tough world out there, one besieged with competition, megastores, mergers, co-op ventures and complex technological changes. The businesses that survive and succeed in this fast-paced and stressful society will be those that focus on technology, knowledge and service, coupled with sound planning and drive. Flying by the seat of your pants is not an option anymore.

Take the right steps—baby steps—one at a time, and you will be successful. This book is designed to help you take the right steps and understand that the decision you have made is one of the biggest of your life. Remember, it takes a good two to three years for the path to become really smooth, but each step taken wisely is a step in the right direction.

I sincerely wish you an exciting trip down the road to success. I hope that this book maps out a safe route for you or enables you to avoid a few potholes. Often, the journey is more exciting than the final destination. Enjoy your trip into the world of entrepreneurship, and never let go of your dreams.

CHAPTER 1

Where do you start?

There are those who dream—and then there are those who make their dream happen.

ARE YOU READY TO BE AN ENTREPRENEUR?

Welcome to the wonderful world of entrepreneurship, one of the leading global trends. What an exciting opportunity to explore your creativity, be your own boss, and build a little gold mine—you hope. It is an exciting challenge, a whole new world of doors and knowledge opening for you. If you do it right, being self-employed can be the most rewarding experience of your life.

It's hard work though, taking commitment, dedication, constant learning and persistence to succeed. With the proliferation of home-based businesses over the last few years, some believe that you can sit in your pyjamas and make a bundle. That idea is a fallacy. Whether you are home-based or operate out of a shopfront, being your own boss requires you to take your business seriously and work to disciplined routines and deadlines.

The failure rate for small businesses is high—in the first few years, as much as 80 to 90 percent. The first two years are traditionally the most difficult. You have to establish a client base, an effective marketing plan, viable products or services and a reputation within your community. This all takes time and patience.

So where do you start? Take a look at what is involved in being an entrepreneur, so you can better assess whether you are ready. When you read of entrepreneurs who are considered successful, they don't talk about money as the focus of their success. Instead, they talk about achieving a balance in their lives, freedom, passion, happiness, excitement, achieving goals, helping others, hard work and focus.

What is an entrepreneur?

Dictionaries describe an entrepreneur as "a person who starts or organizes a business company, especially one involving risk." These days, we tend to associate entrepreneur more with a person striking out on his or her own, usually equating the word with a successful venture. A successful entrepreneur is not a particular type of person, but someone with a well-rounded combination of talents that enables the business to progress.

Some people thrive on the challenge, and some have a natural aptitude for business. Others study hard, take courses and read extensively. A true entrepreneur will have a passion for business and an unquenchable desire to learn, absorb, explore and grow. Anyone can be self-employed, but it takes a certain type to fulfill the true entrepreneurial requirements. An entrepreneur will have, or will develop, some—or all—of these qualities. Figure 1.1 allows you to determine which entrepreneurial traits already apply to you.

Figure 1.1: EIGHT ESSENTIAL ENTREPRENEURIAL TRAITS

Do you have a real entrepreneurial spirit? Are you:

	Yes	No
1. **A risk-taker:** Usually taking calculated risks, an entrepreneur will not hesitate to seize the moment and run with their intuition.	❏	❏
2. **A decision-maker:** The word "procrastination" does not exist in an entrepreneur's vocabulary. They are comfortable with their decisions and know where they are going.	❏	❏
3. **A dream-maker:** Entrepreneurs have their dreams and are aggressive at making those dreams become reality. They don't say "I wish" but instead "I will."	❏	❏
4. **A visionary:** Instead of looking just one step ahead, entrepreneurs can visualize the whole big picture, both now and in the future.	❏	❏

		Yes	No
5.	**Driven:** Because they have a vision and a dream, entrepreneurs are usually driven and motivated people who let nothing stand in the way of their goals.	❏	❏
6.	**Passionate:** Consumed as entrepreneurs are by their dream, passion plays a large part in making their dream become reality. You can feel the passion radiate from a true entrepreneur.	❏	❏
7.	**Confident:** Entrepreneurs know where they are going and why, and are confident that they will succeed.	❏	❏
8.	**Energized:** Full of drive and motivated by their dreams, entrepreneurs usually have an abundance of energy and thrive on seeing each step of their dream take them closer to a reality.	❏	❏

Do you have what it takes?

As you research your business, review these traits and assess whether your business idea generates these feelings in you. If you choose the right business, you should feel passionate and driven to succeed. Having the dream is key, but if you are a procrastinator or not comfortable in making decisions or in taking calculated risks, perhaps you are not cut out to be an entrepreneur. Now is the time to admit to your challenges and decide how you can overcome them.

$UCCE$$ $TRATEGY

LEARN HOW TO THINK ON YOUR FEET: If you lack confidence and communication skills, take a course through Toastmasters. It will teach you the necessary verbal and time management skills, how to think on your feet and carry on a winning conversation—all in a supportive and positive environment. To find out more about Toastmasters, visit *www.toastmasters.org*.

It takes a dedicated person to handle the successful start-up and running of a business, but it's well worth the effort. The rewards of doing it yourself are bountiful. You will gain self-confidence, knowledge and emotional satisfaction. If you love what you are doing and do it well, you will be motivated to persist toward your future goals.

Figure 1.2 lists 30 questions that are designed to give you some insight into the qualities an entrepreneur needs, or should develop. Answer them honestly now, before reading on.

Figure 1.2: YOUR ENTREPRENEURIAL CHECKLIST

Answer the following questions to determine what business qualities you already have and which ones you need to develop.

	Yes	No
1. Are you a timely decision-maker?	❑	❑
2. Do you trust your intuition?	❑	❑
3. Do you relate well to people on all levels?	❑	❑
4. Can you join in a conversation in a room full of strangers and feel at ease?	❑	❑
5. Can you pick up the phone and ask a direct question in an uncomfortable situation?	❑	❑
6. Could you call a client and ask for a late payment?	❑	❑
7. Can you direct others to carry out your orders without being too aggressive or overbearing?	❑	❑
8. Can you start a project and follow it through?	❑	❑
9. Are you a good verbal communicator?	❑	❑
10. Do you like yourself and who you are?	❑	❑
11. Do you start each day in a positive manner?	❑	❑

	Yes	No
12. Can you maintain a positive attitude in adverse situations?	☐	☐
13. Do you have the appropriate technical expertise for the business you are considering?	☐	☐
14. Are you willing to expand on these skills?	☐	☐
15. Do you keep up with global and financial current affairs?	☐	☐
16. Can you cold-call or sell yourself over the phone?	☐	☐
17. Do you have a sound financial knowledge of how a business operates?	☐	☐
18. Can you express yourself well in writing?	☐	☐
19. Can you work without direction?	☐	☐
20. Are you willing to work long, hard hours?	☐	☐
21. Can you work without getting easily distracted?	☐	☐
22. Do you understand terms such as cash flow, assets, liabilities, equity, depreciation and working capital?	☐	☐
23. Do you keep legible notes and pay attention to details?	☐	☐
24. Do you keep appointments and arrive on time?	☐	☐
25. Are you usually well-organized?	☐	☐
26. Do you enjoy people?	☐	☐
27. Do you have patience with people?	☐	☐
28. Do you enjoy meeting new people and networking?	☐	☐
29. Could you keep the pressures of business away from your family life?	☐	☐

	Yes	No
30. Will you continue to pursue your hobbies and interests?	☐	☐

Ideally you have been able to answer yes to at least 20 of these questions. You need a variety of skills so you can control a multi-faceted operation by yourself. If you answered no to any questions, ask yourself how you could improve in these areas, and make a note of them below.

_____

_____

_____

_____

_____

_____

WHY START YOUR OWN BUSINESS?

Self-employment did not evolve in the last century; it is the way people have survived and made money almost since the beginning of time. Small and micro-businesses constitute a huge percentage of Canadian—and global—businesses. When times get tough and the word "recession" emerges, there is usually an increase in self-employment as people can't find a job.

As words such as layoff, downsize, capsize, pint-size and reorganize resound around corporate walls, they all mean the same thing in plain English: "You're fired!" "You're redundant," or "We aren't hiring." People tend to take the skills they have developed over the years to start a business, but sometimes, they are starting in a far from ideal climate.

As the world constantly changes, so do the reasons for business start-ups. The increase in technology and Internet-based businesses means that now millions of workers are telecommuting, working at home, "moonlighting" in a second part-time business, or struggling in their first endeavour.

The downside of self-employment

People who make time to take an in-depth course on self-employment and business management significantly increase their chances of success. The new business that is thrown together on a hope and a dream without being thoroughly researched, or that started without enough working capital, could sadly become a failure statistic.

During the 1990s, self-employment significantly increased in Canada, but as the economy stabilized toward the end of the century, it significantly decreased. Those finding the entrepreneurial road a bumpy one returned to the workforce and a regular paycheque. With the recent unsettled economy, economists predict that self-employment will be on the increase again.

Those people who don't do their homework or learn the appropriate skills too often face business failure, with devastating results. Often, owners are left with huge, high-interest consumer debts to pay off. And who do you think suffers? Not just the family, but the whole economy. A failed business means fewer dollars circulating in the local, provincial and national economy, with suppliers left with bad debts that they can ill afford. Business failure is often the cause of divorce, so the more you are aware of what you are up against, the better armed you will be.

Leaving the traditional workplace

With all these challenges facing aspiring entrepreneurs, why do so many people want to leave their traditional jobs? Here are the most common reasons—and the reality behind them.

1. More work, less pay

Wages have not kept pace with inflation in the last few years, and in some cases, workplace conditions have become unbearably stressful for many employees. Forced to take on increased workloads through layoffs, they have worked under these stressful conditions for long periods. The pressure to have material "stuff" and to keep up with the Joneses is media-driven and relentless. Just visit any shopping mall in the evenings and over the weekend and observe North American "shopaholics" in action.

There comes a point for many when the measly paycheque is not worth the job-related stress. People opt for self-employment with the vision of controlling their destiny and experiencing profitable returns. Even if your new business is well planned, you'll profit only after a couple of years of hard work. If you don't plan properly, you will work even harder than in a salaried position and make less money.

2. Stress-related illness and depression

More employees are now taking stress leave, which has been recognized by doctors and employers as a serious by-product of this new millennium. Heart attacks at an earlier age are often linked to work pressures. Marriage failures are on the increase, one factor being financial problems caused by cutbacks and layoffs.

Unemployment can lead to depression. I can relate, first-hand, to the feelings of worthlessness, futility and good old self-pity. Many people hope that owning their own business will solve their stress problem. However, being your own boss involves a high level of stress too. You have no pension, no employment insurance, and in most cases, no future retirement plans—all good reasons for you to set practical goals for your business and plan it out in detail. Planning will help to reduce negative stress.

3. Unappreciative employers

These days, people with secure positions are considered the lucky few. Some employees are treated abominably. Verbal abuse, sexual harassment and low wages are common complaints in today's workforce. Financial pressures of struggling businesses are passed on to employees, who are not getting the rewards and positive strokes necessary for sustained job motivation. Some corporations are now aware of these effects on employees and are taking steps to increase employee motivation, but many are not. The time eventually comes when one says, "Enough! I'm quitting! I'll start my own business!"

4. Layoffs, downsizing or no work

Canada's large primary resource-based economy is a classic example of one that is fragile and subject to both local and global influences. The United States softwood tariffs in 2002 shut down mills that were the primary employers for many towns, particularly in British Columbia. Government restructuring and changing technology both contribute to corporate downsizing. In these situations, many people turn to self-employment as an opportunity to generate income.

5. Fewer opportunities for youth

For the educated young people, entrepreneurship is an exciting alternative to working for an employer for minimum wages when you have maximum qualifications. Such youth have much to offer our economy with their new and innovative ideas, energy and technological knowledge. There are many subsidized programs that encourage our youth to seek self-employment as a job alternative. However enthusiastic they may be, it is crucial for young people to be business-savvy before they make this important decision.

6. Incompetent employers

Experienced employees often feel that their employers are not particularly competent. Some get tired of working under these conditions, feeling that they have the experience and ability to strike out on their own. However, being an expert in one area does not constitute expertise as a business person. When you switch from a job with one area of responsibility—such as head of human resources—to managing all aspects of your own business, it is quite a change of wardrobes.

7. Family juggling and home-based businesses

Operating a home-based business has become a popular way for people juggling family responsibilities to earn an income and attend to family needs. More women are operating from home and trying to achieve a balancing act. Many find themselves caught up in a constant struggle for time, are usually stressed and are always "too busy." It works for some, but it takes discipline and commitment to strive for that perfect balance. I haven't quite found it yet.

Many baby boomers are also facing the responsibility of looking after ageing parents in their home, and choose self-employment as a way to juggle yet another family ball. Coping with my 93-year-old mother, I can say quite honestly that it is quite a time-consuming responsibility. Home-based businesses are also promoted as great tax write-offs but they do have their disadvantages. See Chapter 12 for an in-depth discussion on this subject.

$UCCE$$ $TRATEGY

GET HELP: If you are starting a business to accommodate juggling family jobs, explore services available in your community to help you. You may need a babysitting exchange, a home-care nurse, or even a "gofer" to do some running around. You cannot do it all, and your business—and you—will suffer if you try.

8. Leaving the boss behind

No one enjoys being told what to do. When you are your own boss, you, and you alone, are responsible for all decisions. There is a certain pride in the words "I have my own business" or "I am going into business for myself." As much as you may not enjoy being told what to do, at least you had direction in your old job. As an entrepreneur, you are the one who makes all the decisions. What a responsibility! Who shoulders the blame when things go wrong? You, of course. That's a heavy load to place upon yourself, so let's hope you are not a procrastinator, and that you have confidence in your business acumen.

9. Fingertip technology

With the advent of the home computer and continual new advances in technology, many new and exciting businesses can be operated from home or with a small capital outlay. With the Internet comes easier accessibility to information, clients and a career for many. Web page design and on-line business-to-business ventures didn't really exist ten years ago. The world is at your fingertips. Using technology to operate your business is essential these days, but if you are looking to start a Web-based business, tread carefully. Remember that many dot.coms are now not-dot.coms.

10. The baby boomer upsurge

Canada and the U.S. are quickly becoming geriatric nations. Many corporations who downsize offer early severance packages to long-term employees, who at 50-something don't feel ready to put up their feet and plant petunias.

To many, self-employment is an attractive option, particularly as they have the time and usually the buyout financial resources to explore this option. The downside is that many have been employees with attractive benefit packages for dozens of years, and the transition to becoming an entrepreneur is a difficult one.

WHY ARE *YOU* STARTING YOUR BUSINESS?

If you start your business for the right reasons, you are on your way to success. But some start for the wrong reasons, making it a difficult road. People starting up out of desperation risk making hasty decisions. Some are just not suited to self-employment. Some have spent many years working for one employer, feeling stressed, unmotivated and depressed, and view self-employment as a solution to all their problems. Some find themselves needing an immediate income replacement when they are often tired and burnt out. What is really needed is a good long rest with time to research their new venture thoroughly. If you are in a similar situation, *please* proceed with caution.

Others may not be used to decision-making after decades of working for an employer who did it all for them. Some have no time to take the necessary courses needed to expand their knowledge. The two most important steps—preparing a proper business plan and thoroughly researching the market—are often not taken, and they jump in with both feet without first checking the depth of the water.

Let's face it, there's no easy way to make money. Business means hard work, diligence, patience and careful planning. That doesn't mean you shouldn't start your own business, but it does mean you must think about what lies ahead. Most important of all, consult professionals for advice.

Analyze yourself

The short questionnaire in Figure 1.3 helps you determine why you are starting your business. Complete it and carefully analyze why you are exploring self-employment. The first eight reasons on this list can create difficulty for you if you are thinking of starting your business to solve these problems. Be sure your reasons are the right ones and that you have the emotional stamina, sufficient financial resources, knowledge and time that this venture requires.

Figure 1.3: WHY I AM STARTING MY BUSINESS?

Answer the following questions honestly to determine why you are starting your own business.

	Yes	No
1. I need more money; my wages don't stretch far enough.	❐	❐
2. I am depressed because I cannot find a job.	❐	❐
3. My work situation is unbearable—my boss doesn't appreciate me.	❐	❐
4. I was laid off and feel that I am ready to be my own boss.	❐	❐
5. I am tired of working for an incompetent boss.	❐	❐
6. I can better organize my family life by working at home.	❐	❐
7. I have to care for my ageing parents at home.	❐	❐
8. I want to be my own boss. I'm tired of working for one.	❐	❐
9. I can start a technology-based business at home.	❐	❐
10. I retired early and have the funds and time to explore this option.	❐	❐
11. I have the experience and the time to research this thoroughly.	❐	❐
12. I have the skills, time, passion and money to start a business.	❐	❐

SEVEN SKILLS FOR SUCCESS

By completing these first exercises, you should now have a better indication of some of the skills necessary for entrepreneurial success. You should also have some idea of your strengths and weaknesses and know where you need to focus your efforts to improve. The key skills you need can be broken down into seven areas as explained in the following list.

1. Interpersonal skills

Owning a business is all about dealing with people, so your number one priority is to determine whether you like people or not. There are many people operating businesses who make it painfully obvious that they are not people persons. Everyone has a story to tell of being treated rudely. Remember four important words: *YOU are your business.* The way you deal with people will determine much of your success. How many times have you decided not to return to a store because the cashier, clerk or manager was rude to you? How many times have you been impressed by a business person going out of his or her way to help you?

$UCCE$$ $TRATEGY

POLITENESS PAYS OFF: Good manners, politeness and attentiveness to your customers' needs ensure repeat business. Customers need to feel that they are important to you. The same principles apply to dealing with your trade suppliers, employees, business contacts and even the competition. Never burn your bridges by treating people badly, and respect those with whom you deal.

With the competitiveness of the big-box stores—who don't always have a reputation for good service—your ace in the hole will be wonderful customer service. You will need to develop patience, as some people are more difficult to please, or even understand, than others. You may be dealing with senior citizens, new immigrants to the country, disgruntled consumers, tradespeople or the mayor of your community. Part of developing your customer service skills will be learning to listen to—not just hear—your customers' needs. Listening is an art, and coupled with great service, you have a winning combination.

A good sense of humour is also an important survival tool, as is a smile. A smile or a little joke in a tense situation can do wonders in turning a problem around. Maintaining a positive outlook will keep you motivated and your customers coming back. No one wants to talk to a negative person. If you maintain a positive outlook, you will transmit this to your customers. They will want to be associated with and do business with you.

> ## CASE STUDY
>
> **GOING THAT EXTRA MILE**
>
> My pride and joy Jeep was involved in an accident in the snow (no, my husband was driving, not me), and the rear panel with a special Grizzly edition sticker had to be replaced.
>
> "Unfortunately, you will lose the sticker," said Lawrence, the owner of Bodycraft Collision. "They aren't available now."
>
> I liked the sticker and repeatedly grumbled about losing it, muttering something about male drivers. When I picked up the Jeep ten days later, beautifully de-dented and shiny, there was a new Grizzly sticker on the back. I was ecstatic! Lawrence had tracked down the manufacturer of the stickers in the U.S. to have one especially made for me. I was so impressed with his service that I tell everyone—including you—about his special caring and attention to detail. Now *that* is wonderful customer service and great listening.

2. Self-confidence

If you suffer from a lack of confidence or self-esteem, entrepreneurship can become a difficult challenge. *You* are the only person who can blow your own horn. Confidence does grow as you establish yourself as an expert and build on the other vital skills. Yet there are many who never make it past first base because they don't have that all-important confidence and self-esteem.

You will spend a great deal of time working alone and do not need negative thoughts to distract you. Sometimes it is difficult to stay motivated. There are many tools, counsellors and courses to help you overcome these stumbling blocks. Hypnotherapy can help to remove negative thoughts and allow you to stay on track and keep positive. Remember, you are selling yourself first to your clients—your business follows.

3. Financial skills

Business is all about dollars and cents. Although you are doing something that you love, the underlying reason is to generate an income. You have to understand financial figures and the business end of business. Most people hate this area and mistakenly avoid it. You don't want to learn the hard way, by making serious mistakes. Your knowledge should include basic accounting, organizational and administrative skills, an understanding of all tax laws, federal and provincial requirements, and an in-depth knowledge of the business that you are about to undertake. (See Chapter 3 for more on financial statements.)

Sounds like a lot to learn, and it is. But take heart—you can learn everything you need to know. No one was born a business hotshot, and there are many courses available offering business management training, most of which can be tailored to fit your schedule.

4. Technical skills

Anyone can hang out their business shingle, but without a sound technical knowledge of your trade or profession, it isn't fair to you or your customers. As a business person, you have a responsibility to perform the best service in an expert manner, so please don't start or purchase a business until you have the necessary skills.

Start in an area where you can best utilize your talents. Your skills may need to be expanded through evening courses or additional reading. Never cease to keep up with the changing technology within your chosen field.

Attend seminars, workshops, trade shows and conferences to add to your knowledge and keep an edge on your competitors. Don't make the mistake of becoming so engrossed in working *at* your business that you forget to work *on* your business.

$UCCE$$ $TRATEGY

AVOID THE "TECHNICIAN TRAP": Michael Gerber wrote in his best-selling book, *The E-Myth Revisited*, that "The typical small business owner is only 10 percent Entrepreneur, 20 percent Manager and 70 percent Technician." He states that an ideal entrepreneur is an equal mix of all three. Read his book as you plan your business. It will help you become more aware of avoiding the "technician trap."

Your customers will look to you as the expert, and that is what you have to be. For example, when you look in the Yellow Pages for a plumber or an electrician, you assume the companies advertised there are run by professional and skilled people. As a consumer, you put your trust in them. Your customers put the same trust in your skills, and you should never let them down. Be the expert, or don't be in business.

5. Communication skills

The secret to both a successful business and an enriching life is learning to effectively communicate. Everything you do is about communicating something to someone in some manner. How you communicate verbally to potential clients will make the difference in whether they choose to do business with you, both now and in the future.

$UCCE$$ $TRATEGY

IMPROVE YOUR WRITING SKILLS: People are quickly judged by their written skills, or the lack of them. When letters or flyers are received with obvious grammatical errors, 99 percent immediately judge that company as unprofessional and recycle the literature. This is your first—and often last—foot in the door. If you need to tune up your written skills, take a course or read books on writing business letters. A course on creative writing can be a tremendous benefit for marketing your business.

In this electronic era, we communicate using voice-mail, faxes, answering machines and e-mail. Therefore, every form of communication that transpires through your office should be polite, professional and positive. Your telephone should always be answered quickly and pleasantly, and any correspondence written without grammatical errors. "Leave a message after the beep" doesn't cut it in business. Voice-mail and answering machine greetings should convey a feeling of "we care" and should imply that messages will be promptly returned, not within a few hours. These days, people are stressed and impatient. They want to talk to you now, so always be available either by pager or cellphone.

You may need to communicate with lawyers, accountants, bank managers, loan companies or venture capitalists. You may have to negotiate leases or contracts and work with building inspectors, municipal officers, government and various tax officials, suppliers, advertising agencies and employees. Some may be difficult to deal with, so good verbal and written communication skills will reduce the chances of being misunderstood.

If you lack confidence, it often shows in your conversations by the overuse of "ers" and "ums." The listener's immediate perception of you is that you lack knowledge. Your messages should be clear, concise, confident and competent. The ability to communicate effectively at a variety of levels in a variety of ways to a variety of people is a skill few people naturally possess, and this is where Toastmasters International can help. Many prominent business people owe a good part of their success to this highly effective organization.

6. Marketing skills

You may have the best business in town, but how are you going to get your message across to potential customers? Marketing is not just putting an advertisement in the local paper or flyers in the mail. In a nutshell, marketing refers to the various strategies you use to reach potential customers, informing them of your products or services. Effective marketing encompasses using communication skills, knowing how to define and target your market, and then utilizing the right marketing mix to reach potential customers.

It's easy to spend valuable dollars on ineffectual methods. Study your competitors and decide if their marketing techniques will work for you. You will have to read books, talk to others in a similar field and observe how other businesses successfully market. No one has the magical marketing answer— usually, effective marketing is a combination of many techniques that can change from time to time. Your job will be to define which works best for you. Marketing is explained in more detail in Chapter 10.

7. Technological skills

Today's businesses must be on-line and technologically terrific. Because time is today's most valuable commodity, most businesses need to use e-mail. Many people now prefer to communicate using e-mail rather than the telephone. I was surprised recently when I used the services of a small business that relies heavily on computers for production purposes, yet which did not use e-mail. Having to save a graphic file on a disk and deliver it is not an acceptable option for today's busy clients.

Consumers like to surf 'n' shop in the evenings on their home computers, so a well-designed Web site can be an important marketing tool. You don't have to sell over the Internet, but your site can describe your service or products and give the consumers what they want—information.

$UCCE$$ $TRATEGY

STAY IN TOUCH: There is nothing more frustrating to a customer than not having telephone calls or e-mails promptly returned. Make it a practice to check messages and e-mails regularly and to return calls. This is an important part of customer service and your customers will appreciate you "going that extra mile."

Word processing and publishing programs allow you to prepare professional letters and marketing information. Accounting and spreadsheet programs allow you to keep your costing, forecasting and bookkeeping up-to-date at the click of a mouse. A database or contact management system streamlines administrative functions and is a wonderful marketing tool. Research which technology will help your business save time and keep current with the business world.

DO YOU HAVE THE MANAGEMENT SKILLS?

To help you identify where you may need to develop your managerial skills, complete Figure 1.4 and see how you score. Do you have what it takes?

Figure 1.4: MANAGEMENT SKILLS CHECKLIST

Using the following questions, determine whether you have the management skills necessary to run your own business.

	Yes	No
1. Could I cope with constant pressures and deadlines?	☐	☐
2. Could I handle stressful situations without "losing my cool"?	☐	☐
3. Could I fire an incompetent employee?	☐	☐
4. Could I maintain strict credit control?	☐	☐
5. Could I refuse credit to a good but slow-paying client?	☐	☐
6. Could I adapt to constant change?	☐	☐
7. Could I maintain control of my daily, weekly and monthly finances?	☐	☐
8. Do I understand how my business is taxed?	☐	☐
9. Do I know what a break-even point is?	☐	☐
10. Could I delegate responsibilities to others?	☐	☐
11. Am I willing to increase my skills in the areas that are lacking?	☐	☐
12. Will I use a business plan and regularly revisit it?	☐	☐

If you didn't answer yes to all the questions in Figure 1.4, you now have a guide as to where to focus your management training efforts. It's important to be the very best manager you can be to ensure that your first business will be an exciting and successful venture.

WHY DO BUSINESSES FAIL?

No one likes to think of failure, yet business failure statistics are high. If you know why businesses fail, you can avoid making these mistakes. There are seven main reasons why the majority of businesses fail:

1. No planning and poor management
2. Lack of cash flow and capital
3. Wrong location
4. Inadequate marketing plan
5. Competition not researched
6. Wrong choice of business
7. Business grows too quickly.

Any one of these reasons can cause your business to fail, but combine two or more and your business will be in hot water. Let's look at each in turn.

1. No planning and poor management

The previous exercises have shown that you need to be multi-faceted in your entrepreneurial abilities. Just as an architect must work to blueprints, so your business must work to a plan. The key to business success is in the development of a sound and well-researched business plan, discussed in Chapter 7.

You only have to drive around your own community to see "the revolving door syndrome" of retail outlets closing down after a few months and a new venture starting. Service industries suffer the same fate. The usual reason for these failures is lack of planning. No matter which business you pursue, it needs a great manager at the helm. Good management encompasses everything from customer service to running an efficient office. Review the strategies below and see if you are ready for this challenge.

What is good business management?

- Providing the right service or product at the right time, in the right location, at the right price
- Knowing that profit margins can support overhead, pay salaries and meet personal commitments

- Ensuring that the business provides a steady year-round income and that you have a "plan B" for quieter months

- Astute inventory management to ensure a regular turnaround

- Keeping accounting records up-to-date and closely monitoring financial figures

- Regularly reviewing marketing strategies for their effectiveness

- Changing with consumer trends, technology and the changing economy

- Making time daily for follow-up, marketing and paperwork

- Monitoring accounts receivable and keeping in touch with slow-paying clients

- Understanding all aspects of your business and the industry

- Providing a better service than your competitors

- Becoming known as "the expert" in your field

- Being an active member in your community

- Diversifying—not putting all your eggs in one basket

- Continual networking and follow-up

- Planning for growth and having an exit strategy.

2. Lack of cash flow and capital

"Cash flow" describes the flow of money within a business. Businesses are often started by people with very little money to invest in the start-up and not enough to see the business through the first two fragile years. Without enough capital investment, important corners are cut. Shoestring budgets make survival and growth difficult. Without money to purchase the necessary equipment, support monthly overhead or spend on marketing to launch the business, the enterprise cannot get off to a positive start.

The average business is started with minimum capital, often borrowed from family, banks, credit cards or high-interest loans. Some people increase home mortgages, an inadvisable step, because if the business fails, the home could be lost and the marriage or other personal relationships really put to the test. Know where your financing will come from, what the terms of repayment will be, and whether the business can afford the repayments. If you can't afford to borrow—then don't. Rethink your business plan.

$UCCE$$ $TRATEGY

START WITH A CAPITAL CUSHION: The very minimum capital you will need is enough to support the business and personal commitments for the first three months—or longer. This is the barest necessity, based on a business that has a guaranteed and immediate cash flow. The ideal would be a financial reserve that covers all expenses for the first nine months.

3. Wrong location

With the competition from big-box stores and large malls, location is key for retail businesses to succeed. Is it practical to have a hairdressing salon in an industrial area? Or a restaurant tucked into a small strip mall frequented mainly by seniors? Despite this self-evident logic, people often locate their businesses in the wrong areas. "But the rent is so cheap!" they cry in delight.

Studies show that the average consumer will travel no more than three blocks out of their way, particularly if the same product can be purchased closer. No amount of advertising will entice customers to an out-of-the-way location if they can buy the product more conveniently elsewhere. Walk-by traffic, visibility and parking are all vital to a retail location. There is no such animal as "cheap rent."

4. Inadequate marketing plan

A marketing plan is an integral part of a business plan, yet many people don't plan how they will market their new business. "Oh, I'll put some flyers out, put an advertisement in the local paper and wait for the phone to ring" is *not* a marketing plan. You need a structured marketing plan—one where you research which marketing techniques best suit your business. With small and home-based businesses, marketing is usually cited as one of the largest hurdles faced by the owners.

$UCCE$$ $TRATEGY

FIND YOUR NICHE: Identify whether your business is filling both a *need* and a *niche* in the marketplace, which you will only discover after thorough market research. Then move on to how you can best fill that niche and attract customers to your business.

5. Competition not researched

Many budding entrepreneurs take their specific talent and dive into starting a business without first assessing their competition. Take the time to thoroughly research this aspect of your business. With the proliferation of home-based service businesses, knowing who and where your competition is can be time-consuming. Your hidden competitors will be the unlicensed ones. Most municipal offices and your chamber of commerce can give you a list of licensed businesses in your field.

Only so much business can be generated in one geographic area. Too many stores offering the same service means that all will struggle to make a living, offering profit-draining specials to entice consumers. Study your town or marketing area intimately *before* starting your business.

Also consider the future. What would happen to your business if a large store selling your product or service cheaper opened up a few blocks away? There are no regulations prohibiting businesses offering similar services from opening up near each other. Just take a look at your own hometown.

$UCCE$$ $TRATEGY

FILL THE INDUSTRY GAPS: Ask yourself two questions: What can I offer that the competition can't? What can they offer that I can't? This will help you to focus on the niche that your business should be filling. Can you compete with large chain stores or well-established smaller businesses? Chapter 4 discusses researching your business in depth.

6. Wrong choice of business

Be an expert in your field and love what you do (you will hear this message many times; it's important). Choosing a business because it seems like an easy way to make money is foolhardy. Review consumer, economic and long-term trends and assess your business community. If you are buying into a "business investment opportunity" or purchasing an existing business, you need an accountant to review the proposal.

Many unprofitable businesses have been positively presented through professional presentation, skilled wording and a good sales pitch. A professional portfolio often glosses over the real reasons for the business sale—lack of profits. Some people think they can take a business and do better than the last person. If it's your first business purchase, don't be so sure that you can create miracles. Advertised promises of a quick return for little outlay and minimal work belong in the fiction section.

7. Business grows too quickly

Business growth doesn't sound like a reason for business failure, but it is often the case. If a business is started with minimum cash flow, particularly one involving a large inventory, rapid growth can create all kinds of problems. Sudden growth may mean that your location is no longer suitable, and moving a business is costly. Additional inventory requirements, staffing, machinery or equipment upgrading must be paid for with profits. There is always a delay between needing extra cash and the eventual cash flow back into the business from sales. Sudden growth puts extra demands on your management abilities as you adjust to the changes.

WHAT IS THE NEXT STEP?

In this chapter you learned about being an entrepreneur, and some of the desirable traits, skills and qualities you should apply to your business. Have you identified some areas where you need to round out your skills? Knowing why businesses fail will help you to avoid pitfalls as you start planning. The next step is to look at the different types of businesses available to you and the steps involved in buying a business.

CHAPTER 2

How do you find the right business?

If it's as easy to make money as the advertisements say,
why aren't we all rich in a year and a day?

WHAT TYPE OF BUSINESSES ARE AVAILABLE?

The business that best suits your needs and experience will take time to research. The more time you spend, the wiser choice you will make, as you will discover that very few will fit your personal criteria. For example, if you don't like cold-calling, opt for an established business with an established clientele. If you are uncomfortable selling to friends and family, don't enter into a multi-level situation. If working seven days a week is not for you, avoid retail.

Businesses come in all shapes and size, with close to 70 percent being in the service sector. Following is an outline of the six main types of businesses:

1. Service

2. Retail

3. Franchising

4. Manufacturing

5. Distribution

6. Multi-level and network marketing.

1. Service businesses

The majority of new entrepreneurs start a service business because it is the easiest way to generate income utilizing their many years of expertise. What is a service business? Quite simply, one that performs a service in return for a fee, which is usually calculated on an hourly or contract fee basis. Service businesses include consulting, accounting, bookkeeping, Web design, all the trades, teaching and tourism, to name just a few. Clients pay for your expertise and knowledge.

Being that expert is a key component to a successful service business. Once you advertise and open the doors, you are representing yourself as a professional in your field. Unless you belong to an accredited association—mandatory for doctors, lawyers and accountants—the consumer has little recourse except to sue if you offer wrong advice or perform inadequately.

A service business should offer just that. Service. Clients expect it, so you'd better be prepared to offer excellent service plus a little bit more at a reasonable price. Guarantee your work, as this gives the message that you stand by and take pride in what you do. Consumers, now more than ever, expect quality service at the best price. Don't hang out your shingle until you are sure you can offer a professional product—*you.*

$UCCE$$ $TRATEGY

ENSURE CUSTOMER SATISFACTION: Punctuality, reliability and follow-up are three major components of a service business. Be on time for appointments. Call if you are unavoidably detained, then always follow up afterwards, asking if everything is to the client's satisfaction. This one call will earn you credit and gives you the opportunity to address any problems before an unsatisfied client starts complaining to others.

Isn't it amazing how one hears the negative service business stories more than the positive ones? We read about home renovators performing substandard work, mechanics who don't adequately fix a vehicle's problem or bookkeepers who operate without proper accounting knowledge. Imagine what could happen if a gas appliance was not properly installed. An improperly wired house could cause a devastating house fire, and a brake failure could cause someone's death.

Your clients should receive the same professional expertise and service that you would expect to receive. You are taking the lives, property and welfare of your clients into your hands. Before you open your doors, consider taking out liability insurance for protection from unforeseen disasters (see Chapter 6). Serious errors can lead to lengthy and costly legal battles, causing irreparable damage to the business.

Service businesses often appear glamorous, but they do have their downside. Review this list of advantages and disadvantages and see which ones may apply to you.

The advantages

- They usually require less start-up capital
- You can apply your skills to generate income
- Many can be operated from a home-based office
- Overhead costs are considerably lower
- You have some flexibility in setting appointments
- You usually don't have to carry a large inventory, if any
- There's less paperwork and accounting.

The disadvantages

- If you are ill or injured, the job doesn't get done
- You work longer hours catching up on administrative functions
- It is easy to become isolated from the business world
- There is a high liability factor involved
- If you make a mistake, your reputation is threatened.

2. Retail

Welcome to the mega-millennium, the world of big-box, humungous, cold, poorly serviced but cheap discount stores. What a difficult climate for small retail stores. All the more reason to do thorough homework before embarking on a retail venture. The competition is fierce, with many small retail businesses hardly making an acceptable living. Retail outlets not only compete with each other, they also compete with large chain stores, manufacturers' outlets, and multi-level, Internet and mail-order sales.

Future trends

However, if you carefully target your market, your chances of success will increase. Future trends indicate that baby boomers are opting for service and stress-free shopping, tired of the mega-monsters. Barbara Caplan, a New York-based consumer trends expert, stated in 2002 that "People want to hit the bull's eye every time they do something or buy something. They want pleasure, enjoyment, connection with people, an experience—and they want to be taken seriously." Caplan calls it the "affluent attitude," and baby boomers, along with teenagers, will drive the future consumer economy.

Although Internet sales are making small inroads into retail shopping, according to an article in the *Vancouver Sun* in early 2002, research indicates that more than 60 percent of potential on-line shoppers abandon a site before buying. Web sites must be easy to use and "surfer-friendly," which many are not. So although retail competition has increased from these two sectors—big-box and the Internet—service is still the winning factor that will entice consumers into your store, because in most cases, you can't compete with pricing.

Here are some factors to consider that are unique to retail stores:

a) Location

Prime retail locations are expensive for a good reason. If a store is located in a large shopping mall, rents can be disproportionately high, with advertising dollars paid to the mall property managers each month. You have to sell a lot of doughnuts to pay $2,000 or $3,000 a month for rent. If your store is located in an out-of-the-way location, you will not experience the volume of walk- and drive-by traffic necessary to generate enough sales. Before deciding on a location, find out how many other stores in that location moved on or closed up shop.

b) Employees

Both you and your employees should have thorough product knowledge. Remember—be the expert. Your employees should also have excellent customer service skills. Consumers expect and demand both. Many customers have been lost to the competition because of incompetent sales staff.

The retail trade requires excellent people skills. You need patience to deal with a variety of temperaments. You will have to serve teenagers, seniors, immigrants, tourists with language difficulties, parents with screaming children and some rather disagreeable customers who seem to enjoy giving sales staff a difficult time.

c) Inventory control

Well-stocked shelves and attractive displays entice customers to browse. A small retail store can easily carry a minimum of $60,000 in inventory, equating to large amounts of cash sitting on the shelves. Poor inventory purchasing means that slow-moving products will eventually have to be discounted. Select your lines carefully to facilitate a quick turnaround. Find out how many times a year your inventory should "turn" or sell by your industry's standards. Monitor your inventory turnover and watch for the slow-moving products.

d) Hours

Retail stores are often open seven days a week, with extended trading hours. You can't work seven days and order supplies, restock shelves and manage all the accounting and administrative work. You need help. First, determine the hours you can manage to work regularly without overextending yourself, decide for which work you are best suited and then fill the gaps with additional staff. Be prepared for long days.

e) Marketing

Many retail stores waste money on ineffective marketing methods. Study how similar stores advertise in your area. Note how their advertising appeals to you as a consumer. Visit the stores both before and during an advertised sale, noting whether traffic has increased or not.

$UCCE$$ $TRATEGY

KNOW YOUR PROFIT MARGINS: You need to use a mix of marketing techniques, including specials, clearance sales and special events, to keep your business in the consumers' eyes. Sales may increase on clearance and sale items, but profit margins will decrease. Calculate how much you can reduce the cost of an item before losing money.

---

f) Consumer spending cycles

Keep up-to-date with consumer trends as they vary with the economic climate. As the nation seems to be working harder and getting poorer, tailor inventory to your target market. Unless you specialize in strictly high-end products, maintain an inventory that appeals to the pockets of lower- and middle-income brackets. Retail outlets are totally vulnerable to consumer spending cycles. Your sales can be affected by weather, post-Christmas financial woes, summer vacations, the back-to-school rush, the economic climate and political changes. Learn the cycles that will both increase and decrease sales so you can better plan your cash flow and marketing strategies.

g) Overhead and profit margins

A good portion of your profit will be going into other people's pockets, particularly to your staff and landlord. If you employ family members, at least the money stays in the family. Standing overhead costs—that is, overhead costs that do not decrease whether or not you make a sale—must still be met. Advertising, rent, telephones, power and wages eat up a good percentage of profits. If you are starting a new store, know the break-even point (the amount of sales you must make each month to cover the bills), calculate how much you must sell and determine how you are going to achieve this figure. (See Chapter 11 for information on calculating your break-even point.)

$UCCE$$ $TRATEGY

MORE IS BETTER: If you are purchasing an existing store, use an accountant to thoroughly review two-years' financial statements, which must be up-to-date and professionally prepared. For example, a store with six-month-old statements could be trying to cover up a recent decrease in sales and profits. Your accountant can compare sales fluctuations and cost variances to reveal the true picture.

h) Pricing

Tough competition in the retail sector means that you must know your prices and regularly review them. Not many businesses can boast total product exclusivity—even specialty stores have competition. A smaller store's buying power is weaker than the larger ones, and you can only corner a certain percentage of the market, unless you sell a unique product line.

Keep normal retail prices in line with the competition. At the same time, they must be high enough to support your overhead. It is easy to fall into the trap of offering continuous sales that realize very little profits. Profit pays for the overhead.

3. Franchising

It seems that everyone is franchising everything these days, from coffee shops to tanning salons. Those with a solid reputation who have perfected their business strategies over the years will be asking a fair price for a franchise. Traditionally, established franchise business failures are significantly rarer than independent business failures because they have designed effective sales, marketing and administration systems. This is what you pay for, along with the company's good name.

Investing in a relatively new franchise company is as risky as starting your own business, as is buying one that is riding a current popular trend. Your market research will indicate whether the trend is predicted to be short-lived or long-term. Definitely consult your accountant before making a decision.

Well-established and profitable franchises are expensive, and there are many reasons for this:

- They have spent the time and money on in-depth marketing research
- They have perfected their marketing and advertising methods
- Locations are researched for viability
- They have built their reputation and are trusted by consumers
- Profit margins, products and operating expenses have been established and refined.

CASE STUDY

LICKED BY ICE CREAM

Norma and Joseph, an early-retired couple, pursued their dream of owning a family business. They purchased an ice cream franchise, thinking it would be a good investment and also create jobs for their teenage children. It was located in a large shopping mall, so they had to be open long hours, pay high rent, advertising and royalty percentages to both the mall and the franchise, and of course, pay top dollars for the business.

After two years of operation, Norma and Joseph were tired—and not any richer. Because of the high overhead costs, after all expenses, the business was making substantially less than $20,000 a year, not an acceptable income for two hard-working people. Disillusioned, they sold the franchise for a loss. It takes a lot of licking ice creams to get rich.

If you have a strong and creative entrepreneurial spirit, you may find a franchise too restrictive and regulated, as you must abide by their rules.

Uniformity is the secret to their success. A McDonald's hamburger in Mexico tastes exactly like a North American one. They have designed an operational plan and a formula that work. Although you are an independent, you are controlled by the head office. You pay for goodwill on purchase, and a percentage of profits or sales volume each year. You must purchase their own brand of supplies and raw materials, paying more than if you shopped around. A good franchise is an expensive proposition, but in most cases, a profitable business is the end result.

4) Manufacturing

Manufacturing is defined as anything produced from raw materials, from candles to cameras. As a manufacturer, you are responsible for the end product and its safety in the marketplace, therefore you should be an expert in the industry. During you market research, check local, North American and overseas markets producing similar products. Often, locally manufactured goods cannot match the prices of internationally produced goods because of our higher salaries and living standards.

Starting a manufacturing business

It takes years to establish a new name in an industry, so you will need enough working capital to maintain the new business for up to two years or until regular profits roll in. There are various government-funded programs available for certain manufacturing businesses, and these can be found in the publication *Overview of Government Assistance Programs for Small Business,* available from the Canada Business Service Centre in your province (see Appendix 1 for phone numbers).

Allow adequate time and money to talk to the various government agencies and to confer with your accountant or a business consultant. You need a sound business plan that you have prepared—with professional advice—so that you are fully conversant with its contents. Manufacturing can require a lot of money, as you may need to purchase tools, packaging supplies and equipment or incur legal costs for patents and trademarks. You will need an experienced team working together to cover production, sales, shipping, marketing and administration.

Buying a manufacturing business

Most vendors will provide a training period after purchase, but their expertise usually comes from many years in the industry. Are they going to take the time and teach you all the tricks of the trade? You may purchase a business with dependable, well-trained employees already in place, but you cannot rely solely on your employees—they are transient. You have to rely on your own experience and good judgment.

$UCCE$$ $TRATEGY

GET THE SCOOP FROM STAFF: Before the purchase, if possible, talk to the key employees. Ascertain their long-term goals with the company and listen to any complaints or suggestions about the current operation. Employees are the backbone of every business and usually know the "inside scoop" that you may not hear from the vendor.

If you plan to export a product or import raw materials, you must learn about the various methods and costs of shipping, customs documentation and letters of credit. Products have to be costed to allow for fluctuations in currencies, particularly as some countries' economies can be unstable, with their currency values changing almost overnight. No matter how small or large your manufacturing business will be, don't do it alone. There is a lot of help available to you through various government agencies (see *http://strategis.ic.gc.ca*). A well-run manufacturing concern can make healthy profits as well as increase the goodwill value over time.

5) Distribution

Distribution (or wholesaling) usually operates on small profit margins, relying on volume to support a profitable business. A distributor acts as a link between the manufacturer and retail outlets. Be knowledgeable about the products you are distributing; most manufacturers offer support or training to their distributors.

The size and variety of lines you distribute will dictate the type and size of the premises you will need. Larger items may require a warehouse, dock-loading facilities, shelving, forklifts, special equipment for moving materials, and an efficient shipping and receiving system with dependable, honest employees.

During the research process, find answers to the questions in Figure 2.1.

Figure 2.1: PRODUCT EVALUATION

A thorough product evaluation requires you to carefully think about each of the following considerations.

	Yes	No
1. Have the products been available for a few years?	☐	☐
2. Could they become obsolete?	☐	☐
3. Does the manufacturer have a good reputation?	☐	☐
4. Do you know how large the market is?	☐	☐
5. Do you know all your major competitors?	☐	☐
6. Are prices competitive?	☐	☐
7. Does the manufacturer honour warranties?	☐	☐
8. Are the products easily serviceable or repairable?	☐	☐
9. Do you know the products' seasonal sales cycles?	☐	☐
10. Are there any reoccurring problems with the products?	☐	☐

If you are purchasing an existing business, the retail client base should be established. You will need to review the financial information to see whether the client base needs expanding, what the current terms of payment are, how slowly clients pay, and whether there are any bad credit risks. If you are starting your own distribution business, you must find potential clients and evaluate their interest in your products. It's no use distributing products that move slowly, as they take up valuable warehouse space and restrict your cash flow.

Profits and overhead costs

Your business plan will help to determine if there is enough profit margin in your products to cover overhead. Average gross profit margins (i.e., profit after the sale less the cost of the product) can range from 10 to 30 percent of selling price. A profit margin of less than 20 percent doesn't leave much room to cover overhead costs. Calculate how much you must sell monthly to cover your break-even costs before making a final decision.

6. Multi-level and network marketing

Starting a multi-level or network marketing business—perhaps part-time at first—is one way to get your feet wet. The start-up costs can be low and the business operated from home. It is a transient type of business. Approximately 0.6 percent of beginners make it to the top level and earn an excellent income. One well-known, reputable direct sales company estimates that they have 30 percent of their people starting the business, 40 percent operating it on a part-time "dabbling" basis, and 30 percent "on their way out."

Very few people stay in these businesses long-term. It is certainly one way of discovering what type of sales and business person you are. You need the type of personality that can sell and total confidence in the products you are selling. Be prepared to market those products at every opportunity. You will need to find people to join your down-line or team, as you earn commission off their sales. This is where the real money kicks in.

It takes commitment

Your social life can be affected. Instead of enjoying a social event, you may instead see a room full of potential clients. You may even find friends avoid you if you constantly grind away at them. If you are outgoing, an extrovert and a person with a lot of business, social and networking contacts, multi-level could be for you. Those who succeed are usually passionate and driven entrepreneurs, committed to their products and their company.

Most multi-level companies require that you attend training sessions, motivational seminars and weekly "bring a friend" sales sessions. Their products are often distributed through in-home parties, so be prepared to work nights and weekends. These companies tend to come and go, so find one with a solid history. There are many disreputable companies distributing through this system—and there are some quite reputable, popular ones that have been around a long time. Talk to others who have been in the same company for a while and listen carefully to their feedback.

Answer the questions in Figure 2.2 before you make a commitment.

Figure 2.2: IS DIRECT SELLING FOR ME?		
Consider the following questions before deciding whether direct selling and the company in question are a good match for you.		
	Yes	**No**
1. Is the company secure?	❏	❏
2. Does it have a good reputation?	❏	❏
3. Do the company principals have sound credentials?	❏	❏
4. Are their track records credible?	❏	❏
5. Does the corporate management regularly change? (If yes, why?)	❏	❏
6. Can I feel comfortable approaching friends and family for sales?	❏	❏
7. Has the company been in business a few years?	❏	❏
8. Are the products of good quality and reasonably priced?	❏	❏
9. Am I confident enough to involve friends and family?	❏	❏
10. Will family life suffer because of evening/weekend commitments?	❏	❏
11. Am I able to attend out-of-town and out-of-country conferences?	❏	❏
12. Can I quickly close a deal?	❏	❏
13. Do I have enough money to purchase the start-up inventory?	❏	❏

Each company has its own set of rules, but usually you will need to buy sample kits or inventory, brochures, videos, magazines and promotional items. You will need credit card facilities and will be charged shipping and handling costs, approximately four percent of the dollar value of the order. Some companies restrict how and where you can sell their products. Some want you to market only through home parties or prohibit displaying at trade shows. Be aware of these restrictions before making a final decision.

Multi-level marketing is like any other self-employed business, with the normal start-up costs and monthly overhead. Talk to a few people who have succeeded in the business and review start-up costs with them, including the continuing costs of remaining successful.

WHICH BUSINESS IS RIGHT FOR *YOU?*

Ultimately, only you can decide which business will work best for you, so the next step is to further narrow down the possibilities by doing more research and evaluating. Figure 2.3 outlines some important considerations to think about as you toss and turn at night, dreaming about owning your first business.

Figure 2.3: TEN FACTORS TO CONSIDER BEFORE DECIDING ON A BUSINESS

1. **Why I want to start a business:** Are you starting for the right reasons? Figure 1.3 in Chapter 1 will help you to better define this.

2. **My health and mental attitude:** Entrepreneurship takes long hours and can be stressful. If you are a "Type A" personality or easily depressed, self-employment can be a challenge.

3. **My future goals:** Be clear about your short-, mid- and long-term goals for yourself, your family and the business. Do you foresee a comfortable work-at-home situation, or do you want to grow? You need these goals to sustain your motivation.

4. **Family and quality of life:** These are the two most important facets of our lives. How will your business detract from or add to both?

5. **Suitability of your skills:** Are you experienced and knowledgeable enough for this business? Are you willing to continually upgrade your expertise and knowledge? Of course, you *love* people—right?

6. **Time:** You need extensive time to research and get this venture going. Then you'll be married to it, particularly for the first year or two. How much time are you prepared to devote to this business?

7. **Industry track record:** It may sound like a wonderful opportunity, but you need to research the past performance of this type of business. Trends come and go.

8. **Current and future trends:** Chapter 4 is devoted to market research and researching trends. You need to know where this business is going in the next decade.

9. **Financial considerations:** How much will you need, when will you need it, and where is it coming from? Chapter 7 addresses these questions.

10. **Personal cash needs:** You will need the business to provide you with an income. Have you reviewed your family and personal budget? Some businesses don't generate a profit for a year or two. How will you manage?

Work with professionals

When a business piques your interest, use professionals to help you make informed decisions. If you feel that you can't afford their fees, then you are not quite ready to start a business. Economizing in the wrong places will cost you later on. You will need the help of an accountant or business consultant, and should use a lawyer for all legal work and to review contracts and leases.

Ask friends in business if they are happy with their accountant, lawyer or consultant. Be careful with referrals though—what works for one person may not be the best for another. Work within your budget, as many professionals charge an expensive hourly rate. If you have access to a Community Futures Development Corporation or a self-help, community business or Economic Development office, call them for advice and referrals. Look in the phone book or visit *www.communityfutures.ca.*

You must feel comfortable with the professional you work with, so don't be scared to ask questions. Remember the old saying, "A question is only a dumb question until you find out the answer." Prepare a list of questions before you meet each time, and write down or record the answers. A good professional will fill in all the other gaps and tell you what you need to know.

WHY ARE BUSINESSES SOLD?

You can purchase two types of businesses, either an existing one or a "business opportunity," which will be discussed next in this chapter. Finding the perfect business is an exercise in patience, time and frustration. Having travelled this road and worked with other entrepreneurs on the same path, I have seen the process take months. It requires professional advice and a practical approach, because the wrong choice may cost you thousands of dollars.

Established businesses sell for a variety of reasons, the most common of which follow.

1. Business runs out of money

Poor planning, administrative difficulties or new competitors are the usual reasons why businesses run out of money. Most small businesses struggle when they first open, and if costs exceed expectations or sales do not meet them, bank accounts quickly deplete. Owners become desperate to sell and will appear eager to persuade you that their business is the best thing since the invention of the microchip.

$UCCE$$ $TRATEGY

KNOW THE DIFFERENCE: Some businesses are excellent opportunities to acquire a business at a fair price. Perhaps all that is needed is a competent manager to turn it around. But first do your homework. It's no use buying someone else's troubles if they can't be remedied.

2. Illness, death or family problems

Illness is a common reason for selling a business, particularly if there are no staff or family members to continue the operation. Seventy-five percent of small businesses close after the principal owner dies or becomes seriously ill. Some businesses cause too much stress on the family relationship, and the decision has to be made between keeping the business or maintaining the family's health. If it is being sold because of family pressures, find out why the work created these pressures in the first place. If the business is so stressful, do you really want to inherit someone else's problems?

3. Business burnout

It happens to many business owners—they just get really tired after many years of doing the same thing. It's like any other job. When the challenge has gone or the daily stresses are too great, the passion is lost. I personally know of many people who have closed up shop for these reasons. Baby boomers are frequently ready for a change of lifestyle. If the business has adequately supported the owner for many years, it may be a worthwhile proposition. It should have a well-established clientele and reputation, along with a solid financial history.

4. Increased competition

It's difficult to keep one step ahead of the competition, particularly for many smaller retail businesses. The arrival of a new supermarket, big-box store or shopping mall is often their ultimate demise. Even if the vendor doesn't admit to this reason, it should be obvious if you thoroughly research the competition. If this appears to be the main reason for selling, pass this one by, because you will only inherit someone else's failing business.

WHAT IS A BUSINESS OPPORTUNITY?

A business opportunity is just that—an opportunity to make money using a concept or idea that someone has developed. Businesses such as multi-level, network marketing, distributorships, vending routes, janitorial contracts, franchises, mail order, Internet or computer-related businesses are considered business opportunities. Many can be operated from home. You purchase a concept that may or may not already be proven. Its success depends entirely on your business acumen and your ability to establish clients. The purchase price usually includes the necessary tools, such as vending machines, inventory or samples.

Many of these businesses will present you with an idea that is made to sound so exciting and profitable, you just can't wait to sink your teeth into it. *Be cautious.* Seek professional advice, as these businesses are advertised in a manner that readily attracts people wanting a quick return and who have little cash. Those promises of big money usually don't pan out.

Beware of scams

Advertisements are designed to focus on five key attractions to potential buyers. They will tout:

- Low start-up costs
- Quick returns with high profits
- Part-time
- No experience necessary
- Work from home.

Take a look in your newspaper under the Business Opportunities section on a Saturday, and read the tempting offers of easy money. Here are just some advertisements, taken from a daily newspaper in one weekend edition:

- **LOOK! A minimum $10K investment can earn $65K** a year immediately. Guaranteed.

- **E-MAIL PROCESSORS** required immediately. Use your own computer to earn income from home. No experience necessary.

- **AMAZING OPPORTUNITY.** Open the hottest franchise in North America. Low investment, high returns.

- Earn up to **2.5 million annually.** Investment required.

- Earn **$900 a month**, work only **10 hours a week.** Up to $2,500 a month for 25 hours' work.

- **Awesome** Internet Business. Home-based, no computer or exp. necessary. Huge profit potential.

- **Retire in three years!** Incredible income, low start-up costs, huge market!

- **$100,000 year** potential, computer earns you money 24 hours a day!

- **$20K investment, six-figure return,** huge market, no selling.

Advertisers reel in unsuspecting victims, preying on their desire for quick, easy cash with minimum investment. People who want to operate a home-based business are often their targets. It's hard for the eager not to get excited with these wonderful promises. But if all these businesses were as simple as they sound, then why aren't more people rich? There are some not-so-honest people who are ready to take your money and run, or sell you an unprofitable business that makes money for no one except the vendors.

Five rules to avoid fraud

If you are not sure about with whom you are dealing, spend some time researching. Follow these five simple rules to put your mind at ease. Even if you are purchasing what appears to be a viable and reputable business, a thorough background check is time well invested.

Rule #1: Perform a company name search

A legitimate business should be registered in your province with the corporate name registry. Are the owners really who they say they are? What is the corporate structure? For a small fee, you can have the business name, structure and owners searched by calling the corporate registry in your province (listed in Appendix 1).

Rule #2: If in doubt, check them out

If you are not sure about the vendor's honesty, play super sleuth. Note the licence plate and personal telephone numbers. See which name the phone line is registered under. If the person claims to own property, do a title search. Ensure you have both their home and business addresses.

Rule #3: Check references

Ask the vendor for both business and personal references, but be wary of personal references unless they come from a reputable source. Friends can provide glowing references for often shady characters. Ask for three recent trade references and ensure that the vendor is paying bills on time. Their bank may provide a credit reference with the vendor's permission. Ask for the vendor's bank manager's name.

Rule #4: Check the vendor's credentials

Checking a vendor's credentials is important, particularly if you are considering investing money into a new venture or a partnership. People seeking venture capital will often tell you anything to get their hands on your money. Some become quite desperate. Ask for a resumé and a list of previous employers, and check all references or contacts.

Rule #5: Check with other agencies

It is a simple procedure to check with the Better Business Bureau (see White Pages) for previous complaints about a business. They will fax you a free report, usually within 24 hours. If you are a member of a credit bureau, have a credit check performed on the company. If the vendor is a member of any associations, call them and ask for a reference. If the vendor is trustworthy, they won't mind you asking these questions. If there is any hesitation, take it as a warning.

HOW DO YOU ASSESS A POTENTIAL BUSINESS?

Study the business proposal

A motivated vendor should have prepared information on the business for sale, called a business proposal. They come in many shapes and sizes, and you may have to wade through a lot of information to find out whether this business is right for you. You will undoubtedly look at many proposals before getting excited about a particular one. As most people can't afford to consult their accountant about each one, learn to first analyze them yourself. Then you can weed out those that do not meet your criteria and give the ones of interest to your accountant.

A well-presented business proposal should contain all or most of the following information:

1. History and detailed operation of the business

2. Profiles and resumés of the company owner(s)

3. Profiles and resumés of key employees, if any

4. Summary of current and future markets

5. Details of relevant competitors

6. Details of property leases, description of location and its benefits

7. Full description of the assets for sale, including any training period and other services or guarantees offered with the business

8. Asking price and terms of payment

9. Financial statements (prepared by a reputable accountant) for the previous two years

10. Projected income and expenses for one to two years

11. Letters of reference from clients and suppliers

12. Any pending contracts or letters of intent from clients.

Many proposals don't contain all this information, so it's up to you to ask the vendor the right questions to fill in the gaps. Bear in mind that the vendor will present the business in its most positive light and probably play down any negative aspects.

Twelve important questions to ask

As you review the proposal, there are twelve significant areas that you need to analyze. Once you feel satisfied that you have answered all the following questions and still feel positive about the proposal, make an appointment with your accountant or business consultant and review the proposal together. If you do not understand some of the terminology, turn to the glossary of terms in Chapter 3.

1. Is this business profitable?

A business' profitability can be greatly determined by interpreting the financial statements. Therefore, ensure that they are prepared by a reputable accounting company. If possible, obtain two years' statements. They will show the assets, liabilities, equity and growth of the business, sales, cost of sales, operating expenses, the wages paid to staff and owners, and subsequent profits or losses. Your accountant can help you analyze them.

> ## $UCCE$$ $TRATEGY
>
> **PAY FOR THE PROFITS:** Be prepared to pay for a well-established, profitable business. It's worth it, because you will have an immediate guaranteed income. Take into account the hard work that someone else has put into the business. They have experienced the mistakes and the learning curves—that alone has to be worth something.

2. Can the business support your wage requirements?

If a business is not incorporated, the financial statements will not show the wages paid to the owners. Instead, the business should reflect a bottom line net profit high enough to satisfy the wage that you would like to take from the business. If it is incorporated, owners' wages will show as management fees. Wages will also be broken down into the various employee categories, such as manufacturing, sales and office.

You will first have to decide which role you and your family or partner will play in the business. Then look at the wages paid out each year on the financial statements. This will give you an idea of how much wage overhead the business can support. Take into account the profits (if any) after all expenses and your wage. They can be used as additional wages, as long as your wage requirement does not negatively affect the business' cash flow.

3. Are sales seasonal, increasing or decreasing?

When you look at the annual sales on a financial statement, they don't reflect seasonal or month-by-month fluctuations. Ask the vendor to supply a two-year monthly sales breakdown so that you can assess seasonal fluctuations and decreases or increases in sales. The case study about Mel's Bookkeeping and Tax Services gives an example.

CASE STUDY

MEL'S BOOKKEEPING AND TAX SERVICES

Mel was selling a small bookkeeping and tax business showing annual sales of $68,500. The business incurred monthly costs of $2,000, and Mel drew $2,500 a month. The sales looked good, but when analyzing them month-by-month, this was the picture.

Monthly Sales for Mel's Bookkeeping and Tax Services

January	$ 6,000	July	$3,500
February	$ 7,000	August	$2,500
March	$ 9,000	September	$4,000
April	$12,000	October	$5,000
May	$ 9,000	November	$3,000
June	$ 6,000	December	$1,500

Analysis

Because the bulk of the bookkeeping income was from small businesses having their annual books and income taxes prepared, the first few months of the year were busy. But for five months, the business did not make enough to cover overhead and wages. Not only would the first six months be stressful with a heavy workload, it would also be difficult to plan cash flow to keep the business going for the rest of the year and plan to pay personal tax installments. One solution would be to train clients to bring in their books quarterly to even out the workload. Many businesses experience these seasonal fluctuations.

4. Are you paying too much for this business?

The sale price of a business is based on the value of the assets—equipment, buildings, furniture and inventory—plus goodwill. The business should reflect the ability to generate a steady wage. There is usually room to negotiate on the pricing, particularly if you and your accountant have performed a thorough analysis of the proposal.

5. Are the assets worth what is being asked?

If you purchased the shares of an incorporated company, the assets are usually sold at book value as listed on the financial statements. Book value is the cost of the assets less accumulated depreciation over the years. With a proprietorship, the vendor may put an unrealistically high value on the assets or show you misleading appraisals for the value of larger equipment. Never pay more than fair market value.

No matter what an appraisal says, equipment is really worth no more than its book value at the time of sale. This is how banks evaluate assets on loan applications. Some vendors and purchasers arrive at an agreed purchase price somewhere between book and market values. Evaluating the inventory will require astute knowledge of what you are buying. People inevitably end up with worthless inventory or overpriced equipment. See Rule #2 under "Seven rules for a successful purchase" later in this chapter for more information.

6. Is the goodwill realistically priced?

Goodwill is the term used to place a value on the intangible worth of the business. The figure is based on the business' reputation, its stability and its ability to generate both profits and a reasonable wage for the owners. Your accountant can help you decide whether the goodwill price is reasonable. If you are purchasing a franchise, the goodwill is usually a set amount and there is little room for negotiation.

One common calculation bases goodwill on the money the business generated as an owner's wage within a one-year period (although some vendors use a two-year calculation), plus any net profits. If the vendor is drawing an annual wage of $40,000, or $65,000 with a spouse, then the goodwill could be as high as $65,000. If the business is still making a profit after these wages are drawn, then the goodwill may be worth even more. If it is losing money after these wages are drawn, then the goodwill amount should be reduced.

7. Do you have the experience to keep the business profitable?

A new business is a challenge, and as the owner, you are responsible for its success. Ask the vendor about the role he or she plays in the business. Can you adequately fill these shoes or afford to pay someone else to? Remember to address those four main roles in business—operations, administration, sales and marketing.

CASE STUDY

MISSING THE MECHANICS OF BUSINESS

Tony and Pradeep purchased a mechanical repair business. Pradeep had some mechanical experience, gained mainly from tinkering and a short night school course, while Tony was meticulous at paperwork. He had operated his own micro-business for many years.

When they took over the store, things didn't go quite as planned. The operation required a vast knowledge of different components, and the paperwork, accounting, inventory management, sales and marketing were more than a full-time job. Extra staff was hired to keep the business operational. The first two years produced a dramatic loss due to mismanagement at all levels. The stress caused Tony and Pradeep to argue and led to the eventual downfall of the business.

8. Could this business be expanded?

Diversification is the key to growth, and planned growth is the key to success. How else could this business expand or diversify into other areas? If it is a retail store, what other lines or services could be introduced? For a service business, how could you expand, increase or improve this service? For a seasonal business, how could you diversify during the quieter periods? If you cannot expand or diversify, what else can you do to increase sales?

9. What mistakes did the owners make that you should avoid?

Your accountant will highlight any areas of concern in the financial statements. The balance sheet may show too much inventory, a growing bank overdraft or perhaps too many outstanding accounts receivables. Government taxes may be overdue. The statement of income and expenses will highlight areas of overspending, such as wages or advertising. The profit margins after cost of sales may not be as high as you have been told. Ask the vendor these questions. From there, you have to decide whether you could run the business more efficiently. What would you change? What can be changed? What will take time to change? What would such changes cost?

10. What is the life expectancy of this business?

Your business needs a built-in longevity to survive. Research the history of the industry, study consumer trends and be reasonably certain that your business will still be performing profitably in the next five to ten years. For example, one long-term business trend is computer servicing, repair and customer education. Few businesses can survive without technology these days, and many owners do not fully understand how to use the various software programs.

Consumers are fickle. They drive the world trends and trends change quickly. Some businesses do not continue to grow because they refuse to keep up with both trends and technology. Is the business you are purchasing keeping up with these changes? How will future trends affect its growth?

11. Who makes the most profit—the franchiser or you?

With a franchise, you need to know exactly what percentage of profits is going into the franchiser's pockets. You will probably pay a percentage of gross sales as a royalty or toward advertising costs. Some franchises require an annual fee for overhead costs. With an existing franchise chain, those numbers will already be available to study.

You will pay a franchise fee, or goodwill on purchase, and depending on the franchise's reputation, this can be tens of thousands of dollars. In some cases, franchises make more money than their operators. Think about how much ice cream or how many cups of coffee you have to sell to cover these costs.

12. Are projections realistic?

Projections of future income, expenses and profits should be based on past performance, factoring in the present and future economy and trends. Few projections live up to their claims because too many factors can change at any moment. So don't take them at face value. It makes more sense to study past financial statements. If they reflect a loss yet the projections reflect healthy profits in the coming year or two, ask what magic formula the business will be using to achieve these figures and market that formula yourself—you'll get rich a lot quicker!

$UCCE$$ $TRATEGY

QUESTION A PROJECTION: Projections are just one person's idea of how the business may perform in the next one or two years. It's amazing what one can do with numbers and a spreadsheet. They are only as good as the substantiated reasoning behind them, so ensure that they are based on past history, current performance, and relevant current and future market trends, expansion potential, and sales and marketing strategies.

Seven rules for a successful purchase

If after answering all these questions, you still have a burning desire to buy this business, the next step is to delve even further. Here are seven rules to help you to further evaluate the business' viability.

Rule #1: Take a thorough inventory of the premises

The reputation of the business in the marketplace is important to your success. A good reputation is based on management and technical expertise, quality products and customer service. If you would be taking over an existing location, it's time for a field trip. Take note of the overall appearance of the premises. They should be a clean, cheery, well decorated and comfortable. Answer the questions in Figure 2.4 on your field trip.

Figure 2.4: HOW TO EVALUATE THE PREMISES

Take an inventory of the premises and ensure all these questions are answered.

	Yes	No
1. Is the staff friendly?	❏	❏
2. Are the products attractively displayed?	❏	❏
3. Do prices seem competitive?	❏	❏
4. Is there sufficient, up-to-date inventory?	❏	❏
5. Are the employees happy in their work?	❏	❏
6. Will they stay on after a change of ownership?	❏	❏
7. Do you know their areas of expertise?	❏	❏
8. Is the location suitable for this type of business?	❏	❏
9. Do you know what improvements are needed?	❏	❏
10. Are these improvements costly?	❏	❏
11. If leased, do you know when the rent will increase?	❏	❏
12. Do you know how long the lease is for?	❏	❏
13. Will you have the first option to renew the lease?	❏	❏

Talk to the employees and ask lots of questions. Take someone experienced with you for a second opinion. You need to be sure that equipment is in good working order and that the internal operation is efficient. Ask to see the lease and talk to the landlord.

$UCCE$$ $TRATEGY

DON'T BUY JUNK: Ensure that the inventory is all marketable and that no obsolete or unsaleable items are included. If there are useless products, make a deal to either purchase them at a low cost or have the book value deleted from the final inventory purchase price. Then it is the vendor's responsibility to dispose of these items.

Rule #2: Perform a physical inventory of the assets

The proposal should contain a list of assets and inventory for sale with the business. Take it with you and physically check each asset, ensuring that you see everything on the list. Note model and serial numbers of larger pieces of equipment. You can phone around later to verify that you are paying a fair price. Ask what type of regular repairs and maintenance the equipment requires and when it last broke down or was serviced.

CASE STUDY

OUTDATED AND OBSOLETE

Sid and Ray were interested in buying a store that carried a large inventory worth nearly $100,000. It was a well-established business, with much of the inventory consisting of rebuilt stock and used spare parts. Their knowledge of this equipment was basic, so under their accountant's advice, they spent three weeks thoroughly physically checking the inventory, finally arriving at a price reduction. What they didn't do was take along someone who had expertise with that type of equipment. After the first year of operation, they realized that much of it was useless. Of the remaining inventory, large, expensive pieces sat on the floor without moving all year. These pieces had to be reduced to cost to regain some cash flow. Sid and Ray finally dumped the old stock at a loss of $30,000.

As a new purchaser, you may not be aware of what sells and what does not. You don't want to purchase inventory that will not turn quickly, as this depletes your operating capital and cash flow. If in doubt, contract a company to evaluate the inventory (see Inventory Services in the Yellow Pages). They may also be able to suggest an appraiser for your equipment.

For example, one client of mine was buying a business including a piece of equipment valued at $6,500. When I requested the financial figures, the equipment turned out to be quite old, having a book value of only $2,300. My client then offered the book value price for the equipment, saving $4,200.

Rule #3: Discuss all information with your accountant

Professionally prepared proposals can boggle your mind with hype, exciting words, facts and figures. Don't buy a business without some pertinent written information and financial figures. Be wary of financial figures prepared by the business, as people can be extremely creative with their accounting. They must use a professional accountant to validate the financial statement's authenticity.

You *have* to use an accountant to review a proposal. He or she will prepare a list of questions to be asked or will ask those questions for you. Accountants can read the whole history of a business in financial statements. Your accountant will contact the accountant who prepared the statements and will know the right questions to ask. As an example, if just one outstanding supplier account for $3,000 is not entered into the books, the profits will be overstated by $3,000.

Rule #4: Have a proper agreement for sale prepared

Don't purchase any business without having a legal agreement for sale prepared. It will protect both you and the vendor. Without this document, you have no recourse when trouble arises—and it can. Your agreement becomes a valuable document in court. (This subject is covered in more depth in Chapter 5.)

Rule #5: Visit your local municipal office

A visit to your local municipal or council office enables you to check that the company has not infringed on or broken any local bylaw or environmental laws. Check pending or possible future bylaws that could be detrimental to the business. Planning and engineering departments can tell you whether there are pending changes to zoning regulations or traffic route changes. New road construction may involve cutting off store access, sending customers to competitors. There may be new malls being built near you. You don't need a new competitor opening a sparkling new store next door a few months down the road.

$UCCE$$ $TRATEGY

FIRST KNOW THE HOME-BASED BYLAWS: If the business you are considering will be home-based, become familiar with the home-based bylaws. Most have restrictions on retail sales, manufacturing, the type of business, traffic generation, office size and building usage. Many home-based businesses have been closed down due to bylaw infractions, and it's usually your friendly neighbour who will report you.

Rule #6: Research your competition and the market

No matter how well the business appears to be doing physically and on paper, presume that the competition is still fierce. Find out who your competitors are, what type of products they sell and what their pricing structures are. What does this business offer that is better than the competition?

The business may be seriously affected by consumer spending trends, continued downturns in the economy, environmental issues or advancing technology. It may have performed adequately to date or may show a slight drop in sales over the previous year or two. No matter what the vendor tells you, thorough market research will indicate current and future trends. (Chapter 4 deals with market research and strategies in depth.)

Rule #7: Don't start a business on a shoestring

Purchasing or starting a business on a shoestring budget or with big loans is usually a formula for disaster. Prepare a business plan that includes projections and cash flow forecasts. See Chapter 7 for more information on business plans. Your business has to meet loan payments one month after you open your doors. Allow time for take-over or start-up, a period when revenues may drop or expenses may be higher than normal. If you ruin your credit rating by defaulting on loan payments, it will take years to repair. You are also threatening the growth and success of your business if you can't spend the necessary dollars to keep it fully operational.

As you research this business, consider the questions in Figure 2.5.

Figure 2.5: BUSINESS PURCHASE CHECKLIST		
Use this checklist to guide you through the purchase.		
	Yes	**No**
1. I've searched the company name and had it validated.	❏	❏
2. I've validated the vendor's personal credentials.	❏	❏
3. I've validated business and trade references.	❏	❏
4. I've researched the business location, the lease and employees.	❏	❏
5. I've evaluated the assets and inventory and they are satisfactory.	❏	❏
6. I've discussed the business proposal with my accountant.	❏	❏
7. My lawyer has prepared the agreement for sale.	❏	❏
8. The municipal approval and research are completed.	❏	❏
9. I've researched the competition and market.	❏	❏
10. I have sufficient funds available to start and operate this business.	❏	❏

	Yes	No
11. This business is definitely a profitable concern.	❑	❑
12. This business can pay me a satisfactory wage.	❑	❑
13. The sales figures are steady and not declining.	❑	❑
14. I can operate the business competently.	❑	❑
15. My accountant agrees that the price is satisfactory.	❑	❑
16. The assets are fairly evaluated.	❑	❑
17. The goodwill is fairly priced.	❑	❑
18. This business could be diversified or expanded.	❑	❑
19. I am aware of mistakes made by the previous owner.	❑	❑
20. This business has a definite long-term life.	❑	❑
21. This franchise makes acceptable profits.	❑	❑
22. The projected returns are realistic and attainable.	❑	❑

WHAT IS THE NEXT STEP?

Before you progress any further, you now need to understand the ins and outs of financial figures, because that's what being in business is all about—making sales and making profits. It is difficult to make informed decisions or prepare a business plan if you don't understand accounting terminology and financial statements. The next chapter will give you a crash course in both these areas. As most people hate accounting, you had better make a fresh cup of coffee and grit your teeth—the more you know, the better prepared you will be for success.

CHAPTER 3

What is a financial statement?

*A balanced life is one where the assets
far outweigh the liabilities.*

WHY DO WE NEED ACCOUNTING?

Accounting is one of the few languages that is universally understood. Businesses throughout the world record their transactions using what is called the double-entry bookkeeping method. I believe this system was invented by an ancient Greek. No wonder people look at their financial statements and mutter, "It all looks like Greek to me." Yet to survive and succeed in business, you should learn this foreign language, its terminology and its unique bookkeeping methods. Once you get the hang of it, it makes a lot of sense.

The majority of business owners glance at their financial statements when their accountant prepares them annually, and then throw them into the filing cabinet, usually after complaining about both their tax and accounting bills. Yet these documents are the lifeline of a business and the only true tool that monitors the performance of a business to the penny—if the bookkeeping is accurate.

Learn to love financial statements

Running a business is no different from running your household. Your home and contents are your assets and the mortgage and unpaid bills are liabilities. The difference between the value of your assets less the debts is called equity. We all know what equity in our home means. Your paycheque is the income which should accommodate the home expenses such as food, mortgage or rent, clothing and utilities. The money you have left over (if any) is your profit.

DEFINITION OF A FINANCIAL STATEMENT

> *A financial statement is a snapshot taken of your business at a given time. Usually this picture is taken at a month-end. It will tell you what the business owns (its assets), what it owes (its liabilities), your capital and equity in the business, what the sales were, what it cost to make those sales, what the business overhead was and how much profit (or loss) the business made.*

Financial statements are essential business management tools because you will be making many decisions based on this information, including whether to buy an existing business or not. Just as you would not buy a used vehicle without having a mechanic do a thorough check or purchase an expensive jewel without an appraisal, you wouldn't buy a business without first establishing the accuracy of the financial figures. Financial statements paint a vivid picture of your business' progress and will guide you toward making sound decisions. So learn to treat them as your friend, not a necessary evil.

$UCCE$$ $TRATEGY

THINK AHEAD: The smart operator will review financial statements at least quarterly. You can catch mistakes and review problem areas before they worsen, and use the statements to plan ahead. They show you sales fluctuations, profit margin changes, cost increases, overhead fluctuations and changes in net profit. They will tell you whether you are further in debt or have too much cash tied up in inventory or receivables. You can plan your personal tax position and strategies for growing your business.

As a consultant, clients don't leave my office until they have received a thorough lesson in interpreting their statements. It may take a few cups of coffee, but you cannot operate a business without understanding what is happening to it.

Financial statements can be prepared monthly, quarterly, half-yearly or annually. Most small businesses only have an annual statement prepared for tax purposes. This is seat-of-the-pants management, which leads to large holes and is one main reason why so many businesses fail. Problem areas develop, but no one takes the time to notice or analyze why.

To make this fun subject a little easier, each term found on a financial statement is defined in this chapter. Understanding financial statements is probably the most difficult subject to digest, so hang in there—the reading gets easier once you have grasped the basic concepts.

How do the figures get there?

Financial statements don't just magically appear at the press of a button. A full accounting cycle must first be completed. To better understand how financial statements are produced and the importance of accurate paperwork and bookkeeping, let's examine the accounting cycle.

1. Source documents

The first rule of accounting is to keep a receipt for everything, from the research stage right through to start-up and onwards. (See Chapter 11 for your record-keeping and accounting lesson.) These papers are called "source documents," and include invoices, cheques, credit card accounts, bank deposits, bills and receipts. Each month, these source documents are recorded into various books, or ledgers, using the double-entry bookkeeping system.

2. Double-entry bookkeeping system

When source documents are recorded into the various ledgers, either manually or using an accounting software program, one entry is always a debit and one a credit. As Figure 3.1 shows, one entry describes the transaction and the other acts as a control, for example, when your cheques are reconciled to the bank statement. At the end of each month, all transactions are totalled, with debit columns equalling credit columns. The balances are then transferred to a general ledger, which is set up in order of the financial statement's accounts. The general ledger is used to prepare financial statements. Figure 3.1 gives an example of paying a telephone account and entering it to the cheque register or disbursements journal.

Date	Paid to	Cheque #	Bank out	Telephone	GST
			(Credit)	(Debit)	(Debit)
06/26/xx	AT&T	7824	176.55	165.00	11.55
			(Control)	**(Expense description)**	

Figure 3.1: PHONE PAYMENT USING DOUBLE-ENTRY BOOKKEEPING

3. The six-step accounting cycle

Without giving you a complete bookkeeping lesson, Figure 3.2 shows how those source documents are turned into a financial statement in six steps.

Figure 3.2: THE SIX-STEP ACCOUNTING CYCLE

1. Source documents are recorded into various journals and balanced at the end of the month.

2. Monthly balances are transferred into the general ledger, which is then balanced.

3. Your accountant usually prepares other entries called general journal entries, such as depreciation.

4. A trial balance is prepared. This is the total of the debits and credits in the general ledger.

5. From these figures, a financial statement is prepared.

6. Income and expense accounts are closed off annually and balance sheet items carried forward to the next fiscal year.

WHAT INFORMATION IS IN A FINANCIAL STATEMENT?

A financial statement follows a set format, consisting of the following sections:

1. Notice to reader or review engagement report

2. Balance sheet

3. Statement of retained earnings (if incorporated)

4. Statement of income and expenses

5. Notes to financial statements

6. Statement of changes in financial position.

1. Notice to reader or review engagement report

A financial statement opens with either a notice to reader or a review engagement report. This is a statement from the accountant to the business owner telling you which method was used to prepare the statements.

A notice to reader states that the accountant has prepared the information provided from the records of the business, but "has not reviewed, audited, or otherwise attempted to verify the accuracy or completeness of such information or determined whether these statements contain departures from generally accepted accounting principles." Some even state that "These statements are for internal use of management and for income tax purposes only. Accordingly, readers are cautioned that these statements may not be appropriate for their purposes."

Most small businesses have a notice to reader prepared, as a review engagement report is a more expensive and time-consuming process, used mainly by larger businesses. For a review engagement report, the accountant performs more in-depth checks and cross-checks.

With a notice to reader, although accountants perform certain checks, they cannot guarantee that the accounting is correct. Bank accounts may be reconciled and all information processed, but the information may not be correctly allocated or information may be missing. If you are buying a business, contact the accountant who prepared the statements to verify the accuracy of the books and records. If the person preparing the books does not have an accounting background, errors are sure to occur.

You will find the word "unaudited" on each statement page. This means that the accountant has not performed a full audit of the books. Audited statements are usually required for non-profit organizations or businesses that have gone public on the stock exchange. They are costly and not necessary for the average business.

2. Balance sheet

A balance sheet reflects the value of the business at a given month-end date: its assets, liabilities and the current equity in the business, as well as how much profit (or loss) the company is making. It reflects the ending balances at the completion of the fiscal period for which the statement was prepared.

3. Statement of retained earnings

Applicable only to incorporated businesses, this page is an ongoing record of the business' profits or losses for both the period in question and since inception. It shows the opening balance for the period and adds or subtracts the current profits or losses, reflecting a new closing balance. These figures are a similar calculation to the equity section of an unincorporated business.

4. Statement of income and expenses

This statement reflects all sales and other income the business has generated for the period, less all expenses. The "bottom line" indicates the net profit or loss the company has incurred for the fiscal year to date. An example is given in Figure 3.4 of this chapter.

5. Notes to financial statements

At the end of the financial statements, the accountant provides details as to how certain figures were calculated. These include how inventory was costed, when the business was incorporated, the rates of depreciation used, the terms of loans and shareholder loans and any other information that Canada Customs and Revenue Agency (CCRA) or banks may need to see.

6. Statement of changes in financial position

A statement of changes in financial position is only prepared for some incorporated businesses. Banks like this type of information. It details where the money came from during the year (profits or loans) and how the money was used (to finance a loss, pay back loans or purchase assets). It shows the working capital of the business and whether it has increased or decreased during the year.

ACCOUNTING TERMS AND DEFINITIONS

During your entrepreneurial career, you will hear many new words and terms. Now is the time to learn what they mean. The terms are explained here, in the same order as they appear on a typical financial statement.

Balance sheet terms

Assets: *Everything the business owns.* These include bank accounts, inventory, accounts receivable, equipment, buildings, vehicles, computers, deposits and investments. Assets are broken down on the balance sheet into current assets and fixed assets.

Current assets: *Any asset the company owns that could be turned into cash within one year.* These are listed in order with the most current, cash in the bank, first.

Cash at bank: *The total cash in all bank accounts.* Each account is reconciled (balanced) with the bank statement or bank book, to the penny. When you read the statements, all bank accounts will be grouped together as one total. If the balance is overdrawn, it will show farther down as a liability.

Accounts receivable: *Uncollected debts owing to the business.* This amount should be balanced to a client list of monies due, called a receivables list or an aged analysis. The age of the debt is separated into current, 30, 60, 90 days and over. This list should be prepared monthly and used to help you collect outstanding accounts.

Prepaid expenses and deposits: *Expenses paid ahead of the statement date and/or funds or deposits in trust.* Examples of prepaid expenses include the last month's rent on a lease, a deposit on hydro service and annual insurance policies.

A policy paid in July with a December business year-end has six months of the policy prepaid, which is an expense for the next fiscal period. Prepaid expenses also include equipment maintenance contracts, vehicle and shop insurance, and property taxes. Your accountant will calculate these figures for you.

Inventory: The value at cost of unsold materials or products. This includes manufacturing raw materials, goods purchased for redistribution or finished goods. An inventory evaluation must be taken when a statement is prepared. Old, obsolete or slow-moving products should be devalued in price at year-end and included in this figure. Assets or consumables, such as stationery, are not considered inventory as they are not resold.

Work in progress: Partially completed contracts, services or manufactured products not yet billed to clients. The value of the work to date is estimated and classified as work in progress instead of being called accounts receivable.

Fixed assets: An asset owned and utilized by the business. These consist of equipment or similar items with a singular value of over $200. Smaller items, for example, a calculator, are overhead expenses. Fixed assets are listed at purchase cost, not appraised value. They include furniture, fittings, computers, cellular phones, buildings, vehicles, manufacturing equipment, land, machinery, telephone systems and leasehold improvements.

Leasehold improvements: A permanent addition to a structure. These are assets that remain in the building if a company closes or moves, and include new carpeting, lighting, shelves or renovations to a building. (See the definitions for depreciation and amortization following to see what happens then.)

Accumulated capital cost allowance (CCA) and depreciation: An allowance made for the wear and tear on a capital item (asset). Each type of fixed asset has a defined rate of depreciation, determined by CCRA. For example, computers depreciate annually at a rate of 30 percent, furniture at 20 percent. Your accountant will depreciate your assets for you and the current year's depreciation shows on the income and expense statement. Accumulated capital cost allowance is the total depreciation claimed since the asset was purchased.

Amortization: The allowance for wear and tear on certain fixed assets. Leasehold improvements are a good example. If you signed a five-year lease and spent $10,000 on improving a building, your accountant would depreciate these leasehold improvements over a five-year period, or at a rate of $2,000 a year.

The balance sheet shows the amount of amortization claimed since the improvements were made.

Net book value: *The difference between the purchase price of an asset less accumulated depreciation.* For example, if equipment is shown at a value of $40,000 and accumulated depreciation is $35,400, the net book value is $4,600. This tells you that the equipment has been around for a long time. Net book value reflects an asset's true value.

Incorporation fees: *Fees paid to incorporate a business.* Although this cost is usually shown under "other assets," some accountants show it as an expense on the statement of income and expenses. Don't query the logic—that's the way it is.

Goodwill: *The intangible dollar value paid for a business.* If a person purchased the business before you, they probably paid a certain amount for goodwill, and in turn will charge you a goodwill sum. It is amortized over a period of years.

Total assets: *The sum of current, fixed and other assets, less accumulated capital cost allowance.* This amount reflects the book value of all assets at the end of the accounting period.

Liabilities: *The total of all debts owing by the business.* These are broken down into current liabilities and long-term liabilities.

Current liabilities: *Debts owed by the business that are due and payable within one year.* These include bank overdrafts, short-term loans, supplier accounts (accounts payable), federal and provincial taxes payable, and employee payroll deductions due to CCRA and Workers' Compensation.

Long-term liabilities: *A debt due and payable over a period of years.* Examples are equipment loans, bank loans, mortgages, loans from friends and shareholders' loans. The principal portion due for each loan within one year is recorded under current liabilities. The remaining balance shows under long-term liabilities. Your accountant calculates these balances for you.

Equity: *The amount of money the business owes the owner.* In a proprietorship, this is the capital put in by the owner less money taken out, plus or minus profits or losses. In an incorporated company, equity consists of the shares issued, plus or minus profits and losses.

The balance sheet equation: Total assets equal the total of liabilities plus equity. This is the magic of double-entry bookkeeping—it really works. Figure 3.3 shows a simple transaction.

Figure 3.3: A SIMPLE BALANCE SHEET EQUATION

Andrew invested $50,000 to start a mobile gymnasium business. He used $20,000 of his own money and borrowed $30,000 from the bank to purchase a vehicle.

His current asset is cash in the bank	$15,000	=	ASSET
His fixed asset is automotive equipment	$35,000	=	ASSET
His long-term liability is a bank loan	$30,000	+	LIABILITY
His capital is his equity	$20,000	+	EQUITY
(Or shareholder's loan if incorporated)			

Balance sheet equation:
Assets ($50,000) = Liabilities ($30,000) + Equity ($20,000)

Cash flow: The movement of money in and out of a business. A business with "poor cash flow" will have trouble paying its bills. "Planning your cash flow" means projecting when and how the money will come into the business and where and when it will be spent. A "healthy cash flow" means a business is operating at peak efficiency and has enough money to pay its liabilities.

Working capital: The difference between the dollar value of current assets and current liabilities. A bank will always look at a business' working capital when considering a loan application. The theory is that if you turned all your current assets into cash and paid off all your current bills, a healthy company should have some cash left over. In many cases, the equation seems to work the other way. Here is an example of healthy working capital:

Current assets:	$27,942
Less current liabilities:	15,355
Working capital:	$12,587

Statement of income and expenses terms

A statement of income and expenses graphically illustrates how a business operates over a given period. It is usually broken down into three or four sections and gives management valuable information. It shows all income, cost of sales, gross and net profits and overhead expenses. Using a furniture store as an example, a statement of income and expenses is given in Figure 3.4.

Income (sales or revenue): The total of all revenue sources earned from a business. Income is mainly derived from sales but also includes interest earned from bank accounts, royalties and commissions. It does not include funds from loans, and can be broken down into various categories to help you further analyze sales.

Cost of sales: The actual costs incurred to generate a sale before operating overhead. Each business incurs different sales costs, dependent on the type of business. They can be broken down into cost of sales and then direct sales costs. Cost of sales usually applies to a business that carries inventory. This calculation is the cost of manufacturing, distributing or retailing a product. A service business, such as consulting, incurs overhead costs only.

Direct or sales costs: The expenses incurred to sell a product. These expenses can be separated from normal cost of sales to analyze expenses applicable to selling products. This is useful as it helps you better monitor your profit margins.

Gross profit: The difference between the selling price and the cost of sales. This is a vital area to monitor, because it is the gross profit that pays for the overhead expenses and your wages. It is expressed as a percentage of sales on a financial statement and should be consistent with your expected profit margins.

Overhead expenses: Costs incurred to sustain the business operation. These expenses include items such as rent, telephones and insurance. Some costs do not change whether sales are made or not. Some increase or decrease depending on sales volume, such as advertising. They are listed in alphabetical order on a financial statement.

Net profit/(loss): The profit (or loss) after all expenses and before corporate or personal taxes. Often referred to as the "bottom line," this is the profit that the business generated after all costs were incurred. An incorporated business or a proprietorship pays tax on this amount. Figure 3.4 shows an example of a furniture store's income and expense statement and a description and analysis of the results.

Figure 3.4: STATEMENT OF INCOME AND EXPENSES FOR JUDY'S HOME FURNISHINGS INC.

Revenue:

By furniture sales	$ 62,000	
By bedding sales	45,000	
By small item sales	18,000	
	$125,000	

Cost of sales:

Opening inventory	$ 12,000	(Furniture in inventory at beginning of period)
Purchases	50,000	(All furniture purchased for the period)
Freight in	1,000	(Freight costs to deliver furniture to store)
Customs & duty	5,000	(Import, customs and brokerage charges)
	68,000	
Less closing inventory	(9,000)	(Cost price of unsold inventory at end of period)
Total cost of sales:	$ 59,000	
Gross profit: (53%)	**$ 66,000**	(Cost of sales subtracted from sales)

(Gross profit is calculated by dividing $66,000 into $125,000 as a percentage. This is the gross profit on retail, not cost price.)

Direct sales costs:

Wages—sales staff	$ 25,000	(Wages paid to sales staff)
Discounts	1,000	(Discounts given on sales)
Damaged goods	500	(Damaged furniture written off)
Delivery expense	3,000	(Delivery costs to clients)
Total direct costs:	$ 29,500	
Gross profit: (29%)	**$ 36,500**	(Direct costs subtracted from gross profit)

Overhead expenses:

Accounting fees	$ 500	(Cost to prepare statement)
Advertising	2,000	(Newspapers, flyers, magazine advertising)
Bad debts	200	(Uncollectible accounts receivables)
Bank charges	500	(Monthly bank and credit card fees)
CPP & EI expense	2,800	(Employer portion of CPP and EI)
Depreciation	2,500	(Allowance for wear and tear of assets)
Fees, licences, dues	300	(Licences, dues to organizations)
Interest, loans	1,500	(Loan interest for period)
Legal fees	400	(Legal fees, excluding incorporation)

Management salaries	15,000	(Shareholders' salaries, incorporated company)
Office stationery	1,500	(Printing, coffee and office supplies)
Office salaries	7,000	(Clerical wages)
Promotion	1,200	(Client gifts, incentives, open houses, etc.)
Rent & taxes	5,000	(Monthly rent and property taxes)
Repairs & maintenance	700	(Store repairs, general maintenance)
Shop supplies	500	(Odds and ends, small tools)
Telephone, cell, computer	800	(Line rentals, long distance, Internet, cellular)
Utilities	1,200	(Light, heat and water)
Workers' Compensation	800	(Workers' Compensation)
Total overhead	$ 44,400	
Net profit/(loss):	**$ ($7,900)**	**Loss**

Analysis of a statement of income and expenses

It appears that Judy's Home Furnishings Inc. has a few problems. The gross profit margin is healthy at $66,000 or 53 percent after cost of sales, but when sales wages and overhead costs are deducted, there is no profit left. Wages total $47,000, or 37.6 percent of costs. The total cost of sales is $88,500 or 71 percent of sales. Add on all wages, and cost of sales plus wages equals $110,500. This leaves a measly 11.6 percent of sales, or $14,500 to cover the overhead costs. This store employs four people—two sales staff, the owner and a bookkeeper. Either the wages are too high or the sales are too low. Perhaps staff hours should be reduced or a better marketing strategy implemented.

The other overhead costs are not far out of line. Marketing is necessary, and as a general rule, four to seven percent of sales should be allocated to promotion, and $2,000 represents only 1.6 percent of sales. Other overhead costs could be slightly trimmed but the main problem appears to be high wages that are not supported by sufficient sales.

HOW TO ANALYZE A FINANCIAL STATEMENT

Learn how to read financial statements and practise interpreting the various pictures that financial statements paint. Practise using the Complete Computer Care Centre's case study. Read the statements in Figure 3.5 and see what they tell you. Write down your observations before reading the analysis.

CASE STUDY

COMPLETE COMPUTER CARE CENTRE

Marcel started a home-based computer sales and service business called Complete Computer Care Centre. At the end of his second year, he took his books to his accountant to have the year-end and taxes prepared. When he started his business, Marcel's idea was to educate and service clients in all facets of computer technology, from designing the right system to suit their needs, purchasing and installation, software education, consulting and problem-solving to equipment service and repair.

He purchased his equipment from a reputable supplier who extended good warranties. Because the industry was so competitive, he knew that his gross margins on equipment were not much over ten percent. But with the busy lifestyle that many of his small business clients led, he hoped to encourage them to hire him to solve all their problems, from installing the new system and software to networking and upgrading their systems with new technology—such as firewalls, new anti-virus software and scanners. Using technology, Marcel could fix many clients' problems by connecting to their computers from his office, saving unnecessary travelling time and costs.

Marcel purchased the latest computer equipment for himself and this year he borrowed money from the bank to buy a used van. His father lent him $15,000 to start the business, which was not due until he had completed four years in business. He purchased some new systems for resale near the end of the year, as they were "a steal" and he knew he could make a better profit on them. He always kept some equipment in inventory.

It was a competitive field and Marcel found that he was busy reading and educating himself to keep up with the latest technological advances. He attended a conference in the U.S. and actively promoted his business through both networking and various marketing strategies. Marcel's hourly billing rate for consulting and service calls was $95, a reasonable industry billing charge. He paid a bookkeeper to prepare his books every three months, and subcontracted out some of the work that he could not handle. He had a new Web page designed and kept it high on the search engines. He was married with a lovely wife and had a second child on the way. Life was hectic. At the end of the year, Figure 3.5 shows how his financial statements looked. What do you observe from these figures?

Figure 3.5: ANALYZING COMPLETE COMPUTER CARE CENTRE'S FINANCIAL STATEMENTS

Complete Computer Care Centre
Balance Sheet
December 31, XXXX
(Unaudited)

ASSETS

Current assets:

Cash at bank	$ 3,237	
Accounts receivable	7,310	
Inventories	18,247	
Prepayments & deposits	310	29,104

Fixed assets:

Computer equipment	25,500	
Office furniture	3,170	
Automotive equipment	15,750	
	44,420	
Less accumulated CCA	(13,263)	
		31,157
Total assets:		**$60,261**

LIABILITIES

Current liabilities:

Accounts payable	$23,862	
GST/HST & provincial taxes	8,198	
Current portion bank loan	3,150	35,210

Long-term liabilities:

Bank loan	14,400	
Loan, R. Matthews	15,000	29,400
		64,610

EQUITY

Balance beginning of period:	$ 1,290	
Contributed capital for period:	1,210	
	2,500	
Net profit for period:	7,757	
	10,257	
Less draws for period:	(14,606)	(4,349)
Total liabilities and equity:		**$60,261**

Complete Computer Care Centre
Statement of Income and Expenses
December 31, XXXX
(Unaudited)

Revenue:

By computer sales	$ 82,250	
By parts and small items	22,978	
By consulting	10,341	
By service repairs	39,021	154,590

Cost of sales:

Opening inventory	7,830	
Purchases	104,175	
Freight in	2,790	
	114,795	
Less closing inventory	(18,247)	
		96,548

Gross profit: (37.5%)   **$58,042**

Overhead expenditure:

Accounting fees	1,800	
Advertising	3,120	
Bad debts	1,170	
Bank & credit card charges	2,635	
Computer supplies	3,470	
Depreciation	11,090	
Discounts	1,020	
Education, books, seminars	3,130	
Fees, licences	980	
Insurance	760	
Internet & Web site	3,210	
Loan interest	1,230	
Office supplies	910	
Promotion & marketing	2,310	
Rent & taxes	2,110	
Repairs & maintenance	790	
Small tools & shop supplies	910	
Subcontract labour	2,100	
Telephones	1,280	
Travel & accommodation	1,210	
Utilities	710	
Vehicle–gas	1,630	
Vehicle–repairs & maintenance	2,710	50,285
Net profit for period:		**$ 7,757**

How did Marcel manage?

When Marcel sat down with his accountant to review his financial statements, here are some of the observations that the accountant made and discussed with him. Did you identify any of these points?

The balance sheet story

Current assets: With little in the bank and $7,310 still to be collected from accounts receivable, Marcel's inventory is tying up much of his cash flow. On reviewing the age of the receivables, some were well over 90 days. Marcel found it difficult to call clients and ask for money, so his accounts payable were mounting up. Some of the accounts could become bad debts if he doesn't diligently pursue his collections.

Fixed assets: Because most of his assets depreciate at a rate of 30 percent a year, their net book value has dropped from $44,420 to $31,157 in two years. Depreciation is a large expense this year, accounting for $11,090.

Current liabilities: Marcel's accounts payable are high because of his large inventory purchase. He also hasn't paid installments on his GST for the year, and must find $8,198 by June 30th. Together, he has $32,060 to pay, and little in the bank. His focus must be to sell as much inventory as possible and collect his unpaid accounts.

Long-term liabilities: His bank loan still has over four years to be paid off, but the monthly loan payment must be made to ensure that he maintains a good credit rating. There is nothing to pay on his father's loan for another two years.

Equity: Marcel's equity in the business started at $1,290 this year, as he suffered a loss in his first year of start-up, which is subtracted from his equity portion. He didn't put much into the business, and only made $7,757 profit. However, he took out $14,606 from the business, double the amount of profit he made. This affects his cash flow and is one reason why his bills are piling up.

Working capital: Current assets are $29,104 and current liabilities $35,210. This affirms that Marcel is definitely experiencing a cash flow problem. With both the business overhead and a family to support, it's time to take a close look at how he is operating the business and how he could become more cost- and time-efficient.

The income and expenses statement story

Revenue: The annual revenue of $154,590 looks healthy for a one-person business, but if you analyze the equipment and parts sales, they constitute $105,228, or 68 percent of his income, which only generated an approximately 10 percent profit of $10,500. His consulting and service revenue totals $49,362, which represents 520 billable hours. If you divide that by 50 weeks, he is only billing 10.4 hours a week or two hours a day—not enough considering the time that he really puts into the business. His concept of "sell them a system and service them forever" is a good one, but perhaps he should work harder to build up his service clientele and then focus on selling new systems when he is generating more billable hours.

Cost of sales: Marcel didn't factor in a freight cost for some of the systems, and by working on such a small gross profit margin, his profit on computer sales was reduced from $11,410 to $8,688 or 8.26 percent. His gross profit looks high at 37.5 percent, but that is because his consulting and service work is included in the figures. Considering the time spent talking with clients, pricing systems, submitting quotations, picking up and delivering—including a free hour for set-up—Marcel is losing money as a systems supplier.

Overhead: Employing a bookkeeper to do the accounting is probably a wise move as accounting is not Marcel's forte; however, using subcontractors for work he doesn't have time for is not so wise. Ignoring collections cost him $1,170 in bad debts, and offering credit card payment options incurred big bank charges. The discounts could be discontinued; most people don't expect them on service accounts.

To keep up with changing technology, success in this industry requires that Marcel spend time and money on books, certification and education. It is a cost of doing business. Perhaps the trip to the U.S. could have been foregone for education closer to home. Most of the other costs are within reason for a small business, as long as Marcel's marketing and advertising are producing the desired results.

Summary: The net profit isn't enough to support Marcel, even adding back the depreciation, which is not a cash expense. He won't be paying any income taxes this year, which is not a healthy sign. It is better to pay taxes on profit earned, particularly as Canada Pension Plan contributions are calculated on this amount and help to provide for future retirement. Marcel needs to seriously rethink how he will focus his business in the coming year, as his cash flow is in a precarious position. His best bet is to revisit, re-evaluate and revise his business plan—and listen closely to his accountant.

The five-minute financial test in Figure 3.6 will test your knowledge of this chapter and the meaning of some of the basic accounting terms. The answers are on the following page, so complete the exercise and no peeking.

Figure 3.6: THE FIVE-MINUTE FINANCIAL TEST

Test your knowledge of basic accounting terminology by filling the blanks as necessary.

1. A computer system is classified as an _____

2. An unpaid bill for stationery is called _____

3. A five-year bank loan is called a _____

4. The difference between sales and cost of sales is called _____

5. Accumulated capital cost allowance is _____

6. In a proprietorship, a loss is _____ from equity.

7. Purchases, freight and duty are all part of _____

8. Advertising, telephone and shop supplies are called _____

9. Current assets and current liabilities are payable within _____

10. In a proprietorship, money contributed by the owner is called _____

11. Working capital is calculated by subtracting _____ from _____

12. Unpaid sales invoices due by clients are called _____

13. The unpaid taxes charged on sales invoices are called _____

14. The annual allowance made for the wear and tear of assets is called _____

15. Net book value is the cost of an asset less _____

ANSWERS TO THE FIVE-MINUTE FINANCIAL TEST

1. Asset

2. Accounts payable

3. Long-term liability

4. Gross profit

5. The amount of depreciation of an asset since purchase

6. Deducted

7. Cost of sales

8. Overhead expenses

9. Twelve months

10. Capital

11. Current liabilities from current assets

12. Accounts receivable

13. Current liabilities

14. Depreciation

15. Accumulated capital cost allowance

WHAT IS THE NEXT STEP?

Now that you have a better understanding of business and accounting terminology, the next step is to start researching the market to see if your business idea will work for you. Until you complete this process, you can't be sure that there is a niche or need to take your concept and turn it into a viable, income-generating business.

CHAPTER 4

How do you research the market?

You have an idea, but will it fly?
Research will confirm your piece of the pie.

DOES YOUR IDEA HAVE MARKET POTENTIAL?

At some point in our lives, many of us have thought of a brilliant business idea. The successful ones are those who take their golden idea and thoroughly research the market. Now it's time to take your dreams and ideas and discover how practically they can be applied to a business. The first step is to identify a *need* and a *niche* in the marketplace. Remember those two words—need and niche. Don't aim for a huge slice of the pie. The next step is to see whether a small slice of the market will support your business idea and your lifestyle.

How many times have you heard people say "I have the greatest idea for a business! This is going to be a winner!" The vision of being their own boss and the dough rolling in blinds many would-be entrepreneurs as they plunge quickly and fruitlessly into a money-losing venture.

Researching a new business' potential is one vital area where many people fall down, cutting the process short in their haste to get started. Doing your homework can be tedious and takes weeks—even months, depending on the size and complexity of the business. But long-term, the efforts are well worth it. Your new business will have greater longevity and success if you know your exact place in the market and the competition that you face.

Keeping up with technology and changing marketing techniques are huge challenges. Those who cater toward long-term future trends will have an excellent starting point. Those who drift into something in an unorganized manner will drop out quickly.

Will your business solve clients' problems?

A business should offer solutions to people's problems. You are not selling a service or a product, you are selling a solution. Change is constant, so factor it into your plans. The most valuable commodity these days is time. The average person is too busy and "stressed out." Technological knowledge is a necessity. How can your business cater to solving these problems? What niche can you fill?

$UCCE$$ $TRATEGY

TAKE YOUR BUSINESS TO THE CUSTOMER: Think how you could simplify the stressed out home-based workers' lives if you brought your business to them or filled a need that isn't being filled. For example, people are now setting up in business as professional "declutterers" and organizers. They recognize the growing needs of busy people. Many large companies now cater to this overworked market, including Staples Business Depot's home delivery program. Home-based business is a growing and permanent long-term trend. Could your business service this market?

An ever-increasing number of people are working from home. They are isolated, coping with multiple tasks, plus juggling work and family. How could you help them? The top home-based businesses in North America are nearly all related to services that small business people need, such as business and financial consulting, Internet and computer services, marketing and advertising, graphics, writing and sales.

My "Top Ten" home-based businesses

As a professional who works long hours in a home office, if the business doesn't come to my home, much of the work is achieved using technology, including remote computer repairs or e-mailing of graphic files. Having personally used all these services, here are my top ten businesses for busy home-based people:

1. Computer and equipment servicing, repairs and cleaning
2. Software program education
3. Office services for editing, data entry, research
4. Gofer (errands, after-school child care and chauffeur)
5. Personal fitness coach
6. Home delivery shopping service
7. Declutterer and organizer, house cleaner
8. Mobile automotive mechanic and car detailer
9. Hairdressing and beauty needs
10. Personal chef, meal delivery service.

As this list implies, maintaining a healthy computer system and knowing how to use the software is imperative for most businesses these days. Time is wasted on mundane office chores and running errands. The busy person has no time for cleaning, cooking and shopping. Keeping fit should be a priority. If the boss isn't healthy, then the family and business won't be either. These types of businesses are all service oriented and don't take a lot of money to get started.

WHAT DO YOU RESEARCH?

You are not just starting or buying a business, you are determining how to generate enough profit to pay you a decent wage and build a healthy business over time. You need to be sure that when those doors open, your business will meet all your expectations. Your market research should explore the following areas:

1. The current and future markets
2. Consumer trends
3. The local market
4. National and international markets
5. Industry knowledge
6. The competition.

> ## CASE STUDY
>
> **PAYING ATTENTION TO DETAIL**
>
> For many years, Mark had been intrigued with the idea of starting a car detailing business and when at age 27 he met someone who had started a "mobile" business, his idea finally clicked. He would fill a need by starting a mobile car detailing business, bringing his service to the homes of busy workers. He spent $500 buying supplies and "jumped right in." Then he was accepted by Community Futures Development Corporation's (CFDC) self-employment program (*www.communityfutures.ca*). Here he learned to research, market, prepare a business plan and develop his business and entrepreneurial skills.
>
> A true entrepreneur, Mark pays attention to the little details. He follows up with clients, uses a referral program, sends thank-you cards with discount coupons, leaves candies with his name in the vehicles and stresses service to the max. He maintains a database with well over 200 clients. He recently won Abbotsford's CFDC's New Entrepreneur of the Year award. By paying attention to the small details while keeping the big picture in mind, Mark is on his way to a successful career as a young entrepreneur.

1. The current and future markets

Your business must withstand the ever-changing consumer and market trends. As the world and technology change, so new businesses are born and old ones die. Look at the new businesses that have evolved recently, including home air filtration systems, Web design, Internet mail-order, digital printing, recycling, bottled water and computer consulting, to name a few. A few products that have died—or are dying—include LP records, typewriters, audio tapes and carbon paper.

The business magazine *Red Herring* (*www.redherring.com*) predicts the top ten business start-ups of the future, and all ten are in these technology sectors—biotechnology, energy, semiconductors, data storage, software, wireless and communications. Obviously, our world will continue to become an even more complex place to do business. Keep informed on future trends through books and the Internet, especially as related to your field.

The extent of your study will be determined by whether you intend to trade locally, nationally or internationally. Answer the questions in Figure 4.1 to start.

Figure 4.1: RESEARCHING YOUR FUTURE MARKET

As you research your new business, be sure to address these important issues.

	Yes	No
1. Will this business be viable within the next five to ten years?	❏	❏
2. Has the history of this industry been stable?	❏	❏
3. Is this industry growing?	❏	❏
4. Is there export potential in the future?	❏	❏
5. Are imported products cheaper and of comparable quality?	❏	❏
6. Is this a short-lived business subject to consumer trends?	❏	❏
7. Could this business be diversified?	❏	❏
8. Can this business offer services/products that others don't?	❏	❏
9. Is this business seasonal?	❏	❏
10. Is there enough cash flow to maintain a sufficient inventory?	❏	❏
11. Will this business be subject to major changes in the next five years?	❏	❏
12. Am I flexible enough to adapt to constant change?	❏	❏

2. Consumer trends

Consumers drive the market, and their needs are constantly changing. For example, take two traditional industries, vacuums and sewing machines. We still need clean houses and our clothes need sewing, so the need for these products has not changed. What has changed are consumers' priorities. Working moms spend less time cleaning, or they hire someone. Products have changed to reflect society's new needs, such as home cleaning equipment that eliminates allergens. Many vacuum dealers have diversified into home air filtration systems due to the significant increase in allergies and worsening air quality.

Where moms used to sew their families' clothes, we have now become the throwaway society. My 93-year-old mom still darns, knits and sews. I either throw the holey socks or ripped clothing away or take the clothes to her to fix. There's no time for sewing now, yet in my past life, I sewed and knitted. Children are rarely taught the art of sewing now as moms are too busy, yet future trends will gear toward catering to the baby boomers who will have both the time and more disposable income.

Health and fitness has become a huge current and no doubt future trend. Companies are catering to the fact that obesity and lack of fitness in both adults and children has become a global concern. Even McDonald's has introduced a line of healthy alternatives, realizing that a large portion of their market is families concerned about their weight and diet. Fitness centres and personal trainers are now integral to many people's lives. These global trends are also an important part of your research.

Current and future trends

Listed here are many trends that will impact the future. Can your business accommodate, cater to or withstand these trends?

- The huge increase in baby boomers with more disposable income
- Baby boomers who are caring for their aged parents
- Lack of facilities and long-term care for ageing seniors
- The environment—chemicals, global warming, pollution, conservation, recycling, endangered species
- The large swing toward self-employment and home-based businesses

- Lack of time to perform basic chores, such as shopping and house cleaning
- Healthier diets—natural foods, less fat, vegetarian meals
- Exercise and fitness
- Housing—multi-unit dwellings, downsizing of homes and numbers of children
- Technology—communications, Internet, computer reliance
- Increased desire and necessity for knowledge and education
- Immigration—changing populations
- Youth—fewer job opportunities
- The huge influence of the media
- The need to be entertained
- Less income as job markets change
- Downsizing of businesses
- The Internet—bringing the world into the average home
- Vitamins, alternative medicines, therapies and remedies
- International economies—their changing structure and currency values
- Cocooning—September 11 created a universal awareness of home and family
- Government cutbacks and privatization policies
- The younger generation's need for everything—*now*.

3. The local market

The majority of small businesses are service businesses that serve their local community. Thorough local research is important, as there can be a lot of hidden competition, namely the many unlicensed home-based businesses that do not openly promote their services yet are still taking a nibble at your slice of the pie. Your municipal office will have some very helpful information, as will chambers of commerce. The municipal office can usually give you a list of the licensed businesses in your field, and from this you can deduce which ones are housed in commercial premises and which ones are home-based.

Chambers of commerce

Well-acquainted with their business sector, the chamber of commerce is a valuable research source. Lynn Whitehouse, executive director of the Greater Langley Chamber of Commerce—an award-winning chamber and one of the largest in B.C.—outlines some of the services that they offer. Most chambers should offer similar services to the following:

- Referrals to reputable realtors for leasing commercial space
- Referrals to reputable goods and services businesses
- Printed information on the demographics of the town and its residents
- A One Stop Business Registration Centre
- Discount packages of coupons for business services
- Business start-up pamphlets and books
- Business library
- Membership business directory for review.

Municipal offices

Your local municipal office is also a mine of research information, and will supply you with the following resources:

- Zoning regulations for businesses
- Home-based business bylaw information
- Business licence directory
- Environmental laws and bylaws
- Local demographics—population, age, male/female ratio, marital status, household sizes, labour force by industry, languages spoken, schooling, businesses in your area
- Some municipalities house a One Stop Business Registration Centre
- Applicable local bylaws and applications for new commercial building permits.

Researching your community

Take a community tour to gather the following information:

- The number of competitors successfully trading in your area

- The accessibility of your potential location

- Where people prefer to shop

- The quiet shopping areas and what type of stores trade there

- How your competitors advertise in the local paper

- What competition is listed in the local Yellow Pages

- Leasing costs of suitable vacant buildings with parking accessibility.

$UCCE$$ $TRATEGY

BE A SUPER SLEUTH: Peruse the businesses for sale classifieds and call ones similar to yours. Try to find out why they are selling, whether their business is successful and how long they have been in business. If you can find an old Yellow Pages (check with your local public library), call businesses in your field and see if they are still operating. You will be surprised how many were listed two years ago that are not listed now. Talk to ones who are still in business or visit their premises to "snoop out" the reason for their success.

4. The national and international market

If you are looking to trade across Canada, you can learn more about the national market by consulting statistical agencies, such as Statistics Canada, and by researching on the Internet. The search engine Google is an excellent source for locating Web sites. (See Appendix 1 for information on useful Web sites.) Contact national associations in your field and visit their Web sites. Attend as many industry-related trade shows as possible for new information and to weigh up the competition.

Exporting

If you are considering manufacturing and exporting, there are government grants available. The federal government is keen to boost export sales, and a sound idea and business plan may qualify you for a loan. Marketing internationally requires knowledge in:

1. Current and future market trends

2. Customs procedures, regulations and paperwork

3. Transportation choices and costs

4. Financial transactions in foreign countries

5. Methods of distribution

6. Locating distributors, manufacturing representatives, buyers and sales agents

7. Packaging and labelling requirements.

Visit an international trade show. You will be exposed to the most current information available, be able to study your competition in depth and research your business potential. Without the latest information, you could be reinventing the wheel.

Resources

Obtain a copy of the publication *Your Guide to Government of Canada Services and Support for Small Businesses* from your local Canada Business Service Centre (see Appendix 1). It details many programs and free services, including Team Canada Inc., who can help you with all facets of exporting. Team Canada can be contacted toll-free at 1-888-811-1119, or visit their Web site at *http://exportsource.gc.ca.*

5. Industry knowledge

The old saying "we learn by our mistakes" will not do your reputation any good if it applies to your lack of expertise. Know your industry inside out so that if problems arise, or a customer asks technical questions, you are knowledgeable enough to resolve these problems and answer their questions competently and confidently.

Product knowledge

If your business sells products, one way to expand your knowledge is to contact the manufacturers or a local distributor. They are usually happy to send you information and answer your questions. Figure 4.2 lists some relevant questions to answer.

Figure 4.2: PRODUCT EVALUATION CHECKLIST

Consider the following questions when evaluating a product you may want to sell.

	Yes	No
1. Are the products well established in the marketplace?	☐	☐
2. Are you aware of their seasonal selling cycles?	☐	☐
3. Are products regularly upgraded or changed?	☐	☐
4. Could you be caught unexpectedly with obsolete inventory?	☐	☐
5. Do the manufacturers offer satisfactory warranties?	☐	☐
6. Are replacement parts readily available?	☐	☐
7. Are the products competitively priced?	☐	☐
8. Are they C.S.A. (Canadian Standards Association) approved?	☐	☐
9. Are buying trends increasing?	☐	☐
10. Are you satisfied with the quality?	☐	☐
11. Are the products comparable to those of the competition?	☐	☐
12. Do you know the age groups that buy these products?	☐	☐
13. Do you know the products' life expectancy?	☐	☐
14. Could they become obsolete due to changing technology?	☐	☐

Your research may determine that your costs or prices will be too high compared to the competition or that over the last five years, demand for the products is declining due to technological changes and shifts in consumer trends. In another five years, the demand may become substantially less. Products may appear of good quality but not be something that you would feel confident in selling. Perhaps the manufacturers' warranties are inadequate or replacement parts expensive and difficult to secure.

Service knowledge

Apart from needing the expertise and the ability to communicate well with people, your service business must offer you some longevity. Be prepared to change as technology changes. For example, in 15 years, accounting has progressed from handwritten ledgers requiring many hours, even days to prepare, to software programs that can post hundreds of entries in seconds. Although highly efficient, accountants had to find more customers to increase their reduced billing hours.

In your research, be sure you can answer yes to the questions in Figure 4.3:

Figure 4.3: SERVICE BUSINESS CHECKLIST

Before you start a service business, use this checklist in the research stages.

	Yes	No
1. Do you have thorough industry knowledge?	❏	❏
2. Are you prepared to keep up-to-date through education?	❏	❏
3. Is your service currently in demand?	❏	❏
4. Will it be needed in the next five to ten years?	❏	❏
5. Can you price your rates competitively without price-cutting?	❏	❏
6. Can your ideal customer afford your service?	❏	❏

		Yes	No
7.	Do you know your competition within a ten-mile radius?	❏	❏
8.	Do you know your geographic boundary?	❏	❏
9.	Do you understand your liability should something go wrong?	❏	❏
10.	Are you aware of potential industry changes in the near future?	❏	❏
11.	Are you prepared to change with industry trends?	❏	❏

6. The competition

Competition is a fact of life, so your business needs an edge to succeed. You may have an excellent idea, but ask yourself, "How much of the market can I expect to capture?" Know as much as possible about your competitors and their marketing strategies. Answer two important questions:

> **WHAT IS MY EDGE?**
> *1. What can I offer that the competition can't?*
> *2. What does the competition offer that I can't?*

Take a field trip

The best way to research the competition is to take a field trip, armed with notepad and sharp pencil. Identify at least five main competitors, both large and small. Act as if you are interested in purchasing a product or using the service. Find answers to the questions outlined in Figure 4.4.

Figure 4.4: CHECK OUT THE COMPETITION

1. What appeals to you most on entering their premises?

2. How large an inventory do they carry?

3. How are products displayed, and are the displays eye-catching?

4. How many customers are in the store, browsing or buying?

5. What attracted the customers who are purchasing products?

6. Were staff friendly and helpful?

7. Are their prices in line with your industry?

8. Are your prices competitive with theirs?

9. Did you wait long to be helped?

10. Was the salesperson knowledgeable?

11. Were they willing to bargain or undercut other competitors?

12. Were take-home brochures or literature available?

13. Do they offer any special services, such as free delivery?

14. Would they replace a faulty product immediately?

15. What could be improved, and how could you improve in these areas?

16. What age group are their customers?

17. What is their return policy or work guarantees?

18. Do they offer credit terms or credit card facilities?

19. What means of promotion do they use
    (e.g., coupons, flyers, free samples)?

$UCCE$$ $TRATEGY

KNOW YOUR COMPETITORS WELL: If you cannot research some of your main competitors due to distance, first check their Web site and then call and ask for information to be mailed. Ask as many of the questions in Figure 4.4 as possible. Build a profile of each main competitor outlining how they market, why customers shop there, their pricing and service policies, what areas need improving and how successfully you can compete with them. At the same time, you will probably glean ideas for promoting or improving your own business.

Prepare a SWOT analysis

Your strength lies in knowing and assessing your competitors' strengths and weaknesses—and your own. Now it is time to analyze. How can you utilize your strengths and overcome your weaknesses? Called a SWOT analysis, it stands for:

Strengths
Weaknesses
Opportunities
Threats

Draw up two lists, one for your SWOT analysis and one for your competitors. Now answer these questions:

- What are my strengths and how can I incorporate them into my business?
- What are my weaknesses and how can I overcome them?
- What are my opportunities and how can I utilize them in my business?
- What are my threats and how can I overcome them?
- What are my competitors' strengths and how will they affect my business?
- What are their weaknesses and how can I take advantage of them?

- What are their opportunities and how will they affect my business?

- What threats do they present to my business?

With a clearer indication of your own strengths, weaknesses, opportunities and threats, you are now better armed to plan your industry niche.

PERFORM A MARKET SURVEY

Now it's time to talk to consumers or potential clients. It's amazing how talking to people will shed new light on your business and affirm your direction. Many people skip this step, yet large and successful businesses would never even contemplate such behaviour.

Design a questionnaire along the lines of Figure 4.5 and hit the streets to get your answers. The more people you talk to, the more confident you will feel. Interview as many targeted people as possible, so choose people who may use your business. Give the participant a little gift or a token of your appreciation, along with your contact information and a discount coupon for when you are open for business. A little "thank-you" goes a long way.

Figure 4.5: SAMPLE CONSUMER MARKET SURVEY

In order that we can offer the best possible service, please complete this short questionnaire. Thanks for your time and input!

1. Why would you use this type of business?

2. How often would you use these products or services?

3. What is the final factor in your buying decision—price or service?

4. What kind of service would you expect?

5. What type of after-sales service or guarantees do you expect?

6. What would you pay for a service/product such as this?

7. Have you heard of this type of business before?

8. Where did you hear about it?

9. Where would you look for this type of business?

10. What services would the ideal business provide to you?

CASE STUDY

THE TEN-QUESTION EYE-OPENER

For three years I have taught Entrepreneurship Skills in the Equine Industry, an accredited 15-week course at Kwantlen University College. The class usually consists mainly of young women who are crazy about horses and who dream of owning a horse-related business. Part of their business plan entails doing a market survey, similar to Figure 4.5, interviewing ten people. The results have been amazing. Many students have commented that talking to people gave them new ideas, confirmed and increased their enthusiasm, or made them realize that they needed a lot more homework on their idea. Some changed their business direction after doing the survey, realizing the impracticality of their original plan. Others realized that they wouldn't make a sufficient living. In all cases, the survey was a tremendous help in formulating their plans and in identifying areas needing re-evaluation.

WHERE DO YOU FIND RESEARCH MATERIAL?

There is so much information available now about starting a business that there is no excuse not to be well informed. Here are some resources to help you.

1. Canada Business Service Centres

Canada Business Service Centres (CBSCs) are located across Canada, and the main offices are listed in Appendix 1. There are many federal departments currently involved in this program, including CBSC's Industry Canada, Strategis (Industry Canada on-line), Regional Economic Development Agencies and Western Economic Diversification.

Information is provided about all government services, programs, regulations and all small business topics, including sample business plans and industry-specific information. Many publications are free of charge. They can also be downloaded as PDF files from their Web site. Other materials include videos, CD-ROM products, external databases, directories and how-to manuals. Visit your local office, browse their library or talk to an information officer. Their Web site address is ***www.cbsc.org.***

2. Business Development Bank of Canada

The BDBC is Canada's small business bank, which focusses on the emerging and exporting sectors of the economy and on delivering financial and management services. They offer business counselling, mentoring, venture capital, term loans and student business loans. Their site has an excellent entrepreneurial assessment quiz plus a business plan that you can download. Call your local branch or visit their Web site at ***www.bdc.ca.***

3. Statistics Canada

If you need demographic, trade, social or economic statistics, call Statistics Canada at 1-800-263-1136. They can provide information by sector, provincially or nationally. They provide statistics from all over Canada, which can be obtained in print, on CD-ROMs, diskettes, microfilm and microfiche, and through their Web site at ***www.statcan.ca***.

4. Yellow Pages

What an information mine! You can research your competitors by studying their advertisements, see how they advertise and what services they offer. Assess how many competitors are in your trading area and get some indication of their size.

5. Chambers of commerce

Your local chamber of commerce is in business to help businesses, both new and established. They supply business start-up kits, which include a resource guide, business plan and cash flow information; business registration forms; and some, one-on-one consulting services. Some house a One Stop Business Registration Centre. As a member, you'll have access to mailing lists, networking opportunities, group medical plans, monthly newsletters and special events.

6. Municipal offices

Visit your municipal office for local statistics, traffic counts, potential re-zoning plans, new building applications, bylaws and other business information.

7. The Internet

When doing research, nothing beats sitting in the comfort of your own home collecting information. There is virtually nothing you can't find on the Internet. It is a powerful, fast, cheap and efficient research tool—in fact, for research, it is indispensable. Many informative small business Web sites can be found in Appendix 1.

8. Trade shows and seminars

Trade shows allow you to be inundated with the most up-to-date information on your industry, helping you to make informed decisions. There are also entrepreneurial trade shows that demonstrate new products and franchises. This is an opportunity to assess new competitors in the market and also promising new businesses. Attend as many business-related seminars as possible. Not only will you learn new skills, you can network with other entrepreneurs and do business with them.

9. Publications

Use Internet listservs, newspapers, flyers, magazines, directories, and trade and financial papers to glean every ounce of information you need. Subscribe to journals and newspapers specifically aimed at your type of business, or borrow them from your local library.

WHAT IS THE NEXT STEP?

Once you have confirmed your niche in the market and feel confident that you have a viable business idea, sometime during business start-up or operation, you will need the services of a lawyer. It may be for signing a lease, a partnership agreement or an employee contract or for purchasing a business. Few of us understand legalese or all that fine print. Some unfortunate people don't use a lawyer and get burned. So next we'll take a look at why you need legal agreements and what a lawyer can do for you.

CHAPTER 5

Why do you need a lawyer?

To save any future fighting,
get it all in writing.

WHAT DOES A LAWYER DO?

Lawyers are in business to protect your rights and to work for you. No matter how small your business, there are numerous areas where you should consult with a lawyer, from purchasing a business to selling one. Very few people understand the fine print on contracts and legal documents, yet once you sign on the dotted line, you have contracted to adhere to specific terms, and these agreements can be upheld in court. To most people, contracts are just a bunch of words in a strange language, and they are often signed without comprehension of their contents.

In business, a verbal agreement or a handshake isn't good enough. Many people have lost money on smiles and handshakes. Although it is human nature to want to trust people, get everything in writing anyway. The most common areas where a lawyer can help you follow:

1. Buy-sell agreements

2. Partnership agreements

3. Building and capital equipment leases

4. Royalty agreements

5. Agent and distributorship agreements

6. Franchise agreements

7. Disputes with clients

8. Corporate affairs.

1. Buy-sell agreements

If you are buying an existing business, have a lawyer review the vendor's agreement, which can be one-sided, with little protection for the buyer. A buy-sell agreement sets out the terms of both the purchase and the sale, setting parameters for both parties (explained later in this chapter).

2. Partnership agreements

Although a partner may seem ideal when starting a business, the percentage of partnerships that succeed is low. (See Chapter 8 for a discussion on partnerships.) A partnership agreement protects both parties by setting down mutual guidelines, parameters, responsibilities and duties.

An agreement will define the shared areas of management that need to be clarified, such as net profits and losses, the injection and withdrawing of capital, interest on capital investments, management duties, banking authorizations, accounting records, salaries, termination or sale, death, disputes and arbitration. Spending the money on a thorough agreement can help prevent bickering and be in place should the time come when the partnership dissolves.

$UCCE$$ $TRATEGY

PLAN FOR THE FUTURE: Your goal as business partners is to build a profitable enterprise, so your agreement should include a clause that clearly sets out the terms and conditions for the business reverting to the other partner. There are many unforeseen reasons why a partnership may dissolve, including ill health. Although the purchase price usually includes asset values, capital investment and profits and losses, decide whether the buyout clause will include a value on intangible assets, such as goodwill or trademarks.

3. Building and capital equipment leases

You have probably already seen—or signed—a lease agreement and noticed but probably not read the pages of fine print. When you sign a rental lease, you are accepting full responsibility to pay for that leased space or equipment for the term of the lease. It is a contractual agreement to adhere to all the terms and conditions until the lease expires. Don't assume, as many people do, that it is a "standard" lease. Have a lawyer review and explain it all to you before you sign. See Chapter 6 for more information about leases.

CASE STUDY

THE LEASE THAT WASN'T

Gordon, Robin and their spouses became partners in a new catering business. Robin professed to be conversant in legal and accounting matters, and so took responsibility for the "legal mumbo-jumbo," while Gordon focussed on getting the operation going. The business thrived, and more money was invested into leasehold fixtures and equipment.

After a year of operation, the building was suddenly foreclosed on. The lease they had signed was in fact only a sublease on which the payments were not being made. In order to save money, Robin had not taken the trouble to have the lease agreement checked by a lawyer. The business was closed down and much of the equipment seized. The partners had borrowed against their mortgages for the business, and they were left with little, except huge bills and business losses. The stress caused Robin's marriage to break up. This could have all been prevented by a visit to a lawyer.

4. Royalty agreements

Your business may involve income from royalties, such as publication of a book or selling the rights of a product to another company. Usually, you are selling a product to another party for them to manufacture and sell, in return for a percentage of the income generated when that product is sold. Royalties can range from 10 to 15 percent of the final sale price of the item.

Be careful what rights you sign away with these agreements and be sure that your product will be manufactured and marketed to your satisfaction. Rights can encompass printed, manufacturing, electronic, national and world rights. Where possible, include a timeline for the length of the agreement and a performance clause. You don't want to sign away your rights forever, particularly if the purchaser is not doing justice to your product.

5. Agent and distributorship agreements

Some businesses may involve the sale of products or services through an agent, for example, authors, actors and professional speakers. You may also engage an agent to distribute your products or services, or you may act as an agent or distributor for other businesses. The agent or distributor earns an income by selling the commodity and receives a fee or a commission, which is a percentage of the sale price. Generally, agents' fees range from 15 percent upwards.

Both parties have certain rights and responsibilities, which should be clearly defined in an agreement. Some agents require exclusivity, so think about including a performance clause and ensure that the agreement can be readily rescinded if either party is not satisfied with the other. Use a lawyer to draft and/or review these agreements before signing.

6. Franchise agreements

There are a myriad of franchises opening, operating and closing, and their agreements are pages of legalese that is often difficult to understand. Some set out stringent terms and conditions and appear to benefit the franchiser more than the franchisee. Don't even try to wade through them by yourself. Seek legal advice and interpretation.

7. Disputes with clients

You hope it never happens—a client decides to sue you for incompetency or damages caused through your services or products. Your first protection against this common occurrence is a good liability insurance policy, discussed in Chapter 6. Your next move is to consult a lawyer to decide on the best form of arbitration. From the initial discussion with an unhappy client to your meeting with a lawyer, keep your cool and document all conversations.

8. Corporate affairs

A lawyer can act on your behalf in corporate matters such as:

- Employment contracts with management staff

- Wrongful dismissal claims

- Patents and trademarks

- Collections

- Intellectual property rights

- Taxation disputes.

HOW DO YOU FIND THE RIGHT LAWYER?

Know your needs

The more people you talk to about finding a lawyer, the more stories you will hear about both good and bad experiences. What works for one person won't necessarily work for another. Perhaps the best advice is don't ask your friends for a referral to "a good lawyer." If the relationship doesn't work out, you may not be friends for long.

Law practices come in all shapes and sizes. Usually, a law firm will focus on one area, such as divorce, immigration or corporate law. You need a lawyer who specializes in corporate law. If you owned a Mercedes, you'd prefer to use a mechanic familiar with Mercedes, not just a general mechanic. Use the same principle when lawyer-shopping.

Lawyers are often active chamber of commerce members, and your local chamber staff get to know many of the professionals in the community. Call and see if they can recommend a corporate lawyer with expertise in the area you require. As with any referral, ask about the services the lawyer performed for them.

Prepare for your consultation

Many lawyers offer a free half-hour consultation. Use this time to establish whether you feel comfortable with the lawyer. Prepare yourself by listing the potential topics, including the fee structure, whether your request can be processed in your desired time frame and whether the lawyer can provide you with references. After your consultation, decide whether this lawyer meets all your criteria. Remember—you are paying good money for someone's services. It is your right to pick and choose whom you hire, so if you feel the need, interview three or four before choosing one.

Here are two useful lawyer referral Web sites that may help you:

- *Find Me a Lawyer Service:* A lawyer referral service on CanLaw, the Canadian Lawyer Index. ***www.canlaw.com.***

- *Canadian Bar Association:* Operated by the B.C. branch of the Canadian Bar Association, this site gives you a list of all the lawyer referral services across Canada. ***www.bccba.org.***

As you formulate your business plan, use Figure 5.1 to remind you of areas where you may need a lawyer. This will help in both planning your budget and your first consultation.

Figure 5.1: DO YOU NEED A LAWYER CHECKLIST

Enlist the services of a lawyer if you are considering any of the following activities:

1. To review a buy-sell agreement on purchasing a business ☐
2. To advise and prepare a partnership agreement ☐
3. To review a lease for a building ☐
4. To review a lease for a vehicle or equipment ☐
5. To review a royalty agreement ☐
6. To prepare or review an agent/distributorship agreement ☐
7. To review a franchise agreement ☐
8. To advise on or prepare an employment contract ☐
9. To advise on or register patents and trademarks ☐
10. To advise on intellectual property rights and contracts ☐
11. To advise on collections procedures ☐
12. To advise on general corporate matters. ☐

WHAT IS A BUY-SELL AGREEMENT?

A buy-sell agreement is drawn up between two parties when a business is sold to protect you both. When you engage a lawyer to review an agreement, they will perform many searches and checks to ensure that what you think you are buying is in fact what you are getting. Some vendors make verbal promises that they have no intention of keeping. They tend to play down the negatives of the business and sometimes forget to mention important factors.

$UCCE$$ $TRATEGY

GET EVERYTHING IN WRITING: If you consider verbal offers and promises made by the vendor important to your purchase, ensure that these points are all documented in the agreement, no matter how trivial they may appear, and no matter how sincere the vendor appears to be.

If a vendor promises to train you full-time for a month, get it in writing. If the vendor suggested that the business should generate a certain annual sales volume, get that in writing too. Then, if you are doing everything right and the business fails to meet certain expectations, you have a signed document and legal recourse.

A buy-sell agreement sets out the full terms of the purchase, the goods and services to be purchased, payment conditions and all other conditions. It covers areas which you, as a layperson, would not even think to consider. See the example in Figure 5.2 at the end of this chapter. Some vendors will prepare their own agreements, expecting you to eagerly sign on the dotted line. If a vendor or his or her lawyer has prepared an agreement, ask your lawyer to review it. If you prepare your own agreement, have it checked by a lawyer. It doesn't matter how small the business, an agreement will protect you, particularly if the deal turns sour.

A lawyer will thoroughly investigate and advise you on the following areas before letting you enter into an agreement. These are particularly important if you are buying an established business or any business where assets are part of the purchase price.

1. Searches

The first step a lawyer will take is to undertake the following searches:

- A search and review of the company minute books (if incorporated)
- A check with municipal authorities regarding taxes, zoning and licensing
- Searches through special registries (depending on the nature of the business) and with the various government agencies, such as Canada Customs and Revenue Agency (CCRA), Workers' Compensation Board and the GST/HST office
- A check that there are no infringements of registered patent trademarks or copyrights, or infringements of any laws, statutes or other regulations.

2. Tax considerations

Taxes have an important bearing on the purchase of an existing company, and your lawyer will investigate on your behalf:

- *Assets:* If the company has assets that are a large portion of the purchase price, you must know their tax position and whether they have already been depreciated.
- *Tax history:* There should be representations and warranties regarding any previous problems with the tax authorities. There may be tax benefits and previous losses to be considered in the purchase price.
- *Taxes payable:* When a business is sold, provincial taxes and GST/HST are usually payable on the sale of the assets.
- *Other:* Other tax issues might include whether the vendor or purchaser is filing taxes and remittances for that particular year, or on any land, or on a particular asset that is being transferred for sale.

3. Incorporated businesses

With the purchase of an incorporated business, you usually purchase the shares of the company at a certain value, and the assets and the liabilities of the business remain at book value. Your lawyer will research the following:

- Representations and warranties regarding the shares
- Representations whether it is a reporting company or not

- Where the company is registered and where it does business

- When and where the last annual report was filed. (If it has been two years since the last annual report was filed, the *Escheat Act* allows the government to seize the assets of the company.)

- How many authorized or common shares the company has issued, and how many shares are validly issued and outstanding

- Whether the vendor has authority under the terms of the memorandum and articles of the company to sell shares or capitals, as well as a list of directors and officers of the company.

4. Competition

How would you feel if after nine months of purchasing your business, the vendor opened a similar business close to you? It has been done. The vendor could be forced into opening another business to survive, and will start where they have the expertise and business contacts.

A competition clause will prevent this, usually by prohibiting the vendor from participating in, setting up or operating a business similar to the one you have purchased within the next two to five years, within a given geographical boundary (typically a five- or ten-mile radius). This comforting clause should be standard in most agreements.

5. Exclusivity

If this business involves handling an exclusive product line or service, include an exclusivity clause to prevent the vendor from selling the same product, right or service to other people later. An exclusive product or service makes a business more financially viable to the purchaser.

6. Records and documentation

Certain items belong to and should remain with the business after the sale; specifically, all company records and documentation. These include client lists, sales, marketing and costing information, accounting records, files, working papers, supplier information, lists of information sources, correspondence and all business records required for the day-to-day operation. Unfortunately, nothing can prevent the vendor from keeping copies of records of client contact information, and computers make it so easy. But your agreement can legally prevent the vendor from using the information.

7. Licences and rights

Your lawyer will ensure that any licences, area or other business rights, designs or trademarks being purchased with the business are noted in the agreement. If the business is limited to a specified geographic area, such as with dealerships or franchises, clearly identify this area with a map in an appendix. In one case, a new dealership did not honour the promises of certain area rights written into their distributorship agreement. But the agreement was not clearly worded and ultimately, the disappointed distributor had little recourse.

8. Insurance

It is the vendor's responsibility to insure the assets until you have purchased the business. If there is any damage to the assets before you take possession, it is the vendor's responsibility to compensate for damages. Clearly stipulate who is responsible for maintaining insurance and whether the purchaser has an obligation to maintain certain insurance policies.

9. Other considerations

Following are some other considerations that may apply to your purchase:

- *Employees:* If the business already has employees, obtain a vendor's statement detailing the number of employees and whether they have a collective agreement. There may be obligations to long-term employees, which require extensive notice on termination. Unpaid employee vacation pay, sales bonus plans or incentive schemes at the takeover date must also be considered. How will these projected future expenses be accommodated in the buy-sell agreement?

- *Company debts:* Your lawyer should research the company's debts or contractual obligations.

‣ *Financial assistance:* If the vendor is offering financial assistance in the form of a loan to the purchaser, two issues could be relevant:

a) provincial legislation that does not allow financial assistance if the loan would render the company insolvent

b) short-term loans may constitute a criminal rate of interest if the various fees total more than 60 percent a year.

‣ *Support documentation:* Enclose a list of documents to be transferred at closing, especially if there are corporate records, business licences or non-competition agreements, resignations of the previous directors of the company and transfers of title. Appendices to the agreement may include a list of property being transferred, leases, licences, types of insurance coverage, contracts as well as financial statements.

‣ *General provisions:* At the end of the agreement, there is a section of general provisions which includes a statement that both the vendor's and purchaser's liability remain in force after the agreement has been closed. This clause is inserted for future protection.

Another provision should state that "This agreement contains the whole agreement between the vendor and the purchaser, and this supersedes all other previous agreements; there are no representations other than those contained in this agreement, and the purchasers or vendors have relied on these representations."

What if legal problems arise?

Once your agreement is signed, dated and the takeover date completed, the business is yours. If a serious problem arises that cannot be resolved, seek your lawyer's advice. If the agreement has been broken and settlement cannot be reached, the court will make a ruling, based on the agreement and the events.

Practice shows that the person with the most detailed documentation has a better chance of winning a court case. A judge can only base his or her opinion on the evidence presented. Cases are built around evidence—not hearsay (i.e., any statements quoted by a third party). For statements to be admitted as evidence, the person must be called as a witness. Written statements and usually audio tapes are not acceptable evidence.

$UCCE$$ $TRATEGY

DOCUMENT DETAILS: Keep a log of events, phone calls, meetings and statements made by vendors and their associates. If the need arises, these people can be called to the stand to testify. Your documentation will allow for thorough questioning and a better chance of winning your case.

If the business is being adversely affected by this disagreement, document as much information as possible. Compensation may be awarded for loss of profits. Your agreement will be written proof of a contract between the parties involved. Without it, you do not have grounds for a court case.

WHAT DO THOSE LEGAL TERMS MEAN?

The legal profession speaks its own unique language in most contracts and agreements. A glossary of common legal terminology follows:

Assign: To give someone else your property or rights under a contract

Assurance: A positive declaration

Authorize: To commission or allow

Case: A disagreement settled in court

Consideration: Payment for something given, including money, services or promises

Contract: An agreement between two people which can be enforced

Covenant: An oath, promise, pledge or vow

Deed: A document in which an owner transfers ownership of an asset

Default: Failure to act or meet one's obligations

Encumbrance: An impediment, usually a loan or mortgage on a property

Hereafter: In the future

Herein: In this place

Hereinafter: Below

Heretofore: Formerly, once

Herewith: With this

Indemnify: Exempt from a penalty, or to compensate

Lien: A hold on another person's property until an outstanding debt is paid

Memorandum: Notes or records made for future business use

Misrepresent: Falsify or distort facts

Statute: A written law

Vendor: Seller

Vested: Placing of the right to

Warranties: Agreements, guarantees, pledges or assurances.

Figure 5.2 gives an example of a simple buy-sell agreement, outlining the sale of a gift shop. This is only a sample agreement to demonstrate which areas legal agreements should cover. Consult a lawyer when having your legal agreement prepared, and listen to his or her advice.

WHAT IS THE NEXT STEP?

Once you understand the legal aspects of your business, you should start preparing a business plan, but first you must research start-up expenses. You won't get too far without knowing exactly what you need and how much it costs. Sometimes, it's surprisingly expensive, particularly if you are leasing commercial premises, so next we'll explore basic start-up costs.

Figure 5.2: A SIMPLE BUY-SELL AGREEMENT

THIS AGREEMENT made the *Twenty-ninth* Day of *July, 2003*

BETWEEN:

> *Peter James Turnbull*, Businessman, of *9291 - 295th Street, Vancouver* in the municipality of *Vancouver*, in the Province of British Columbia.
>
> > (Hereinafter called the "Vendor")
> > **OF THE FIRST PART**

AND:

> *Sarah Elizabeth Scott*, Businesswoman, of *19775 - 26th Avenue, Burnaby* in the municipality of *Burnaby*, in the Province of British Columbia.
>
> > (Hereinafter called the "Purchaser")
> > **OF THE SECOND PART**

WHEREAS:

a.   The Vendor carries on the business of selling retail gifts to the general public under the business name "Artsy and Crafty," (hereinafter called the "Business") and operates the said business in Willowdale Mall, in Burnaby, in the Province of British Columbia, and in connection therewith owns certain records, supplies, and other assets at the aforesaid address.

b.   The Vendor has agreed to sell the Business as a going concern and to sell the said assets and the Purchaser has agreed to buy the same on the terms and conditions hereinafter set forth.

PURCHASE AND SALE

1.   Subject to the terms and conditions of this Agreement and based on the warranties and representations herein contained, the Vendor agrees to sell and the Purchaser agrees to purchase all the property, rights, undertakings and assets as listed in Appendix A (except as hereinafter provided), belonging to or used in the Business, as a going concern, including but without limiting the foregoing:

(a) The goodwill of the Business, together with all trademarks, designs, licences, Authorities and other rights used in connection with the Business, and all records, documentation, correspondence, and other property related to the Business.

(b) The Vendor agrees to provide one month's full-time training to the Purchaser at no extra cost.

(c) The Vendor agrees to bear the cost of having the lease changed into the Purchaser's name.

> (All of which property, undertakings, and assets are hereinafter called the "Assets")

VENDOR'S REPRESENTATIONS

2.   The Vendor represents, warrants, and agrees that:

(a)   The Vendor has the power, authority, and capacity to enter into this Agreement and to carry out the transactions contemplated hereby, all of which have been duly and validly authorized.

(b)   The completion of the transactions contemplated hereby will not constitute a breach by the Vendor of any statute, bylaw, or regulation or of any contract or Agreement to which the Vendor is a party or by which it is bound or which would result in the creation of any lien, encumbrance, or other charge on any of the Assets.

(c)   The Vendor has good and marketable title to the Assets, free and clear of all liens, mortgages, encumbrances, equities or claims of every kind and nature whatsoever.

(d)   The vendor is not in default and has received no notice of default of any term or condition of any statute, bylaw, or regulation to its Business.

(e)   The Vendor has no indebtedness to any person, firm, or corporation which might, by operation of law or other else, hereafter constitute a lien, charge, or encumbrance upon any of the Assets.

PURCHASE PRICE AND PAYMENT

3.   The Purchase price payable by the Purchaser to the Vendor for the Assets (the "Purchase Price") will be One Hundred and Twenty-Five Thousand Dollars ($125,000.00).

4.   The Purchase Price shall be paid as follows:

(a)   Twenty-five Thousand Dollars ($25,000.00) shall be paid directly to the Vendor's solicitor upon execution of this Agreement, as a deposit in trust.

(b)   Fifty Thousand Dollars ($50,000.00) shall be paid to the Vendor's solicitor on the date of occupation, which shall be no later than August 1, 2003.

(c)   Fifty Thousand Dollars ($50,000.00) shall be paid to the Vendor's solicitor in trust in monthly installments of $2,083.33 for a period of Twenty-Four (24) months, plus interest of Nine Percent (9%) per annum, payable in one cheque each year on the Thirty-First of August, 2004 and 2005. These payments will be made by way of post-dated cheques to the Vendor no later than August 31, 2003.

5.   Upon execution of this Agreement, the Purchaser shall deliver to the Vendor:

(a)   A certified cheque or bank draft in the amount of Twenty-Five Thousand Dollars ($25,000.00).

(b) A certified cheque or bank draft in the amount of Fifty Thousand Dollars ($50,000.00), dated August 1, 2003, to be held in trust by the Vendor's solicitor.

(c) Twenty-four (24) postdated cheques in the amount of Two Thousand and Eighty-Three Dollars and Thirty-Three cents ($2,083.33), the first cheque to be dated August 31, 2003, and every month thereafter, to be held in trust until the Execution of this Agreement by the Vendor's solicitor.

(d) A Promissory Note for the annual interest, which will be Four Thousand Five Hundred Dollars ($4,500.00), due August 31, 2004, and Two Thousand Two Hundred and Fifty Dollars ($2,250.00), due August 31, 2005.

VENDOR'S COVENANTS

6. The Vendor will:

(a) Take or cause to be taken all proper steps, actions, and proceedings on its part to enable it to vest a good marketable title in the Purchaser to the Assets, free and clear of all liens, mortgages, encumbrances, equities, or claims of every nature and kind whatsoever and shall deliver, upon date of execution, such bills of sale, transfer, assignments, and consents (including consents by Creditors of the Vendor under, or other evidence in compliance with, the Sale of Goods in Bulk Act, if required), and consents to transfer of licences, leases, contracts, and rights as the solicitor for the Purchaser may require;

(b) To deliver possession of the Assets to the Purchaser on execution of this Agreement;

(c) From the date of execution of this Agreement to the date of removal, maintain in force policies of insurance heretofore maintained, and obtain and maintain such additional policies of insurance as may be required to insure the Assets, in the amount against such perils as are customary in other similar businesses;

(d) From the date of execution of this Agreement to the date of removal, take good care of the Assets and take all reasonable care to protect and safeguard all Assets;

(e) Execute and do all such further acts, deeds, things, and assurances as may be requisite in the opinion of the solicitor for the Purchaser for more perfectly and absolutely assigning, transferring, assuring to, and vesting in the Purchaser titles to the Assets, free and clear of all liens, mortgages, encumbrances, equities, and claims of any nature and kind whatsoever;

(f) Not from the date of execution of this Agreement to date of removal, sell, consume, or dispose of or transfer possession of any of the Assets;

(g) Not from the date of execution of this Agreement, and for a further period of Five (5) years, start or operate a business involved in the wholesale or retail selling of arts, crafts, and similar items, within a Ten (10) mile/Sixteen (16) kilometre radius of the Willowdale Mall in Burnaby, British Columbia.

PURCHASER'S CONDITIONS

7.   Notwithstanding anything herein contained, the obligation of the Purchaser to complete the purchase hereunder shall be subject to the following conditions:

(a)   The representations and warranties of the Vendor contained in this Agreement shall be true on and as of the date of execution.

(b)   All of the covenants and Agreements of the Vendor to be performed on or before the date of execution pursuant to the terms and conditions of this Agreement shall have been duly performed.

(c)   No substantial loss or destruction of or damage to any of the Assets shall have occurred on or before the date of execution.

(d)   The Purchaser shall have received from her solicitor an opinion to the effect that a good and valid title to the will vest is vested in the Purchaser, free and clear of all liens, encumbrances, equities, or claims of every nature or kind whatsoever.

The foregoing conditions are for the sole and exclusive benefit of the Purchaser and may be waived in whole or in part by the Purchaser.

VENDOR'S CONDITIONS

8.   The obligation of the Vendor to complete the sale under this Agreement shall be subject to the condition that on the date of execution the Purchaser pay to the Vendor all monies due to be paid to the Vendor under this Agreement.

POST-EXECUTION AGREEMENT

9.   If the Purchaser shall fail to make all or any part of any payment to be made pursuant to paragraphs 5(a), (b), and (c) herein, and such default shall continue for a period of seven (7) days, the Vendor may, by notice in writing to the Purchaser, declare the full balance owing under paragraphs 5 (a), (b), and (c) immediately due and payable.

10.   If the Purchaser shall fail to pay the balance owing, as demanded in writing by the Vendor pursuant to paragraph 9 herein, and such further default shall continue for a further period of seven (7) days, then the Vendor's solicitor is hereby authorized by each party hereto to take all necessary steps to recover the promised funds.

GENERAL PROVISIONS

11. All transactions in the Business, on or after the date of execution, shall be for the account of the Purchaser.

12. The Assets shall be at the risk of the Vendor up to the date of execution of this Agreement and shall be at the risk of the Purchaser on or after the date of execution of this Agreement.

13. All representations, warranties, covenants, and Agreements of the parties contained herein shall survive the execution date of this Agreement and the payment of the Purchase Price.

14. The Vendor shall indemnify and save the Purchaser harmless from all loss, damage, cost, actions, and suits arising out of or in connection with any breach of misrepresentation, warranty, covenant, agreement, or condition contained in this Agreement.

15. If prior to the date of execution of this Agreement, there shall have been any loss or damage to any of the Assets, and the Vendor shall be entitled to receive monies as a result of such damage or loss, the Purchase Price shall be reduced by an amount equal to that portion of the Purchase Price allocated to the asset totally destroyed, or if the asset is only damaged or partially destroyed, the reduction in the Purchase Price shall equal the amount of the insurance paid to the Vendor with respect hereto.

16. Time shall be of essence in this Agreement.

17. The purchase and sale of Assets herein contemplated shall take effect as of and no later than the opening of business on the **Twenty-ninth** Day of **July,** 2003.

18. Any notice required or permitted to be given hereunder may be effectively given by prepaid post addressed to the Vendor at:

> 9291 - 295th Street, Vancouver, British Columbia V3P 2Y6

and prepaid post addressed to the Purchaser at:

> 19775 - 26th Avenue, Burnaby, British Columbia V7A 4P5

And if given aforesaid, any notice shall be deemed to have been given seventy-two (72) hours following such posting.

19. This Agreement shall enure to the benefit of and be binding upon the respective successors and assigns of the parties hereto, **PROVIDED THAT** this Agreement shall not be assigned by the Purchaser without the Vendor's consent, which consent shall not be unreasonably withheld.

20. Both the Vendor's liabilities and the Purchaser's liabilities as contained herein shall remain in force after the execution of this agreement.

21. This Agreement contains the whole Agreement between the Vendor and the Purchaser, and this Agreement supersedes all other previous Agreements. Both the Vendor and the Purchaser state that there are no representations other than those contained in this Agreement.

IN WITNESS WHEREOF the parties hereto have hereunto set their hands and seals on the day and year first above written.

SIGNED, SEALED AND DELIVERED	)
by the Vendor in the presence of:	)
	)
Mary Jane Whitehead	)
NAME	)
5751 Central Road, Richmond, B.C	)
ADDRESS	) *Peter James Turnbull*
Housewife	)
OCCUPATION	)
SIGNED, SEALED AND DELIVERED	)
by the Purchaser in the presence of:	)
	)
Russell Brian Smithers	)
NAME	)
19834 Oak Street, Vancouver, B.C.	)
ADDRESS	) *Sarah Elizabeth Scott*
Businessman	)
OCCUPATION	)

APPENDIX "A"
LISTING OF ASSETS, ARTSY AND CRAFTY GIFT SHOP

ITEM	PURCHASE PRICE
Two Electronic Cash Registers, "Cashall" brand	$ 4,200.00
Six six-foot counters with shelves underneath	2,700.00
300 feet glass wall shelving	2,500.00
Crystal chandelier	800.00
Persian display rug	750.00
Carpets, lighting fixtures	4,100.00
Coldasair refrigerator	400.00
Quickcook Microwave oven	250.00
Coffee pot, cups and cutlery, miscellaneous plates	50.00
Kitchen table with four chairs	100.00
12 Brass display stands, various sizes	1,200.00
Lateral four-drawer filing cabinet	400.00
Pentium Computer, hard drive, keyboard,	
Laser printer, 17" flat screen monitor	2,400.00
Computer desk, adding machine &	
miscellaneous stationery	750.00
Inventory as listed on Appendix "B" at cost	
(to be adjusted at date of takeover by Purchaser)	65,400.00
One month full-time training by Vendor	.00
Goodwill value	39,000.00
TOTAL PURCHASE PRICE:	**$125,000.00**

CHAPTER 6

What start-up expenses will you incur?

It's a brand-new business, so much to do.
Let's buy everything sparkling new!

WHAT TYPE OF BUILDING SHOULD YOU LEASE?

Oh the excitement of getting everything ready for your new business. There is so much to do and so much to buy, and of course, you want to create a professional image. It's fun to shop for new equipment and stationery or plan the design of your new retail store. But slow down...it is so easy to make hasty and expensive decisions at this stage. This is the beauty of preparing a business plan—if you first research all costs, you can then tailor them to suit your budget, one of the largest expenses being the leasing and outfitting of a building.

Selecting and leasing a building

Without serious homework, many people mistakenly consider only price, ignoring other factors vital to the smooth long-term operation of the business, including the following.

1. Size and growth

As most of us are not clairvoyants, choosing the right-sized building is difficult. Lease charges are based on square footage, with added costs for taxes and amenities. Costs dramatically increase with the addition of just a few hundred square feet.

$UCCE$$ $TRATEGY

FIRST PLAN ON PAPER: Make a scale drawing of your ideal building, allowing room for equipment and machinery or retail shelf space, work and bench space, storage facilities, vehicles, lunchroom, washrooms and office space. This should indicate the required minimum square footage to comfortably house your operation.

Budget permitting, allow for a 20 percent increase in growth in the first two years. If the budget is tight, you may have to limit this luxury, keeping in mind that if the business is successful, you may have to make other arrangements.

2. Industrial locations

Manufacturing and distribution premises require research in the following areas:

● *Utilities:* Research the cost of extra plumbing or electrical work and the monthly utilities charges before the lease is signed. Your utility company can give you monthly readouts from the preceding year. Buildings can use considerable power during colder months because they are not economically heated or insulated. You may want to consider a more effective heating method. Don't forget to budget for a deposit on utilities.

● *Warehouse or storage space:* Consider the building's accessibility and manoeuvrability in relationship to its usage and the equipment or products you are housing. You may need racking or shelving to store inventory. Some real bargains can be found at liquidation centres. If you are shipping and receiving large products, you need adequate dock and loading facilities. Maximize your efficiency by having the right equipment to do the job.

● *Ventilation:* Windows may not supply enough ventilation during summer, making working conditions oppressive, particularly upstairs. This affects employees' productivity, as will extreme cold. You may have to install air conditioning.

> ## CASE STUDY
>
> **RAISING THE ROOFTOP**
> I once worked for a satellite distributorship (before the days of cable TV) which leased a large upper floor of a building because the rent was cheap. No one thought about the logistics of moving or housing the rather large satellite dishes, which even when broken down into pieces, were too wide to pass through the stairwell. A roof hatch was built and the dishes had to be lifted up to the roof and then lowered into the building. Apart from the inconvenience, the roof hatch was difficult to secure, and the building was broken into several times.

◆ *Security:* Deadbolts are necessary on exterior doors, bars on windows, and a monitored alarm system is essential.

3. Business and retail locations

Perhaps the biggest mistake made when leasing a retail location is to look for "cheap rent." If a retail location is wrong for your business, you are almost signing a death warrant when you sign the lease. Be prepared to pay higher rent for a prime location. Costs are usually indicative of a location's visibility and viability. Here's how to avoid some common mistakes:

◆ Research should pinpoint the competition in the area, so don't lease a building close to them. You'll waste money on advertising trying to attract customers.

◆ Customers need easy accessibility. We live "life in the fast lane," so ensure there is ample parking or they will go elsewhere.

◆ Don't lease a "cheap" retail building in an industrial area, as people visiting industrial areas are on business and not in the mood for retail shopping.

◆ Moving a business when it has outgrown its premises is costly, so look for a location that will suit your needs for the first five years. Your first two years will not generate enough profit to finance a move, which usually involves extensive, non-recoverable renovation costs.

- Save time physically hunting for the ideal location by using the Internet to locate realtors and potential premises in your desired area.

- If you lease space in a shopping mall, be prepared to pay a percentage of gross sales to the mall managers toward their "communal" advertising costs.

$UCCE$$ $TRATEGY

STUDY THE CUSTOMER: Study the patterns of walk- and drive-by traffic. Note people's reactions as they walk past other stores. If a store attracts their attention, find out why. Drive past your potential location. Is it visible to customers? Note stores and businesses that catch your eye. What attracted your attention? A field trip will give you ideas for displays, colour schemes and effective marketing techniques.

4. Signing a lease

A lease is a legal and binding agreement between the landlord (the lessor) and the renter (the lessee) for the term of the lease. Because a lease is a complex agreement, have your lawyer explain it to you before signing.

During negotiations, estimate how long you will need the building, and ask for "first right of refusal," which gives you the first option to renew the lease. Any terms and conditions agreed upon by the landlord should be documented in the lease, as verbal agreements can be forgotten. For example, when a three-year lease is signed, it must stipulate if and when there will be any rent increases. Usually, you will pay the first and last month's rent in advance, so include this in your projections. The last month's rent is held in trust—and should be interest-bearing—until the lease expires.

Property taxes, shared janitorial, maintenance and strata fees should be included in the cost of the lease. Ask about these extras and budget for them. You are responsible for the monthly rent for the term of the lease, so include a subletting clause as a backup. Most landlords are cooperative and prefer contented, prompt-paying tenants. Talk to your lawyer before signing the lease.

5. Building renovations

Plan your cash flow by dividing renovation costs into priorities: renovations that must be immediately completed, those that can wait a few months and those that can be deferred until the profits start rolling in. Give your business a chance to get started before spending working capital on major cosmetic facelifts to someone else's building. Get three quotes and look for quality work that comes with a guarantee.

$UCCE$$ $TRATEGY

RENOVATE AND REDUCE YOUR RENT: Landlords are often happy to negotiate. A building may need repairs or painting, and some landlords will trade a few months' rent in return for these improvements. A note of caution: installing permanent fixtures is like throwing money out the window, particularly in a short-term lease, as most fixtures cannot be removed after you leave. Clarify this issue with your landlord.

6. Exterior signs

Unless your business is home-based (only small exterior signs allowed by most municipalities) you need signage, a costly addition to your budget. Both your municipality and landlord should be consulted as local bylaws often restrict exterior signs, and your landlord may require signs that conform to certain specifications.

Before deciding, drive around and look for signs that catch your eye. Start with the basics—you can always add more later. Flashing neon signs can be expensive, depending on their type and size, and come with a monthly rental contract. Portable flashing signs are highly visible and eye-catching, particularly for advertising a special event or sale. Vinyl banners are reasonably priced and can also be used in trade shows. As this is a competitive industry, once you know what you want, obtain at least three quotations before making a decision.

WHAT COMMUNICATIONS SYSTEMS SHOULD YOU USE?

Consumers have become impatient, demanding answers and service *now*. They are also sick of unanswered voice-mails. Therefore, it is in your best interests to be available to clients. As technology becomes more complex, the cost of keeping in touch has become a major expense. Because technology is changing so rapidly, it is difficult to advise new businesses, but here are some basic requirements.

1. Telephones

There is an abundance of sophisticated telephones available, so choose one to suit your needs. If you move around in your business, you might carry a cordless telephone to ensure that you do not miss calls. Call display and call alert services allow you to identify first and second callers.

Telephone lines

If you do not require a listing in the Yellow Pages, home-based businesses can operate efficiently using a residential line; otherwise, order a business line at a monthly cost of $60 to $80. If you also use a cellular phone, this number can be used to advertise in the Yellow Pages and save yourself the cost of a business line. For a business requiring more than one telephone, phone systems can be leased or purchased. They are expensive, so plan carefully before ordering.

A second ringing tone using a different number on the same residential line can be used for either a fax or family line. The ring tone for each number is distinctly different. If you use your residential line for Internet access, an incoming call under the call-waiting service may terminate your connection. You can disable call waiting—consult your telephone company for advice. If you do not use high-speed Internet access or a fax modem, a home-based system should include two residential lines—one for day-to-day business and one for the fax and Internet. Voice-mail, call waiting, a cellular phone or a pager may also be necessary.

Add-on services

There are numerous bundles and packages available from your telephone company, including that much-hated voice-mail. As we can't always be available to answer the telephone, voice-mail is a necessary evil, ensuring that clients can reach you. Other options are available, but may be rarely used and add significantly to your monthly account.

$UCCE$$ $TRATEGY

RETURN CALLS PROMPTLY: Any business communication should be professional, including your voice-mail message. "Bill is not available, leave a message after the beep" doesn't cut it in business. Leave a positive, courteous message that informs callers that their call is important to you and that you will return it promptly. If you are going out of town or will be unavailable for a while, change your voice-mail message to let callers know that you are "unavailable" for a certain period, and where possible, leave an emergency contact number.

Long distance

If you regularly call long distance, there are some cheap rates available—often up to half what you would pay through your regular phone service. If you move your long-distance calling only to another company, some phone companies will substantially increase the cost of your package, so ask before making a choice. Choose a long-distance package that will allow cheap rates during business hours, and check with your provider every few months, as they often change rates without letting their customers know.

2. Fax machines

Sending e-mails with attachments has quickly replaced the need for a fax machine; in fact these days, most incoming faxes are junk mail. If you use a fax modem, you have the ability to view and delete faxes before printing. In most cases, a scanner can eliminate the need to fax original documents. Fax capacity is now an integral part of many printer/scanners (see the section on computer equipment later in this chapter), so evaluate your need for a stand-alone fax carefully—they cost anywhere from $120 upwards.

3. Cellular phones

They are attached to everyone's ears, and have become an integral piece of business equipment. Cellphones have so many options that most people could never hope to understand how to fully utilize them. If you are regularly away from your business, you need one to check messages (or e-mails) and for call forwarding. Another toy that quickly racks up the charges, be aware of expensive "roaming" long-distance costs when you are out of the normal reception area. If you don't like to pull over in your car when the phone rings, either purchase a hands-free unit or, for $50, purchase an in-ear microphone to use for hands-free conversations while driving.

It's a competitive business, so shop around. Many companies offer free phones if you sign a three-year contract, with attractive offers such as the first 150 minutes free for as low as $20 a month. You will also pay a monthly CRTC access fee of approximately $7, plus taxes. Before you commit, remember that if your business doesn't succeed, you will be stuck with the phone. Buyout lease costs are approximately $20 a month for each unused month. Some businesses use a pager service (as cheap as $10 a month) coupled with a cellphone, for situations when one can't answer the phone.

CASE STUDY

STUCK WITH THE BILLS BUT NO PHONE

Perry's landscaping business was quickly growing, and he realized the need for a salesperson to help with the quoting, marketing and selling. He hired what appeared to be Mr. Right, who insisted he needed a cellphone. When the first bill came in, Mr. Right had obviously been making mountains of personal calls. After discovering other indiscretions, Perry fired him. The season was coming to a close, so Perry didn't rehire, but still had to pay for the phone. Early into the next season, he severely injured his back and had to close the business. He found a "friend" to sublease the phone, but she didn't pay the bills and moved out of town—with the phone. Poor Perry was stuck with months of unpaid bills, a two-and-a-half-year lease buyout and no phone.

4. Internet access and e-mail

Nowadays, it seems that if you don't have a dot.com or at least an e-mail address, you aren't considered a real business. There are many books on this subject, but here are some factors to consider before hooking up.

Internet access

There are two choices for Internet service, slow- or high-speed. A dial-up service ideally requires a separate telephone line to keep the business line free. The connection time can take 15 to 30 seconds using a modem in your computer. Most small businesses pay about $20 to $25 a month for up to 200 hours' use. High-speed access, either through your local cable or telephone company, is instant and usually dependable but comes at a higher cost. Monthly charges are approximately $35 with unlimited usage and may cost more if you network other computers. After recently changing from dial-up to high-speed cable, I am absolutely sold. The extra cost is more than negated by the time and frustration saved.

Web site

A Web site acts as a 24/7 silent advertisement and most businesses have one. You can design one yourself or spend tens of thousands of dollars; bells and whistles run the full gamut. An ideal site offers your product or service information, a corporate profile and consumer information. If you are considering a Web site to complement your marketing, study others in similar businesses and talk to people who have good sites to see what type of traffic they draw and what they are spending to achieve their results.

If you design your own site, ensure that it is professional or you will turn potential customers away. You will have to register your domain name as either a .com, .ca, .net or .org, to name a few, with an annual fee of approximately $75 U.S. Monthly hosting fees run about $50, plus the cost of updating, which can range from $50 to $95 an hour. If you regularly submit your name to search engines, this too is an added cost. Know why you want a site and what you expect from it, and allow plenty of time to have the right one designed for you. Consult with three different Web design companies before making a final decision.

WHAT OFFICE AND COMPUTER EQUIPMENT IS NEEDED?

Office equipment

Certain furniture and equipment are standard business requirements. If you don't have anything, starting from scratch can be expensive. Shop around at the various used furniture and larger office stores or through a "buy-and-sell" classified newspaper. The larger stores have on-line and printed catalogues to use as a guideline. If you are setting up an office where clients come to visit, make it comfortable, tidy, professional, yet inviting. Figure 6.1 outlines some of the basic costs.

Figure 6.1: THE COST OF FURNISHING YOUR OFFICE

	Low end	High end
Office desk	$ 120	$ 700
Computer workstation	100	600
Chair for desk/computer	130	700
Four-drawer vertical file cabinet	180	450
Four-drawer lateral cabinet	450	700
Hanging frames (four)	40	60
Fax machine	130	500
Adding machine with tape	80	150
Bookshelf or storage unit	35	200
Guest chairs	25	200
Total outlay:	**$1,290**	**$4,260**

(This list does not include a computer system—that is extra.)

Computer equipment

To be competitive, a business needs a computer system that encompasses accounting, word processing, some graphic abilities, a database and Internet access for research, e-mail and marketing. A small service business might escape the traumas of becoming computer-literate, but progressive companies will ensure they are plugged in and on-line. The new millennium is all about knowledge, information and fast communication. If you don't understand computers, part of your business education should be to attend evening classes so you can learn what your computer can do for your business. Consult an expert so that you purchase what you really need and no more.

Basic system requirements

It seems that the moment you buy a state-of-the-art computer system with peripherals, it becomes obsolete. The trick is to buy one that remains efficient for at least three years; only the software may need upgrading. The market is extremely volatile. One computer expert recently informed me that prices on new products decrease by an average of five percent a month. The cost of a system can range from $1,500 to $6,000.

Dependent on your usage and work, a system should include:

▶ *Hard drive:* A Pentium 4, 80GB hard drive with 512MB RAM memory should handle most businesses' needs for a few years but will set you back $1,800. Smaller hard drives are cheaper but may need upgrading or replacing sooner. This amount includes a CD-ROM drive, but add a CD-ROM writer for copying files or downloading Internet information. DVD drives are also available.

▶ *Monitor:* A 15-inch screen is bad for your eyes if you spend copious time at the screen. Opt for a 17-inch (flat screen, $360). LCD liquid crystal flat screens are now available up to 21 inches or more in size. They are expensive (up to $2,500) but save the eyes and free up desk space.

▶ *Scanner:* An inexpensive and useful tool for preparing marketing information, copying pictures and graphics and scanning original documents, a scanner can range in price from $100 to $750.

▶ *Keyboard and mouse:* Be kind to your hands and use an ergonomic keyboard and mouse. Remote models are available for $150 for the two, or keyboard ($50) and mouse ($35) and upwards.

▶ *Printer:* A quality laser printer is an essential and worthwhile investment for professional presentations. They cost at least $500, with toner cartridges costing up to $100 (about 2,500 copies, dependent on the brand). Inkjet colour printers are cheap to buy ($140 to $750) but expensive to operate because of the cost of the ink cartridges. Only buy one if colour copies are essential to your business.

- *Multi-functional printers/copiers:* For many small businesses, buying a multi-functional black and white printer is the most economical way to go. These machines are a space-saving combination of printer, copier, stand-alone fax, PC fax and scanner. Their prices range from $600 to $850. Some models require a drum replacement after a certain usage at a cost of up to $300.

- *Extras:* There will always be extras you need to complete your system, such as a good-quality power surge bar ($30), a firewall ($60), a networking adapter for more than one computer ($25), a modem ($30), extra cables ($20) and a Zip drive plus disk for backup ($200), so include these in your budget.

- *Software:* Your computer will likely come with a Windows operating system, and which version you use will depend on your needs. If you install Microsoft's Office Suite, it will talk a universal language to people who send you documents by e-mail and has enough programs to satisfy most basic office needs. Some users prefer Corel WordPerfect Office Suite, which I use, so if you use Corel, install Microsoft Word as well for receiving e-mail word documents. Use a good anti-virus program immediately; Norton is excellent ($70), easy to use and can be programmed to do a daily virus scan and automatic live updates.

- *Accounting software:* If you process a volume of monthly sales invoices, use accounting software such as Simply Accounting, Mind Your Own Business or QuickBooks. These programs are designed to handle accounts payable, accounts receivable, invoicing, inventory and payroll. With a well-designed accounting system (consult your accountant for advice here), you have instant access to accounting records. Sales information can tell you how much each product is selling in dollar value. These figures are helpful when reordering inventory or comparing product profits. GST/HST and provincial tax figures are also instantly available.

If you use an accounts receivable system, accounting software maintains a separate record for each client and gives you an instant "aged analysis," showing the age of all outstanding accounts and how much is owed. This information is invaluable for monitoring potential bad debts and for collection purposes.

$UCCE$$ $TRATEGY

DON'T COOK THE BOOKS: If you don't understand figures, either take an in-depth bookkeeping course, use an accounting service or hire a part-time bookkeeper. An accounting program does not make you a competent accountant. The old saying "garbage in, garbage out" holds true when you don't understand why you debit or credit an account. Financial information will be incorrect, and it is expensive having an accountant repair the damage.

WHAT OFFICE SUPPLIES ARE NEEDED?

"Brand" yourself first

Before ordering office stationery, your first step is to "brand" yourself by deciding on a corporate theme, which then appears on all correspondence and marketing materials. Branding consists of four main elements, which are discussed in detail in Chapter 10:

1. Logo

2. Slogan

3. Mission statement

4. Corporate design and colour theme.

$UCCE$$ $TRATEGY

USE A GRAPHIC ARTIST: Your branding should appear on all stationery, signs and marketing materials—even shipping labels—so you are promoting your business image at all times. Budget to have a graphic artist design a logo and corporate theme. Many people design their own and the result is unprofessional, discouraging potential clients.

Office supplies

Budget $200 to $500 for suspension files, file folders, stapler and staples, three-hole punch, paper clips, pins, envelopes, stamps, bulldog clips, pens, pencils, highlighters, rulers, adding machine tape, notepads, laser or photocopier paper, pens, correction fluid, daybook, self-inking or rubber stamps, self-stick notes, extra toner and file trays, to name just the basics.

Sales invoices

Where retail stores use cash register tapes and credit card receipts to record sales, all other businesses need sales invoices for recording each transaction. It is a CCRA tax auditing requirement that invoices be numbered and a numerical copy maintained in accounting records. An extra copy for clients' files can be a valuable reference, so decide on two- or three-part invoices printed on NCR (carbonless) paper. If you cancel an invoice, mark it "void" and keep all copies in the numerical file. Have a printer drill two or three holes for filing in binders.

CASE STUDY

HELPING THEMSELVES TO THE PROFITS

One small business employed three salespeople who decided they would help themselves to inventory, sell it and pocket the funds. The business didn't have stringent inventory control or accounting checks in place. The salespeople took a bunch of invoices with them on the road "in case they made a sale along the way"— which they did. They gave "deals" if the purchasers paid cash and the money went into their own pockets. Eventually the financial figures reflected an unaccountable loss, and a numerical invoice and strict inventory check was undertaken. The missing invoice numbers were tracked down to the three salespeople, who claimed that they either lost them in the car or cancelled them and tore them up. Nothing could be proven and they were never charged with theft, which amounted to nearly $50,000.

Some invoicing options are:

- *Pre-numbered invoice books* stamped with your name on the top can be purchased at a stationery store. It's not consistent with a professional image but it works for some, particularly contractors.

- *Custom-designed invoices* with the help of a printer and graphic artist can reflect a professional, corporate theme. An economic ordering quantity is usually 500 or more.

- *Designing your own invoices* (with professional advice) and taking a good copy of the master to an instant printing service can work. Some businesses print their invoices straight onto letterhead and then copy them.

- *Computer-generated invoices* may be an option if you use a software program for billing. Research the national forms companies for designs that are compatible with your program.

Letterhead, envelopes and business cards

Maintaining your corporate theme, have a simple letterhead designed and avoid using too many colours or large fonts. Stationery costs vary depending on paper stock, logos, colours used and quantities ordered. A neat, well-written letter has more impact on the reader than a badly worded one presented on embossed letterhead with gold printing. If you keep to one colour, printing costs are lower. A textured and coloured paper stock, such as cream or parchment, can present a professional image at an affordable cost. Printed envelopes are costly—you could use an adhesive address label that doubles as a shipping address label.

When you order stationery, the shorter the print run, the higher per sheet cost, so obtain a quotation in quantities of 500 and 1,000. However, don't order 1,000 letterhead just because it's cheap; you may have enough stock to last for 20 years. Some people print their own business cards, and as there is a lot of competition in the printing and office supply industry, it pays to shop around. Digital printing now allows for more customized, print-on-demand short runs, so explore this option.

WHAT INSURANCE POLICIES DO YOU NEED?

Most people don't think twice about the price of insuring their vehicle. Yet many business owners neglect incorporating a comprehensive insurance strategy that includes insuring their most valuable asset—themselves. There is a myriad of policies and coverage available, so let's demystify the most important ones.

Business and liability insurance

Fire, theft and damage

Businesses contained in a commercial building need adequate fire, theft and damage coverage, just as you would insure your home. With fire, water or sewer damage or vandalism, buildings and equipment can be replaced, but not the cost of reconstructing files, documents and accounting records. A commercial policy can be designed to suit all of these needs, including window and glass breakage, employee theft, business interruption, contractor's equipment, fleet insurance, even kidnap and ransom. Policy price is dependent on your individual business requirements, but a basic commercial policy costs in the vicinity of $600.

CASE STUDY

UPPING THE ANTE

Working as a consulting controller for a personnel agency employing temporary staff, I reviewed their insurance policies. I discovered that the computer equipment was woefully under-insured, as was the employee theft coverage at only $5,000. On my recommendation, the equipment insurance was upgraded, and employee theft coverage increased to $25,000. An employee later stole $500 while on assignment, and after I completed my contract, another employee embezzled nearly $10,000. Had the policy not been upgraded, the business would have suffered a substantial loss.

Liability insurance

Professionals should insure for "errors and omissions" and professional liability. Special policies are available for doctors, accountants and lawyers. We all hear about clients suing businesses for malpractice, faulty products and liability through accidents. Ensure you have adequate coverage for your trade or profession. Ask your insurance agent to help you establish a comprehensive policy.

Also discuss "care, custody and control inclusion." Without coverage, even if an employee is working on a client's problem and it is under your control, you are not covered against potential damages caused by your employee. If you cannot get this coverage, know the risks when you send people onto a job. For example, if your employee steam-cleaned a $3,000 couch and damaged the upholstery, your business will get sued. Without "care, custody and control" coverage, the insurance company will not cover you. Not only will you have the damages to pay, but also the legal costs.

Home-based businesses

Home-based business insurance is a rider added to your existing home policy and is restrictive in its coverage. These policies insure equipment and inventory to a certain value in the home, usually up to $20,000, and $2,500 for goods off premises. Client liability to $1,000,000 is included. A policy like this costs approximately $220 a year. Then, if a client comes to your house, trips over the dog and breaks a leg, you will be covered if you are sued.

Other commercial policy coverage is not usually available in home-based policies. Insurance companies have now recognized the need to cater to the home-based sector, so shop around. Some professions are not covered and you may have to take out a commercial business policy to fully protect your business.

Personal insurance

Not only are you the most important asset to your business, you are even more important to your family, so ensure that you are well-insured and that their needs are also taken care of. Here are some policy types to consider and their benefits.

Life insurance

Life insurance has three primary purposes: to provide cash for dependents to settle your debts; to supplement the family income; and for estate and retirement planning. Seek professional advice for the latter as it usually involves purchasing permanent insurance, such as universal life policies. These policies have considerable benefits. If your policy is convertible, you can convert to a universal life policy without a medical assessment.

To provide sufficient cash for family and business purposes, when calculating how much insurance you need for the family, consider how long your dependents will need extra money. This depends on your spouse's ability to earn an income and your financial obligations. For example, a single person starting a business may only need enough to pay off the company debts, while a family person with a spouse who stays home will need $1,000,000 or more to pay off personal debts, provide for the family and possibly plan for retirement, depending on the spouse's age and earning potential.

Your insurance agent can prepare a Financial Needs Analysis to help determine the amount you need. Factor in inflation when doing this calculation. At three percent inflation, a need to supplement income by $25,000 will grow to $50,000 in 24 years. The amount of insurance required for the business will depend on several factors:

- If family members are involved in the business, how easy will it be for them to find another similar-paying job if the business fails?

- If family members can take over the business, coverage is required to bridge the time required to recover and get the business going again. In addition, the bank will probably like to see any loans paid out.

- If the business has to be sold, the chance of realizing its true value is remote. Creditors can attack life insurance intended for the family if one spouse has signed personal guarantees, which is common. For example, if you have a lease or bank loan that is guaranteed by the surviving spouse, the landlord and bank can come after the life insurance proceeds to satisfy the amount owed.

- If the business is a partnership or corporation, it is important that there is insurance in place to enable the surviving partners or shareholders to buy out the surviving spouse's interest. Seek advice on who should own the insurance, as there are significant tax implications if the insurance is corporate or personally owned.

Term insurance

Term insurance is affordable and comes in five- to 20-year terms. Premiums are guaranteed for that period of time and automatically renew at a higher, set rate for the next term.

$UCCE$$ $TRATEGY

SHOP AROUND TO RENEW: Do not automatically renew if your health is good, as the renewal rates can be 25 to 100 percent more than the premiums if you shop around for a new policy. The assumption is that you only renew if you are too sick to get a new policy.

Term insurance meets the need for cash as you build your business and provides for your family's needs. The most cost-effective term insurance is a guaranteed renewable and convertible ten-year term. Much of the competition is focussed on this type, which consequently has the lowest premiums. There are also preferred and regular rates. A 35-year-old can purchase $500,000 for about $35 a month at regular rates, where the preferred rates would be approximately $25. For more information visit *www.lifeinsurancequote.com.*

Disability insurance

If you suffer a serious accident, injury or illness that prevents you from working for an extended period of time, the financial risks to your business and family are significant. Current and future income stops while business and personal expenses continue. Workers' Compensation pays a percentage of your income, but only eight percent of disabilities are usually covered, as accidents often occur off the job or illness is involved, and payments will likely fall short of what you will need. One of the leading causes of divorce is long-term illnesses and the associated financial stress.

Provide some protection with a good disability insurance policy. Although it is designed to protect your income, if you are starting out, there is no income to protect. Consequently, you will only qualify for a minimal amount—possibly $1,000 a month or less. There are policies available for whatever amount you want up to $3,000 or more monthly, but the company performs an income test at time of claim, reviews your actual income and pays approximately 66 percent.

$UCCE$$ $TRATEGY

PLAN WELL AHEAD: One possibility is to purchase a personal disability policy based on your income at least one year before you plan to start a business. Most applications query your intention to leave the current company within a year. A "yes" answer and you don't get the insurance. Ensure that the policy covers you if you change jobs and that the coverage is underwritten when you take out the policy. This means they will pay what you have purchased and will not do another income check at time of claim.

Talk to an expert and ask how you will be paid if you can do part of your job, or as you regain your health. There are usually residual or partial disability payments when you start back but benefits can vary. Further, do you want to wait 30, 60 or 90 days before payments start? The premiums are about twice the cost for 30 days as compared to 90 days. Some disability policies cover your "out of pocket" business expenses, and you can add this rider regardless of how much income you have.

Critical illness insurance

A new insurance called critical illness coverage pays a lump sum of $50,000 or more 30 days after you are diagnosed with a life-threatening illness, such as heart attack, stroke or cancer. Many people recover from these critical illnesses but not until they have experienced considerable emotional and physical health problems, causing significant financial stress. The premiums are lower than for disability insurance and the amount you purchase is not as limited. Many business owners return to work within three months from most injuries or simple illnesses and would not collect much on a disability insurance policy. Critical illnesses keep them off the job much longer and the money is paid out after 30 days. For more information, visit *www.critical-illness-insurance.com*.

Plan an exit strategy

As the business increases in value, consider either disability buyout insurance or critical illness insurance on each partner or shareholder. Few businesses can carry an ill partner for an extended period of time—you need an exit strategy. Set out the conditions in a shareholder or partnership agreement and ensure that the funds to make it happen are insured. If you have insurance owned and paid for by your company, check the tax implications with your accountant. Use a well-recognized insurance professional with at least five years of experience.

WHAT IS RISK MANAGEMENT?

Starting a business involves taking certain risks, some so remote that it is not necessary to plan for their occurrence. Other risks may concern you, but are too costly to protect yourself against. Others are affordable to insure against.

CASE STUDY

PAYING THROUGH THE ROOF

John, a small, unincorporated contractor, hired a subcontracting company to replace the roof of a condominium he was contracted to repair. A freak storm caused $200,000 damage to the condominiums on the top floors. The subcontractor who performed the work did not have insurance to cover this damage, so the insurance company that paid for the repairs successfully sued John for the $200,000. He was forced to sell all his RRSPs and never quite recovered financially from this experience.

This risk could have been eliminated in three ways. First, John should have checked that the subcontractor had the necessary insurance; if not, he could have ensured that his liability insurance included subcontractors; or, if he had his RRSPs invested in segregated rather than mutual funds, they would have been creditor-protected, and the insurance company would not have had access to them. Segregated funds are similar to mutual funds but are sold through insurance companies, thus they have the same creditor protection as an insurance policy.

Figure 6.2 outlines some common business risks, their significance and what can be done to protect yourself against these situations. If you choose not to cover these risks, then you are assuming the risk and ensuing financial consequences yourself. Consider the assessment of the risk and then explore the cost to insure against it.

Figure 6.2: HOW TO REDUCE BUSINESS RISK

Risk	Significance	What you can do
Business failure	Unlikely but would have serious financial consequences: • Property, home, investments • Mutual fund investments	Incorporate • Transfer ownership to others • Transfer to segregated funds
Theft, fire liability, water damage	Low risks that a good business insurance policy will cover.	Consult an experienced insurance broker for a comprehensive policy.
Employee on-the-job accident	What is your liability if you hire someone who is then injured on the job?	Without Workers' Compensation, you may be personally liable for medical and future income costs.
Death	Highly unlikely yet still a possibility.	Term or life insurance to provide for debts and family.
Disability or illness	A real risk. Long hours and stress take their toll.	Disability and/or critical illness insurance.
Key employee or partner is injured or dies	Some employees or partners are critical to your overall business success.	Obtain life, disability or critical illness insurance on them. Insurance can provide a lump sum to buy out a partner if disabled for over a year.

STEP-BY-STEP START-UP CHECKLISTS

As you establish each start-up cost for your new business, use the checklist in Figure 6.3 as a guide to the overall cost. Then transfer these figures to the appropriate places in your business plan.

Figure 6.3: ESTIMATED BUSINESS START-UP COSTS	
Type of Expense	**Estimated Cost**
1. Consultations with accountant	$_____
2. Consultations with lawyer	_____
3. Lawyer's fees to prepare buy-sell agreement	_____
4. Purchase price of business	_____
5. Incorporation fees	_____
6. Business plan preparation	_____
7. Loan application and financing fees	_____
8. First and last month's rent	_____
9. Renovations to office space	_____
10. Utility deposits	_____
11. Municipal business licence	_____
12. Other licences	_____
13. Telephone, fax line and Internet installations	_____
14. Cellular phone purchase and access fee	_____
15. Interior and exterior signs	_____
16. Computer system	_____
17. Printing and stationery	_____
18. Office furniture and equipment	_____
19. Marketing costs	_____
20. Office supplies and miscellaneous	_____
21. Business and life/disability insurance	_____
22. Other: _____	_____
TOTAL:	$_____

Your start-up checklist

Figure 6.4 is a checklist in order of priority of the steps you should take when setting up your business. Use it to keep track of where you are and don't miss any important steps. If your business is home-based, some of these steps will not apply to you.

Figure 6.4: BUSINESS START-UP CHECKLIST		
Step	**Procedure**	**Check**
1.	Decide which type of business is right for me	☐
2.	Research the market and the competition	☐
3.	Take vendor's proposal to accountant for review	☐
4.	Visit municipality to review bylaws and regulations	☐
5.	Research other licensing requirements	☐
6.	Contact lawyer to review/prepare buy-sell agreement	☐
7.	Prepare business plan and projections	☐
8.	Find suitable location for business	☐
9.	Research costs of all renovations to office	☐
10.	Contact lawyer to have lease reviewed	☐
11.	Talk to bank manager about financing requirements	☐
12.	Choose three names and register business name	☐
13.	Have incorporation papers prepared	☐
14.	Call telephone company for phone requirements	☐
15.	Order cellular phone (you will need all your phone numbers so that stationery can be ordered)	☐
16.	Apply for necessary business licences	☐

17. Open business accounts and credit card applications ☐

18. Apply for GST/HST registration ☐

19. Apply for provincial sales tax number ☐

20. Apply for payroll registration and information ☐

21. Register with Workers' Compensation Board ☐

22. Prepare marketing and advertising campaign ☐

23. Research computer requirements and prices ☐

24. Talk to accountant about accounting system ☐

25. Obtain quotations on exterior and interior sign work ☐

26. Obtain quotations on printing requirements ☐

27. Contact insurance broker ☐

Other: _____ ☐

_____ ☐

_____ ☐

_____ ☐

_____ ☐

_____ ☐

_____ ☐

_____ ☐

_____ ☐

_____ ☐

WHAT IS THE NEXT STEP?

You have a great idea, it's been well researched, and you know your approximate start-up costs. Things are looking good, so now it's time to start putting together a formal business plan to see how viable this idea really is. Where will you borrow money? How much will you need? Will your ideas transfer into a viable business concern? Now is the time to put all those ideas on paper, document your research and do some serious number crunching. The following chapter walks you through the various components of a business plan.

CHAPTER 7

What is a business plan?

Success doesn't just happen—it usually takes thorough planning, and of course, money always helps.

WHY DO YOU NEED A BUSINESS PLAN?

You have probably discovered by now that there is more to starting a business than you first thought. There is so much to learn and gather that it can become quite overwhelming. Have you assessed whether you are an entrepreneur at heart and ready for the challenge? Do you have a good indication of the type of business you want? This next step will test your theories and indicate whether to proceed further.

A business plan is a necessary tool for all businesses. Just as a home is not built without blueprints or a movie made without a script, you don't start a business without a sound and workable blueprint. You now take the information you have gathered and put those ideas formally onto paper.

Without a business plan, banks or investors will not entertain the thought of financing your business. It is your only foot in the door, so make sure it shines. You will learn how much you need to borrow, whether you can afford to borrow, your break-even point and whether the business can afford to pay you a satisfactory wage. People often prepare a plan and start crunching numbers, only to discover that their idea needs reworking or is not financially viable. It is better to discover this on paper rather than after you've started.

Where do you find help with business plan information?

With the Internet, sample plans can be freely downloaded and used as a reference. Most banks and large accounting companies have publications or CD-ROMs to help you. As well, try the following resources:

◆ *Canada Business Service Centre:* An on-line interactive business planner that allows you to complete your plan using a template.
Web site: *www.cbsc.org.*

◆ *Royal Bank:* Their small business resource centre includes three sample plans which can be downloaded, along with other resource information.
Web site: *www.royalbank.ca/sme/bigidea.*

◆ *Small Business Development Center:* Offers over 30 industry-specific business plans, both U.S. and Canadian.
Web site: *http://sbdcnet.utsa.edu.SBIC/bplans.htm.*

◆ *Small Business Information Canada:* This site offers extensive business plan information.
Web site: *http://sbinfocanada.about.com/cs/businessplans.*

◆ *Business Plans.com:* This site offers over 250 plans, many of them industry specific and some Canadian. A mine of information.
Web site: *www.bplans.com.*

◆ *GlobalStar Software Ltd.:* Retails excellent business planning software, Business Suite Deluxe and Business Plan Deluxe, which includes hundreds of business forms, marketing plans and office templates, plus a free copy of *Business for Beginners,* available in retail office and computer stores.
Web site: *www.globalstarsoftware.com.*

$UCCE$$ $TRATEGY

GET PROFESSIONAL ADVICE: Enlist a consultant or accountant's help in compiling the information into the correct format, and have him or her review it after both the first and final drafts. Putting it all together can be challenging. A bank would prefer to see that you have involved a professional—it helps to validate the contents.

Expect to spend anywhere from two weeks to a few months in completing research and putting the plan together. Some people hire a consultant or accountant to prepare their whole plan, which isn't a good idea, because *you* need to have answers to all the questions to operate your business successfully—and to satisfy a lender or investor.

WHAT IS IN A BUSINESS PLAN?

Follow a plan format that ensures you research all the important areas of your business, and if it is being used for lending or investment purposes, that you have provided all the information that lenders need. Your first task is to decide why you are preparing this plan. Answer these questions:

- Why am I preparing this plan?
- Who else will be reading it?
- Why will they be reading it?
- What do they need to know?

The size of the final document will be dependent on the size and complexity of your business and whether you are looking for outside funding. The end result should be professionally presented, with typewritten pages and a table of contents, and securely bound. Include the following sections.

1. Executive summary

The executive summary should be no longer than two pages. Prepare it after the plan is completed, as it summarizes the whole plan in a nutshell. Make it dynamic and exciting, to generate the reader's interest. Loans officers or investors have read copious plans and tend to skip through them if they get bored.

$UCCE$$ $TRATEGY

KNOW YOUR GOALS AND OBJECTIVES: By knowing why you are preparing this plan, you can save time and effort by focussing on the important areas. Business plans often contain "filler" information that is not pertinent. Look at sample plans from the sites mentioned earlier to get an idea. If you need to borrow funds, ask the lending institution exactly what is required.

2. The company

Introduce the business in more detail, outlining your type of business, giving its history (if you are purchasing an existing business) or an outline of the new business' products or services. With an existing business, highlight any recent special achievements. This section should be broken down into the following subsections:

a) *General business overview:* A description of the business, where it fits into the marketplace, what needs it will be filling and how it will fill those needs. Describe the markets that will use your business and include any business history.

b) *Company structure:* Outline the corporate structure of the business. Include a list of shareholders or partners and incorporation information.

c) *Location:* Describe the location, its benefits, amenities and accessibility to customer traffic. Include freight routes if it's a manufacturing or wholesale business, traffic statistics if available from your local municipality, and area demographics and growth rate. Detail parking and zoning information, the cost and terms of the lease, taxes and utilities. List any foreseeable disadvantages to your location, and explain why you chose it. Detail office space, storage and operational facilities. List any renovations or alterations that need to be completed.

d) *Key personnel:* Include a brief profile of all key partners or employees, their duties and experience, and include their resumés in the appendix. Highlight their education and expertise, business qualifications, history and references if available.

$UCCE$$ $TRATEGY

COVER ALL BASES: Lenders look for sound managerial experience in the key areas of sales and marketing, accounting and technical operations. A gap in any one area will count as a strike against the business. Ensure you have covered all these bases in your plan. Competent managers are a strong indication that the business will be in good hands.

e) *Goals and objectives:* Outline your goals and objectives, both long- and short-term. Many people neglect this area, failing to think past the start-up stage. Your goals and objectives should be explained in more detail in other sections of your plan and be considered when preparing financial figures.

f) *Strengths and weaknesses:* Blow your horn and detail the business' strengths. Stress where and why you excel in these areas, whether it be great customer service, pricing or a strong distribution base. Don't include marketing strengths and weaknesses—this will be covered in the marketing section. Discuss your weaknesses and how you plan to overcome them.

g) *Mission and vision statements:* A mission statement describes your company philosophy in a few sentences. A vision statement describes how you see your company in the future. Think carefully about each one. Study other mission statements and design one that is uniquely yours. A mission statement shows your commitment to the business and its customers and gives you a written promise to uphold.

3. Products and services

Your business is all about selling services or products, so ensure that what you are offering is marketable and profitable. Use the following headings to detail this information.

a) *Product description:* Describe your products or services, their benefits and how they fill a need in the marketplace. Show your advantage over the competition and the volume you can output. Describe your business' developmental stage. List potential or current contracts. Refer to any letters of intent from prospective clients and include these in the appendix.

b) *Cost of sales:* The basis of your business is profit margins. Show what products sell for and provide the costs of raw materials, freight, packaging, wages, etc. Note the expected gross profit margins and whether they will change if you diversify or expand. Clearly explain how the manufacturing or distribution process will operate, remembering that a lender may not be familiar with your type of business.

c) *Future projections:* If you plan future expansion, research or development, include this information. List any potential threats or opportunities.

d) *Legal concerns:* If your business entails legal considerations such as patents, copyrights, trademarks or special licences, include relevant information.

4. Marketing strategies

Refer to both market research (Chapter 4) and how you plan to market your business (Chapter 10). As marketing is a key component to the success of your business, prepare this section in depth. Ensure that the following topics are included.

a) *Market research:* Break this section down into the following subsections:

- An analysis of today's market and trends
- Past and future industry, global and consumer trends
- Your target market, its size and demographics
- Your ideal consumer profile
- Your projected share of the market
- Geographic boundaries
- Seasonal trends
- Customer service policies
- Strengths and weaknesses
- Market survey results.

$UCCE$$ $TRATEGY

SHOW YOU DID YOUR HOMEWORK: Include a summary of your market survey results including how many people you contacted, the questions you asked and their responses. Note if you have changed your strategy based on these results. Convert answers into percentages, for example, "75 percent of respondents said they would use my service at least four times a year."

b) ***The competition:*** Both you and the lender must understand the strength of your competitors. Your field trips and research should allow you to address the following topics:

- The current competition, their size and market share
- Future competition
- The strengths and weaknesses of the competition
- How you can overcome their strengths and capitalize on their weaknesses
- Your strengths and weaknesses (use the SWOT analysis in Chapter 4)
- Your edge over the competition
- Your cost to stay competitive.

c) ***Marketing and sales strategies:*** Part of your business plan will be a marketing plan, which details how you will find potential customers. A sound marketing plan includes a mix of methods, including using various media, promotional methods and one-on-one techniques. Address these topics:

- Promotional and media methods you will use
- Special services or policies
- The target market these methods will reach
- The effectiveness of each method
- The frequency of use
- How you will sell your products/service (agents, representatives, staff)
- Incentive or sales bonus schemes
- The reach of your sales force.

5. Operational information

Plan how you will operate your business, from overhead costs to distribution channels. Include the following information:

a) ***Overhead costs:*** Explain your estimated overhead costs and demonstrate a break-even point. If future plans involve expansion, reflect these costs. A detailed explanation of these costs will be included in your projections, so don't go into great detail here.

b) ***Suppliers:*** List your major suppliers, their terms of credit and their product availability. Note whether you have to sign any personal guarantees to obtain credit from them.

c) ***Quality control:*** Describe your policies on quality control, any relevant hazards or environmental risks and how you propose to overcome these obstacles. Mention any specific safety procedures relevant to your operation.

d) ***Distribution:*** Outline how your products will be distributed or delivered and any competitive advantages to your methods.

e) ***Employees:*** List the staff positions along with their job descriptions, areas of responsibility and expected salaries.

f) ***Assets and equipment:*** Note any equipment on hand or to be purchased, its value or cost and its life expectancy.

g) ***Insurance policies:*** List the various insurance policies you will take out, including liability, theft and fire, workers' compensation, and key management and employee insurance.

h) ***Licences and permits:*** List any licences or permits that your business requires to operate, and their cost.

6. Financial information

The viability of your new venture will culminate when you prepare projections of income and expenses, cash flow forecasts and when you review how much money you may require. Even if you are not borrowing money, projections and cash flows facilitate making many future decisions.

If you are attempting to borrow money, the financial section should include the following:

a) ***Projections of income and expenses:*** Projections are a month-by-month estimation of sales and expenses, including start-up costs, itemized in the month the revenue was earned and the costs were incurred. Prepare the first year in months, and by quarters or annually for the following two to five years. The bottom line reflects profits or losses. Include notes to substantiate the numbers—it's easy to create figures out of thin air. Be conservative with revenues and practical with expenses.

b) *Cash flow forecasts:* The projections should be accompanied by cash flow forecasts for the corresponding periods. A cash flow forecast differs from projections, as it estimates when revenues will be received and when expenses will be paid, and includes income from loans and other sources. Samples can be found later in this chapter.

c) *Financial statements:* Banks require a projected balance sheet and, if you are purchasing a business, past financial statements for the last two to four years.

d) *Capital expenses:* Include a list of capital spending, such as asset purchases or building renovations. When a lender considers a proposal, these values help determine how a loan will be used and secured.

e) *Net worth statement:* Lenders require personal statements of net worth from owners, partners or shareholders. Loans are often personally secured, and this statement lists your personal assets, liabilities and net worth. Net worth statements also indicate the stability of the key management players.

7. Funding requirements

This section is devoted to the sum you need to borrow, how you expect to repay it and over what time period. Your projections and cash flow forecasts should have indicated how much the business needs and can afford to repay. The total monthly loan payment shows on the cash flow forecast and loan interest only on the projections. How you intend to secure the loan and with what assets should be explained. If you are looking for an investment partner, note the share of the company available in return for their investment.

Outline the following:

- When you need the money and how much
- The type of loan you are applying for
- The desired terms of repayment
- A breakdown of how you will use the funds
- Future funding requirements, if any.

8. Appendix

Include *copies* of any documents that back up and strengthen the information in your business plan, including:

- Up-to-date financial statements from the business you are purchasing
- Personal statements of net worth
- Letters of reference and letters of intent
- Product pictures or relevant newspaper articles
- Resumés of key employees or partners
- Incorporation or business registration papers

CASE STUDY

PLANNING FOR SUCCESS

Mary Jane Stenberg had no concept of a business plan until she participated in a nine-month Step Into Business program, sponsored by the Business Development Bank of Canada. Her fledgling Langley, B.C., company, Stenberg and Associates, provides employment training for a variety of career opportunities. After two years in business, she already employed five people. Mary Jane paid bills and drew a salary, but her dreams were to expand—yet she didn't know how to start.

Now, eight years later, she heads a highly successful business with two locations offering 14 training programs and employing 37 people. How did she grow her business so rapidly and successfully? Mary Jane attributes her success to always using a business plan before making any decisions.

"I followed the business plan I had learned to prepare during the course, and used the template for other things, such as expansion," she explains. "I learned so much. Whenever I wanted to get larger, I revisited and revised my plan. You have to have your plan and abide by it, but don't be afraid to change it."

- Cash flow and projection forecasts
- Permits, licences, trademarks or patents
- Market surveys
- Equipment and asset appraisals
- Partnership or employee agreements
- Insurance policies and leases.

HOW DO YOU PREPARE PROJECTIONS?

Working through the numbers with Phenomenal Flowers Inc.

Following are examples of three months of a twelve-month income and expense projection, a corresponding cash flow forecast and reconciliation of the two. Jasmine is the proprietor of Phenomenal Flowers Inc. and wants to borrow $12,500 from the bank to open a retail outlet. She prepared draft projections and discussed the results with her accountant.

Projections of sales and expenses

Figure 7.1 demonstrates the projected (estimated) sales and expenses for the store. Jasmine made the following assumptions:

- The gross profit margin after purchases and wastage is 45 percent of retail price.
- One full-time employee is paid $1,800 a month.
- Start-up expenses include consulting with an accountant, insurance policies, renovations and repairs to the store, marketing, advertising, phone line installation and office supplies.
- The employee will use Jasmine's van for deliveries.
- If the business starts in March, it can capitalize on Easter in April and Mother's Day in May.
- Jasmine doesn't expect a steady customer base for six to 12 months.

Figure 7.1: PROJECTIONS OF SALES AND EXPENSES

PHENOMENAL FLOWERS INC.
Twelve Months Projected Sales and Expenses

Description	March	April	May
Sales	$ 4,500	$ 9,000	$12,150
Cost of sales:			
Purchases	2,350	4,600	6,300
Wastage	125	350	380
	2,475	4,950	6,680
Gross profit	**2,025**	**4,050**	**5,470**
Overhead expenses:			
Accounting fees	1,500	200	200
Advertising	775	750	850
Bank charges	65	65	70
Fees & licences	230	45	0
Insurance	2,400	0	0
Loan interest	100	100	100
Office supplies	923	180	90
Promotion/marketing	400	500	450
Rent	1,250	1,250	1,250
Repairs & maintenance	1,780	200	100
Telephone	410	125	125
Utilities	300	300	300
Vehicle–gas	100	100	100
Vehicle–repairs & maintenance	130	130	130
Workers' Compensation	65	65	65
Wages	1,800	1,800	1,800
	12,228	5,810	5,630
Profit/(loss)	**(10,203)**	**(1,760)**	**(160)**
Accumulated	**($10,203)**	**($11,963)**	**($12,123)**

Cash flow forecast

In preparing the cash flow forecast (Figure 7.2), Jasmine assumed the following:

- The bank would loan her $12,500 on an unsecured line of credit, which she wants to pay off quickly. She would put $5,000 into the business.

- Half of her sales would be on account, receiving half in 30 days and half in 60 days.

- Her floral supplies would be paid for by cash at the auctions, which she would charge to her Visa and pay off the monthly balances in 30 days.

- Smaller trade accounts would be paid in 30 days.

- Bank charges, loan interest, rent and utilities would be paid when due.

- Repairs, renovations, marketing and insurance would be paid immediately.

Figure 7.2: CASH FLOW FORECAST

PHENOMENAL FLOWERS INC.
Twelve Months Cash Flow Projections

Description	March	April	May
Cash receipts in:			
Cash sales	$ 2,700	$ 5,400	$ 7,290
Receivables–30 days	0	900	1,800
Receivables–60 days	0	0	900
Loan proceeds	12,500	0	0
Total cash:	**15,200**	**6,300**	**9,990**
Cash disbursed:			
Cost of sales	0	2,475	4,950
Accounting fees	0	1,500	200
Advertising	0	775	750
Bank charges	65	65	70
Fees & licences	230	45	0
Insurance	2,400	0	0
Loan interest	0	100	100
Loan principal	0	700	700
Office expenses	300	473	180
Promotion/marketing	400	500	450
Rent & taxes	1,250	1,250	1,250
Repairs & maintenance	1,780	200	100
Telephone	0	410	125
Utilities	0	300	300
Vehicle–gas	100	100	100
Vehicle–repairs & maintenance	130	130	130
Workers' Compensation	0	0	195
Wages	1,800	1,800	1,800
	8,455	10,823	11,400
Surplus/(deficit):	**6,745**	**(4,523)**	**(1,410)**
Opening balance:	5,000	11,745	7,222
+ cash receipts	15,200	6,300	9,990
– cash disbursed	8,455	10,823	11,400
Closing balance	**$11,745**	**$ 7,222**	**$ 5,812**

Reconciliation

To understand how the projections relate to the cash flow, Figure 7.3 shows the outstanding monies due to and by the business at the end of the three-month period. This figure agrees with the projected sales and expense statement.

Figure 7.3: RECONCILIATION OF CASH FLOW WITH PROJECTIONS

PHENOMENAL FLOWERS INC.
Reconciliation of Sales Projections with Cash Flow

Accounts receivable balance due:	$ 6,660
Less accounts payable balance due:	7,095
Shortfall:	435
Loan due:	12,500
Contributed capital:	5,000
Current debts:	17,935
Less cash on hand after three months:	(5,812)
Reconciliation with loss:	**(12,123)**
Less loan principal repaid:	$ 1,400
(Non-operational cost)	

What her accountant noticed

Jasmine's accountant was somewhat concerned with the projections. Month three reflects the store's break-even point, yet until Christmas, the retail floral trade is relatively quiet. With the business heading into summer, no amount of marketing is going to bring in customers when they are on vacation. With the store costing $5,630 in monthly overhead, how are the sales going to be sustained to pay the bills?

Jasmine may have to consider hiring a part-time employee and not taking wages from the business for up to a year. She should reduce her loan principal payments to the standard three percent of the outstanding balance, plus inter-est, and reduce her marketing costs over the summer, saving the marketing push until later in the year. These measures would reduce overhead to approxi-mately $4,000 and help with cash flow, but the store still has to generate $9,000 a month in sales to break even. Jasmine's accountant felt that the bank would not give her a loan based on these projections and advised her against opening the store until she could devise a more profitable solution—or business.

WHO WILL LEND YOU MONEY?

If you have a viable business plan, the ability to repay and, most important, security for the loan—you have the right formula. Deciding what type of money to borrow and from whom is the next hurdle. Many businesses do not require large sums to get them started, and often, people can't get a small loan from the bank, so they look elsewhere. Be aware of the pros and cons of non-traditional financing before you make your decision. With all potential lenders, consider the ten tips for borrowing in Figure 7.4.

Figure 7.4: TEN TIPS FOR BORROWING

1. Don't approach a lender for "working capital." Loans are usually given for tangible assets that can be secured.

2. Don't expect a lender to finance your whole venture. The owner is expected to invest money, at least one-third of the start-up cost.

3. When you call for an appointment, ask what information will be needed so you are well prepared.

4. Dress smartly. Jeans and sneakers are out. Don't chew gum.

5. Research the various government-funded grants and loans before deciding on a lender.

6. Have an experienced third party critique your business plan before presenting it to a lender.

7. Have the approval of your spouse or partner before committing to financial obligations.

8. If you are initially turned down, take the lender's advice and rework your plan.

9. Discuss with your accountant whom you should approach for money and what type of loan may best suit your requirements.

10. In your interview, be a good listener. Don't try to hold the floor and convince the lender how great you are. He or she can tell this by your manner, presentation and business plan.

Traditional financing options

You have a sound business plan and are ready to approach a lending institution for financing. Following are your traditional options.

1. Canada Small Business Financing Program

Small business loans of up to $250,000 are available through this federally secured loans program. Qualifying small businesses include proprietorships and partnerships. The loan will finance up to 90 percent of asset purchases, including new or used equipment and leasehold or property improvements. Financing is also available for capital leases for vehicles and certain equipment. Security is required, and personal guarantees cannot exceed 25 percent of the loan.

The interest rate on commercial loans can be fixed or floating, but should not exceed the lender's residential mortgage interest rate by more than three percent. Lease rates are higher. The interest rate includes a 1.25 percent administration fee. There is a two percent registration fee and loans cannot extend longer than ten years. These loans are administered through your local financial institution. A sound business plan is a firm requirement. For more information, contact your local bank or visit their Web site at *http://strategis.gc.ca/csbfa.*

2. Bank unsecured lines of credit

For loans under $25,000, a line of credit is a source of reasonably priced financing. Interest rates fluctuate, based on current rates, and are usually two percent higher than a mortgage. A line of credit is usually repaid at a minimum of three percent of the loan, so on $25,000 you have to pay at least $750 a month. This option can work if you are sure the business can meet the monthly payments.

3. Bank secured lines of credit

This is riskier financing, because banks require security, usually in the form of a mortgage on your home. The upside is that as you are getting established, you have the option of paying only the monthly interest. The downside is that you are threatening the security of your family if the business doesn't perform as projected. Unless you are 100 percent sure that the business will be profitable in a short time frame, think carefully before putting your home on the line.

CASE STUDY

NICE MORTGAGE—NO BUSINESS

Jean-Guy, a new entrepreneur, remortgaged his home to open a retail furniture store. Thinking that he knew everything about running a store because he had competently managed one for many years, he leased a cheap building, completed renovations and advertising and opened the doors. Jean-Guy forgot one very important start-up step—his business licence. When the bylaws officer visited, he told Jean-Guy that he was contravening the bylaws because the property was not zoned for retail sales. He fought hard, but the municipality would not budge, and he had to close the store.

Jean-Guy couldn't raise enough capital to move to another location. He returned his inventory, lost a 15 percent restocking fee of $7,500 and the last month's rent on the lease. He also suffered the cost of all the renovations, advertising and signage. The final loss amounted to nearly $30,000. He will now be paying off his mortgage for the next 20 years.

4. Alternative lending programs

There is a myriad of loan programs designed to help small businesses get off the ground. They vary from province to province, aiding everyone from students to women, First Nations peoples and youth. Banks and credit unions now recognize that many entrepreneurs need only small loans, and are catering more to this market. Some alternative financing programs include:

- Community Futures Development Corporation (national)
- Women's Enterprise Society (western provinces)
- Canadian Business Youth Foundation (national)
- Calmeadow (national)
- BDC Student Business Loans Program (national).

To learn more about these and other programs, check out ***http://sbinfo-canada.about.com*** and click on "financing."

$UCCE$$ $TRATEGY

VISIT YOUR LOCAL CBSC: The Canada Business Service Centre is in business to help start-ups and growing businesses. Offices are located across Canada and through the Internet at ***www.cbsc.org***. Talk to an information officer, as they are conversant with the loans programs in your province.

"Risky" financing alternatives

When traditional financing is not an option, some eager entrepreneurs seek riskier financing. This route may be destined for failure, because if traditional financing is denied, there is usually a good reason—this is a warning to revisit the business plan and the whole business idea. Here are some options to consider and the risks involved.

1. Family or friends

It's easy to approach parents or family for a loan, but not so easy explaining to them why you can't repay them. Before you consider this option, clarify how they would feel should the business not be profitable and the loan not paid back as per the agreed terms. The benefit to these loans is that family can be flexible if repayments are late, and loans can be interest-free or low interest. If the loan could jeopardize family relationships, perhaps it isn't advisable.

The same principle applies to friends. Which do you value the most? Your business or your friendship? There is no better way to ruin a good friendship than by not repaying debts. Don't ask friends to guarantee a loan for you either. This too ruins friendships. I once guaranteed a small loan for a friend who didn't honour some payments. I made the payments but it caused the demise of a long-time relationship.

2. Second or increased home mortgages

Similar to a secured line of credit, an increased or second mortgage is risky financing for a new business. It's a long-term battle to regain home equity if the business doesn't succeed. You will be left with a large mortgage payment, business debts and the possibility of the bank foreclosing on your home. Many marriages have dissolved for this reason. Business is a gamble, even when you have a good poker hand.

3. Credit cards

For short-term financing, credit cards come in handy—but at what price? They give you a false sense of security because they allow you to make minimum monthly payments. At the same time, high interest rates compound at an alarming rate. Many businesses use credit cards to pay for supplies and start-up costs, so if you have to use them, keep strict control over your spending habits. Use them as a 30-day, interest-free, short-term business loan. Pay off the full balance each month. Collect points but not interest charges. If you have trouble controlling your plastic purchases, cut up your cards or freeze them in a block of ice—it's called freezing your liabilities.

4. Redeeming RRSPs

It's difficult enough to save for an RRSP, and even more difficult to put the money back, once it is withdrawn. There are also tax consequences, so discuss this with your accountant. Redeem them only if you are *sure* that you can replace them by February of the following year. An extra tax burden is the last thing you need in your first year of business.

5. Finance companies and brokers

Finance companies and brokers are often willing to lend money with fewer security requirements than a bank demands, but you may pay exorbitant interest rates. Some people have obtained second mortgages from finance companies, ultimately paying just interest without reducing the principal amount. Treat these loans as you would treat credit cards—proceed with caution and preferably, avoid this type of financing.

CASE STUDY

THE ETERNAL LOAN

Terry and Marianna were in dire straits with their business. Terry spent freely while Marianna lay awake worrying about the mounting debts. Their home was mortgaged to the hilt; the bank would not lend them more. Terry finally persuaded Marianna that if they took out a second mortgage for $50,000, the bills could be paid off. The monthly payments would only be $400. In a moment of weakness, Marianna agreed. They signed with a broker for a two-year-term loan, paying interest only. They paid over $9,000 in interest without reducing the principal. Terry didn't change his spending habits and at the end of two years, they still owed $50,000 and had to sign for another two-year term.

6. Venture capital and loans

Venture capital is money obtained through investors who, in return for their investment, expect a share of your business and usually a say in its management. Expect to spend time looking for this type of financing. Venture capitalists usually only consider investing amounts from $100,000 and upwards. An excellent site for more information is *www.acoa-apeca.gc.ca*.

DOING IT RIGHT: YOUR BUSINESS PLAN CHECKLIST

As you prepare your business plan, use the checklist in Figure 7.5 on page 165 to review your progress through the various stages.

WHAT IS THE NEXT STEP?

A business plan is a true blueprint for your business. The next important step is determining the corporate structure of your business. Many people start as proprietorships and later incorporate. Others incorporate when they didn't need to. Looking at the pros and cons of both, you can decide—with the help of your accountant—which best suits your needs.

Figure 7.5: BUSINESS PLAN CHECKLIST

Ensure that you have completed all the following tasks when creating your business plan.

1. *Before starting my plan:*
   - ❐ I have looked at sample plans to use as resources
   - ❐ I know why and for whom I am preparing this plan
   - ❐ I have clear and defined goals and objectives
   - ❐ I asked the lending institution what they need.

2. *I have researched and documented the company with regard to the:*
   - ❐ General business overview
   - ❐ Company structure
   - ❐ Location
   - ❐ Key personnel
   - ❐ Goals and objectives
   - ❐ Strengths and weaknesses
   - ❐ Mission and vision statements.

3. *I have researched and documented the products and services:*
   - ❐ Product/service description
   - ❐ Cost of sales
   - ❐ Future projections
   - ❐ Legal concerns.

4. *I have researched and documented the marketing strategies:*
   - ❐ The competition
   - ❐ Marketing strengths and weaknesses
   - ❐ Marketing and sales strategies.

5. *I have researched and documented the operational information:*
   - ❐ Overhead costs
   - ❐ Suppliers
   - ❐ Quality control
   - ❐ Distribution
   - ❐ Employees
   - ❐ Assets and equipment

□ Insurance policies

□ Licences and permits.

6. *I have researched and documented the financial information:*

□ Projections of income and expenses

□ Cash flow forecasts

□ Financial statements

□ List of capital expenses

□ Net worth statements.

7. *I have researched and documented the funding requirements:*

□ How much, terms, type of loan, use of funds.

8. *I have provided an executive summary:*

□ Synopsis of all of the above.

9. *I have provided an appendix:*

□ Included all relevant documents.

10. *Now that the first draft is completed, I have:*

□ Typed my plan neatly

□ Discussed it with my accountant

□ Made suggested revisions

□ Completed the final draft

□ Shown it to my accountant

□ Had it proofread and edited, made corrections

□ Shown it to an experienced person for critiquing

□ Completed the final copy (at last)

□ Made an appointment to present it to the lender.

CHAPTER 8

Should you incorporate your business?

If you plan for success and plan to grow,
incorporation may be the route to go.

WHAT IS A PROPRIETORSHIP OR PARTNERSHIP?

Because starting a business is an expensive proposition, most start-ups—approximately two-thirds—tend to be proprietorships or partnerships. While this route is initially cheaper, those businesses seriously planning for growth should consider the benefits of incorporation. For a small business consisting of the owner and perhaps one employee, a proprietorship is the simplest way to start. Only a business licence and name registration fees are necessary.

A sole proprietorship is a business owned by one person. A partnership is owned by two or more people. Anyone can set up, register a name and become a proprietorship. You are considered self-employed, not an employee of the company as with an incorporated business.

What are the advantages of a proprietorship?

For small businesses that do not intend to have offices outside the province or aspirations of large profit, a proprietorship can be ideal. The advantages are:

1.   *Less paperwork:* Once the name registration and business licence are obtained, you are a legal entity. All businesses are required to keep proper accounting records, but a proprietorship doesn't have to have a full financial statement prepared at year-end. Therefore accounting and record keeping is relatively simple.

2.   Tax benefit to start-up losses: It's not uncommon to experience losses in the first year, and these losses can be used to reduce income from other sources. You are personally taxed on the net profit from a proprietorship, so if a loss cannot be used this year, it can be carried back three years or forward seven.

3.   Easy to wind down: If you choose not to continue with the business, it is simple tax-wise to close the business down. Seek your accountant's advice.

4.   Incorporation can be a future option: When the business grows to the point that incorporating is sensible, it is not difficult. The assets of the proprietorship are rolled over into the newly incorporated company, and depending on the time of the year, you may have to file both a proprietorship and an incorporated company tax return.

What are the disadvantages of a proprietorship?

In their haste to save money at start-up, some people regret their decision later on. Take into consideration:

1.   No name protection: Even once you have registered your business name, there is no protection from another person registering your name as an incorporated business. Your thriving, well-known business name is vulnerable to being "stolen."

2.   Liability: Because you are self-employed, you are the business, and therefore responsible for all the business debts. If you suffer cash flow problems, the financial security of your home and family are at risk.

3.   Higher taxes: Corporations pay taxes at a lesser rate than proprietorships. Because you are taxed on the profit you make, many proprietors make the mistake of looking for "write-offs" or doing cash-under-the-table transactions, both detrimental to growing your business. There is more flexibility to utilizing profits in an incorporated structure. Once a business is consistently netting over $45,000 a year and growing, incorporation is a wise choice.

CASE STUDY

WHAT'S IN A NAME?

Anthony became well respected and well known in the graphics industry. His proprietorship, Cutting Edge Graphic Creations, had been in business four years. He considered incorporation, but had not found the time to do the paperwork.

He received a call asking if this was the Cutting Edge Graphic Corporation, and he informed the prospective client of the correct name. The caller apologized, said he had the wrong company and hung up. Anthony's curiosity was piqued. He found no business in the phone book under that name, then asked the directory operator if there was a new listing and there was—Cutting Edge Graphics Corporation Ltd. There was nothing Anthony could do. He realized that by delaying incorporation, he would now be confused with another business and potentially lose clients to them.

4. *More difficult to borrow money:* Because traditionally proprietorships don't show much profit on their tax returns due to both size and "write-off" practices, it is often difficult to borrow money from the bank without substantial personal guarantees. Banks prefer to do business with incorporated companies.

5. *Lack of credibility:* Some clients prefer to do business with a company that has "Inc." or "Ltd." after its name. Proprietorships often have that "mom and pop" or fly-by-night connotation. The consumers' concept is that an incorporated business is a "real" one.

IS A PARTNERSHIP A GOOD IDEA?

How do you choose a partner?

A partnership can bring a combination of talent and experience to enhance your business—two heads are usually better than one. For example, if you are impulsive and creative, seek a partner who is level-headed and practical to help keep your feet on the ground. Choose your partner as carefully as you would choose a spouse. You will spend copious time together, and just as you and your spouse no doubt agree to disagree at times, so will the partnership experience disagreements.

$UCCE$$ $TRATEGY

USE A PARTNERSHIP AGREEMENT: As discussed in Chapter 5, protect both partners by having a lawyer draw up a partnership agreement. Unfortunately, few partnerships weather long-term relationships without financial and emotional stress to both parties. A written agreement can reduce these stresses, should the relationship dissolve.

Seek a partner seek who has the following:

1. Business experience: Your partner should have experience in areas that you don't. There's little use having two salespeople alone. Between you, the technical, management and marketing roles should be filled. Clearly define job roles and responsibilities in the partnership agreement.

2. Money: Deals such as "you put in the money, I'll put in the time" don't usually work. Both partners should contribute equally to the business. Without the financial commitment, a partner may not be sufficiently motivated to make the business succeed, and the lack of commitment could lead to arguments over who isn't doing or paying enough. You've probably had similar arguments with your spouse.

3. Compatibility: Partners must be emotionally compatible, able to communicate honestly and openly and express their feelings when they don't agree. Don't "marry" for money or brains alone.

What are the advantages of a partnership?

A proprietorship can be a lonely experience. It's rather like being single—it suits some people but not others. Working together with the right partner has these advantages:

1.   *Reduces isolation, increases contacts:* Proprietors often complain about being isolated from others. With a partnership, you have someone to brainstorm with and to complain to. A partner will bring networking contacts, information and ideas. You have someone to lean on and to share the workload with—most beneficial when errands need doing, clients need visiting or an emergency arises.

2.   *Shared financial responsibility:* You are not left shouldering the full responsibility of raising start-up and working capital. Partners share not only profits but equal financial responsibilities. The combined assets and two incomes are more desirable to banks if you are seeking financing.

3.   *Expertise:* A proprietor has 60 different jobs to do, quite a load to carry by yourself. A partner brings experience and expertise in areas different from your own. As you work together, you will learn from each other and broaden your own skill set.

What are the disadvantages of a partnership?

Think about it—you will be working together for up to 12 hours a day, 60 hours a week for 50 weeks of the year. It almost sounds like a life sentence. While many husband-wife partnerships are successful, bringing a stranger into your business does have its downside. The main disadvantages are:

1.   *Lack of long-term compatibility:* In all the years spent in business accounting and consulting, I have seen few partnerships succeed. The usual reason is incompatibility—partners chosen for the wrong reason. Choose carefully and have the protection of an agreement in place.

2.   *Financial problems:* Money problems always cause arguments, and constant arguing between partners invariably leads to one threatening to walk out (just like a bad marriage scene). If a satisfactory resolution can't be reached, the conflict usually terminates what could have been a successful business venture.

3.   Uneven workload: It's important to equally share the workload to avoid conflict over who is doing the most work. You must work together as a team.

WHAT IS AN INCORPORATED BUSINESS?

An incorporated business is a separate legal entity. Shareholders purchase shares in the business and are responsible for its operation. You can incorporate a one-person business, and many people do. The company has a president, and if more than one person is involved, a secretary-treasurer and directors who can vote on corporate policies.

The company owns all the assets and liabilities, and in some cases is responsible for debts incurred. This is called "limited liability" because it limits the shareholders' personal liabilities. Incorporation allows for better tax planning and use of profits. If you think incorporation is right for your business, consult with your accountant after completing Figure 8.2 at the end of this chapter.

$UCCE$$ $TRATEGY

BE PREPARED TO DO YOUR HOMEWORK: Because there are so many factors to consider before incorporating, take time to research both your options and the ensuing ramifications. The library section of the Web site *www.arvic.com* offers an extensive checklist when considering incorporation. The checklist will highlight questions that you may not have thought about.

What are the advantages of incorporating?

For a business planning to hire employees, incur larger trade debts, borrow money, trade nationally or internationally and to grow larger, incorporation is the best solution. Here's why:

1.   Credibility: Incorporation demonstrates to lending institutions, suppliers, potential clients and investors that you are serious about this business. Where a proprietor may have difficulty in obtaining a loan, a lending institution will look more favourably at an incorporated structure, particularly if there are shareholders involved.

2.   *Limited liability:* Some trade debts of an incorporated company are not the shareholders' responsibility should bankruptcy occur, unless personal guarantees have been signed. Many people incorporate for this reason. People have been known to walk away from one incorporated business and start another one the next day, sometimes repeatedly.

However, there are certain debts that shareholders are responsible for, including employee deductions, GST/HST and provincial sales tax. Banks rarely lend money without some guaranteed security, and because people use incorporation to reduce their personal liability, more trade suppliers are asking for personal guarantees.

CASE STUDY

NOT TAKING CARE OF BUSINESS

Kenneth and Marie were married for many years with three children, and successfully operated two retail appliance stores. They had two faithful employees who helped with each store, which made a small profit. The couple had a yen to travel the world, and decided to scale back to one store, managed by the employees.

Immersed in their travel adventure, Kenneth and Marie forgot about the store, except for drawing a healthy monthly wage. Meanwhile, back at the store, the wages being drawn by the travellers were depleting the cash flow. Tax commitments fell behind, as did trade supplier accounts. Ignoring the long-distance warnings from both their accountant and employees, they continued to travel.

Finally, the employees tired of the situation, as did the suppliers, who backed up their trucks and emptied the store of inventory. When the couple did return, there was no business left and they had to declare corporate bankruptcy. The stress caused the marriage to dissolve. Because they were responsible for the provincial and federal taxes, they also had to declare personal bankruptcy, losing their property and most of their possessions.

3. Growth and tax planning: Incorporation provides more room to plan future growth. You can add to shareholders, as the structure is already in place. As employees of an incorporated company, they can draw a regular salary, contribute to Canada Pension Plan and make tax deductions, and at year-end, they receive a T4 for tax purposes. You can better manipulate profits and plan your tax situation. If the company is making profits, your accountant may consider paying out dividends, bonuses or extra salaries to reduce profits.

$UCCE$$ $TRATEGY

INVESTIGATE EI ELIGIBILITY: If there are three or more shareholders in a company, you may qualify for Employment Insurance (EI) contributions. This can be particularly useful to a seasonal business to supplement shareholders' wages when there is little or no work. Before making EI deductions, contact the Human Resources Development Centre office near you (in the blue pages) and ask for a ruling, as each situation is different.

4. Corporate tax benefits: Corporations qualify for many tax credits that a proprietorship does not enjoy. The small business corporate tax rate is lower than personal taxes, there is a large capital gains exemption, and there are tax credits for manufacturing, research and development, donations and political contributions, to name a few. Ask your accountant.

5. Personal tax benefits: If you borrowed money to invest into the incorporated business, the interest on shareholders' loans is deductible on personal tax returns. So not only does an incorporated business keep personal taxes more organized, if you draw a regular wage, you could get a tax refund.

What are the disadvantages of incorporating?

An incorporated company is subject to stricter reporting procedures in both legal and accounting matters. Consider these:

1. Higher accounting costs, more paperwork: Incorporating a business does generate more paperwork. First, the incorporation papers have to be prepared. For a small company, you can prepare your own by purchasing Self-Counsel Press' do-it-yourself incorporation guide and kit from your local bookstore or stationers. Incorporation costs approximately $300, depending on your jurisdiction.

Once registered, share certificates and articles of incorporation must be completed. Policies and decisions should be recorded in the company minute book, and an annual general meeting held. An annual report must be filed (fee approximately $35) to list any changes in directors or shareholders, or their addresses.

Maintain scrupulous accounting records and documentation as the books could be audited at any time. Because a formal financial statement must be prepared and filed with corporate taxes, accounting costs are expensive. Even if you prepare your own books during the year, the cost could be a minimum of $800—and more.

2. Payroll records are required: As an employee of the company, you will have to register with Canada Customs and Revenue Agency (CCRA) to make regular, monthly payroll deductions on your salary and maintain payroll records. At year-end, T4s or T4As will need to be prepared. Make timely remittances to CCRA as penalties and interest are charged on late filing. Because you are acting as a federal tax collector, CCRA's attitude is not too friendly if payments are late. They have the power to garnishee bank accounts.

HOW DO PROPRIETORSHIPS AND INCORPORATIONS DIFFER?

From an accounting perspective, the financial statements for proprietorships and incorporations vary, as certain transactions are recorded differently, explained following.

1. Shareholder's loan and equity

Proprietorship: Money put into a business is called capital. Money withdrawn reduces the proprietor's capital.

Incorporation: Money put into a business is called a shareholder's loan and can be repaid as the company agrees. It is classified as a liability, not as equity or capital.

2. Profits, losses and net earnings

Proprietorship: A proprietorship's profit or loss is added to or subtracted from the capital. The profit is called "net earnings" or "taxable income," and this is the sum a proprietor is personally taxed on.

Incorporation: The profit or loss is added to or subtracted from the retained earnings. A loss is referred to as a deficit.

3. Wage structure

Proprietorship: "Wage" withdrawals by a proprietor are not considered a business expense, not are they taxed. Withdrawals reduce the equity in the business.

Incorporation: The shareholders' salaries are a management wage and are a business expense. The company pays corporate taxes on the net profit after all wages.

4. Legal fees for incorporation

Proprietorship: Legal fees incurred in the business start-up are always considered an expense.

Incorporation: The cost of preparing the incorporation is usually shown under "other assets" on the balance sheet and remains there for the life of the corporation.

5. Share issue

Proprietorship: No shares are issued.

Incorporation: A share structure is decided upon by the shareholders (with the help of their accountant or lawyer). Various share structures are available, depending on the complexity of the business and its long-term goals. A certain number of shares are authorized for the business and a certain number issued to the shareholders, which are proportionate to their percentage of ownership of the business.

Shares are issued both with and without par value. There are different classes of shares, as well as voting, non-voting and preferred shares. Your advisor will suggest the best format for your business. Most small businesses use a simple structure, which appears on a balance sheet in the following format:

Share capital:
Authorized: 10,000 Class A common shares with no par value
                       10,000 Class B common shares with no par value
Issued: 100 Class A shares at $1 each
                       100 Class B shares at $1 each

Comparing balance sheet differences

Figure 8.1 demonstrates a balance sheet for Jason's Garden Service, shown as both an incorporated business and a proprietorship. Changes in format are highlighted in italics. You will notice quite a different format in the equity section. The difference in the GST/HST account is the GST/HST charged on the legal fees for incorporation.

With the loss of $9,960, Jason's equity in the proprietorship has been reduced from $22,000 to $10,749. The incorporated company's loss is greater, as Jason's management wage of $1,291 shows on the income statement as an expense. The incorporated company will continue to reflect the loss of $11,251 on the financial statements until future profits exceed the loss amount.

Figure 8.1: BALANCE SHEET COMPARISON

JASON'S GARDEN SERVICE (LTD.)
BALANCE SHEET
DECEMBER 31, XXXX
(Unaudited)

	Incorporated	Proprietorship
ASSETS		
Current assets:		
Cash at bank	$ 11,019	$11,019
Accounts receivable	3,551	3,551
Inventories	6,245	6,245
Prepayments & deposits	1,080	1,080
	21,895	21,895
Fixed assets:		
Automotive–trucks	85,000	85,000
Office equipment	1,550	1,550
Office furniture	850	850
	87,400	87,400
Less accumulated CCA	(21,000)	(21,000)
	66,400	66,400
Other assets:		
Incorporation fees	*700*	0
TOTAL ASSETS:	**$ 88,995**	**$88,295**
LIABILITIES		
Current liabilities:		
Accounts payable	$ 10,520	$10,520
PST payable	315	315
GST/HST payable	*(5,342)*	(5,289)
Current portion bank loan	12,000	12,000
	17,493	17,546
Long-term liabilities:		
Bank loan	32,000	32,000
Loan, R. Davies	28,000	28,000
Shareholder's loan	*22,653*	0
	82,653	60,000
TOTAL LIABILITIES:	**$100,146**	**$77,546**

	Incorporated	Proprietorship
EQUITY		
Share capital:		
Authorized:		
10,000 Class A common voting shares		
with no par value		
Issued:		
100 Class A shares @ $1	*100*	0
Contributed capital for period:	0	*22,000*
Draws for period:	0	*(1,291)*
Profit/loss for period:	0	*(9,960)*
Retained earnings (deficit)	*(11,251)*	0
	(11,151)	*10,749*
TOTAL LIABILITIES & EQUITY:	**$ 88,995**	**$88,295**

SHOULD YOU INCORPORATE YOUR BUSINESS?

Incorporating a business needs some serious consideration before you take this step. The questions in Figure 8.2 on page 180 will help you determine whether incorporation is right for your business.

WHAT IS THE NEXT STEP?

Once you have decided on the structure of your business, the next step is to research and become familiar with the myriad of rules, regulations, red tape, laws and legalities that are involved in operating a business. Armed with this knowledge, you can better plan your time frame and budget, and be mentally prepared to face the paperwork jungle.

Figure 8.2: SHOULD I INCORPORATE MY BUSINESS?

If you answer yes to more than three of these statements, consider incorporation as a suitable and safer method of structuring your new business.

	Yes	No
I have future plans to expand.	❏	❏
I will need to borrow funds for this expansion.	❏	❏
I will carry a large inventory, over $10,000.	❏	❏
I will incur accounts receivable.	❏	❏
I will incur accounts payable.	❏	❏
I will work with a partner.	❏	❏
My business is retail, wholesale or manufacturing.	❏	❏
I need my personal finances to be well organized.	❏	❏
I will be susceptible to liability.	❏	❏
I will be hiring employees.	❏	❏
I plan to build the business and sell in a few years.	❏	❏
Sales will be over $100,000 a year.	❏	❏

CHAPTER 9

What are you required to do by law?

Dot your i's and cross all your t's.
Fill out all the forms in triplicate please.

Before you read this chapter, make a fresh pot of coffee to keep your brain cells alert. There is a right and a wrong way to proceed legally with your business, and a step in the wrong direction will create time delays and, possibly, major setbacks. To make things easier, here is the task sequence and some helpful hints. Additional resources are listed in Appendix 1.

MUNICIPAL APPROVALS

Before you start your business, check with your local municipality for bylaw and zoning requirements, and for information on environmental and other restrictions on home-based businesses. Be sure your business conforms with the many regulations, as your municipality can deny you a business licence.

Municipal licensing and inspections

Before a licence is issued, your premises may have to be inspected by some of the following departments, so know which apply before you start your business:

- Fire department
- Health department
- Local pollution control ministry

- Provincial motor carrier licensing

- Property use and building inspector

- Provincial waste management

- Provincial motor dealer licensing.

Home-based businesses

Currently referred to as "accessory home occupations," today's home-based businesses are considered incubators for growing a thriving business. Many progressive local governments are realizing the need to review their bylaws and to encourage small home businesses to succeed. Many people contravene the bylaws and hide their operations from the community. This means there is less chance to market their businesses, so many don't succeed. Don't take any chances; familiarize yourself with and comply with local regulations.

$UCCE$$ $TRATEGY

BE A LEADER: If your local bylaws do not accommodate your home-based business, approach your local chamber of commerce to see if they can work with the municipality to revise its bylaws. The Greater Langley Chamber of Commerce did this through their Small Business Advancement Committee, which I chaired, and although it took two years, the bylaws are so user-friendly that they are being used as a model for other municipalities and earned the chamber one of three national "Most Friendly Home-Based Business Community" awards in 2000. Home-based businesses in Langley can now hire employees, use more space and, in certain areas, make structural changes to buildings.

Your municipality's bylaws may differ considerably from those of neighbouring municipalities. Many local governments require the following:

- The business should be contained to the residence, and no structural alterations or additions to the residence can be made for business purposes.

- The business should not use more than 20 percent of the residential space.

- There should be no evidence of the business being operated from the residence, such as exterior storage or exterior operation, and no sign identifying the business. (If you drive past the house, you shouldn't notice that a business is being operated.)

- The home-based business is restricted to office use only. No retail sales can be made from the premises, and clients may not visit the home to purchase goods.

- The business can be conducted by a resident or members of the family only. No one else can be employed by the business.

- Generating noise, electrical interference, reoccurring ground vibrations, and noxious emissions, odours or vapours is prohibited.

- No commercial vehicles can be operated by the home business.

- The business may not generate special traffic beyond normal traffic volume.

CASE STUDY

SELLING HIMSELF SHORT

Danny opened a small store on his property, selling hay, feed and retail agricultural products. He didn't apply for a business licence, thinking that selling agricultural products in an agricultural area wouldn't cause any problems. Someone reported him to the municipality—perhaps an envious rival or neighbour. Despite his best efforts to save the business, Danny did not succeed. He was selling retail products from his home that were not produced on the farm and had contravened the local home business bylaws. Although he had invested a great deal of money, he was forced to close down.

NAME REGISTRATION

Once you are sure your business conforms with municipal regulations, register your business name. If you are unincorporated, name registration is not necessary but is a good idea. If you are incorporated, name registration is required by law. If you choose a name with the words "and Associates" or "and Company," or if you are involved in a partnership, you must register your business name.

1. What are the advantages of name registration?

Registering your company name makes it easier for the public to find and remember you. Your proprietorship may grow so quickly that you need to incorporate. You could build a well-known and reputable business, but if your name isn't registered, another business can register yours and use it, and there is little you can do.

Sometimes, people will try to register a name similar to that of another successful business with the intention of creating confusion. Name registration ensures that your name remains distinct and protects your business.

2. How do you register your business name?

To register your name, choose three names in order of preference and submit them for approval to the corporate registry (see Appendix 1). The fee varies, starting from $30 and up. Approval should only take a few days, depending on where you live and whether you register in person, by mail, or on-line. Once the name is approved, submit a name registration form, enclosing the prescribed fee.

$UCCE$$ $TRATEGY

USE ON-LINE REGISTRATION: Many provinces now have on-line registration in place, with approval taking approximately 24 hours. Call your local chamber of commerce or Canada Business Service Centre to find the closest on-line business centre near you, or visit *www.bsa.cbsc.org*, where Internet registration can be completed for every Canadian province.

INCORPORATION

You may then proceed with incorporation, as explained in Chapter 8. Until your incorporation papers are approved (ten days to two weeks), you cannot order stationery, have licences approved or open bank accounts, because you'll need the incorporation papers. CCRA requires copies of the certificate to issue a business number and approve payroll and GST/HST registrations. If you are not incorporating your business, you can pass go.

BUSINESS LICENCES

When your company name has been approved and the business is incorporated, you can apply for a business licence at your municipality and complete any other licensing requirements. Fees vary depending on the type of business and where you live. Usually, municipalities approve a licence without delay. Even if you do not register your business name, you must get a business licence from your municipality.

BANK ACCOUNTS

Opening your business accounts may take a few days. Allow up to two weeks if you need Visa or MasterCard facilities. Pay for as many expenses as possible by cheque; it makes for easier bookkeeping as cash receipts can get lost and credit cards make for complex accounting. A cheque is a written record of each transaction and will suffice in an audit as proof of payment.

Order a two- or three-ringed cheque binder and make sure the cheque stubs are large enough to record daily deposits, expense details, computer codes and the GST/HST amount. Use your personal chequing account as little as possible—expenses can be forgotten and it appears unprofessional.

PROVINCIAL TAXES

Most provinces require that a provincial sales tax be collected on goods purchased or imported for use or consumption. The tax is always collected by the retail outlet or by the final vendor. Additional taxes are levied against hotel rooms, tobacco and motor fuels.

In certain circumstances, you may be exempt from collecting the provincial sales tax; check with the provincial sales tax office listed in Appendix 1.

If you are the final vendor, you must collect tax on all applicable sales, keep proper records and submit the tax monthly. In some provinces, you deduct a commission for collecting the tax. Submit these taxes on time—penalties for late filing can be hefty. Certain customers—such as First Nations peoples—are exempt from provincial taxes and must quote an exemption number. Record these numbers on your invoices for audit purposes.

GOODS AND SERVICES TAX/HARMONIZED SALES TAX (GST/HST)

When should you register for GST?

The GST/HST tax confuses many people, particularly those who are unsure of their first year's gross revenue. When you reach $30,000 in sales during any business year, call your nearest CCRA office and ask to be registered. You should start charging GST the following month. If you earn under $30,000 a year, you don't have to worry about GST registration.

Even if your annual sales are less than $30,000, there are benefits to registering. In your first year of business, you incur expensive start-up costs which include GST/HST. If you register for the GST/HST, you are eligible to claim back all the GST that you have paid out, and this can be a benefit, as you only remit the difference between what you charge in GST and what you pay.

For example, you may have purchased a business or franchise and paid GST/HST on the purchase price. A business costing $35,000 will incur GST of $2,450. GST is also charged on equipment, legal and accounting fees, telephone systems, computers, stationery and more. You may be eligible for a refund after the first three months, particularly if sales were low and expenses high.

$UCCE$$ $TRATEGY

FILE GST QUARTERLY: Small businesses have the option of filing one annual GST return which is due by June 30th of the following year and making quarterly installments. To keep your accounting up-to-date and your liabilities paid on time, when you register, elect to file quarterly.

What is the harmonized sales tax (HST)?

As of April 1, 1997, Nova Scotia, New Brunswick and Newfoundland combined their provincial sales tax with the GST. This value-added tax is called the harmonized sales tax. Because this is a complicated area for many business people, contact your local GST office for an information package on how this tax could affect your potential business.

How do you account for the GST?

Recording the GST definitely increases bookkeeping time and costs, but up-to-date accounting records are essential for monitoring your business. To record GST paid, purchases must be broken down into three entries—the cheque, expense and GST amount. The same applies for recording GST collected—the sale amount before taxes, the GST and provincial sales tax and the total. It's a lot of extra work. Unfortunately, you don't get paid to collect the GST, so you have to absorb the additional bookkeeping costs. (See Appendix 2 for how to fill out the form.)

$UCCE$$ $TRATEGY

BANK IT: The average business owner has trouble paying the quarterly GST, as all too often, the tax collected gets munched into the daily cash flow and is quickly spent. Businesses have been closed down for not paying their taxes. To avoid this, take five percent of each bank deposit (to cover GST collected and paid), and transfer it to a GST savings account. If you are collecting HST or provincial sales taxes, add in the applicable percentage. The money will be there when you need it.

Is everything GST/HST taxable?

No. There are some "zero-rated goods" on which GST/HST is not charged. These include farm produce, basic groceries, most livestock, fish and seafood for human consumption, medical services, prescriptions and exported goods.

Some services are GST exempt, and if this applies to your business, you cannot claim the tax paid nor charge it. These services include daycare, most financial services and long-term home rentals. In certain circumstances, legal aid, educational services, health and dental services, non-profit and charitable activities, and government and certain public services are exempt. Call your local CCRA office and learn how these taxes will affect your business.

BUSINESS NUMBERS, PAYROLL AND CCRA

Canada Customs and Revenue Agency issues you a business identification number and information booklet when you register for GST, corporate or payroll taxes. This number identifies all your tax accounts. You must register with CCRA if you have employees. Some businesses try to avoid any complications by subcontracting or using casual labour instead of putting workers on a regular payroll. This practice is illegal. For more information, contact CCRA or visit their Web site at *www.ccra-adrc.gc.ca* and order their publication *Employee or Self Employed, R CH110.*

As a rough guide, if a person works more than 40 percent of one's working hours for one employer, he or she is considered a part-time or full-time employee and is eligible for employee benefits. These include Canada Pension Plan, employment insurance, tax deductions, statutory holidays and vacation pay. Your employee is protected by the provincial and sometimes federal labour laws.

What are your responsibilities as an employer?

CCRA will send you a start-up kit including TD1 forms for the employees to complete, information booklets and taxation schedules (also available on disk). It is your responsibility to deduct the correct CPP, employment insurance and tax and to maintain proper payroll records. Easy-to-follow payroll books are available at stationery stores.

Each employee needs an individual payroll record with the full name, address, social insurance number, starting date and wages. Each pay period, you record the daily hours worked, wages and all deductions. At month-end, the CPP, employment insurance and tax deducted are totalled, and the employer's portion is calculated. The whole amount must be submitted to CCRA by the 15th of the following month. Figure 9.1 demonstrates this calculation.

Figure 9.1: CALCULATING A MONTHLY PAYROLL REMITTANCE	
Employee's CPP deduction	$ 40.00
Employer's CPP contribution	40.00
Employee's EI deduction	19.00
Employer's EI deduction (x 1.4)	26.60
Employee's tax deduction	140.00
Total remittance:	**$265.60**

How much does an employee really cost?

Hiring an employee is a big decision and a big expense; in fact, most employers agree that finding the right person is a headache. Read Chapter 7 in *Big Ideas for Growing Your Small Business* (McGraw-Hill Ryerson, 2001) for more information on your options, from commissioned salespeople to a full-time employee.

Be aware of all the costs involved when preparing projections. The hourly rate is just one part of the expense. Figure 9.2 breaks down the costs of an employee earning $15 an hour over one month. Add benefits, parking, uniforms, sick time and downtime, and an employee becomes a costly expense.

Figure 9.2: THE REAL COST OF HIRING	
40 hours a week x 4.33 weeks per month:	173.20 hours
173.2 hours x $15	$2,598.00
4 percent vacation pay	103.92
4.7 percent Canada Pension Plan	132.63
2.2 percent Employment Insurance x 1.4	86.91
One statutory holiday	120.00
Workers' Comp. (average rate of $3.50/$100)	90.94
Total monthly employee cost:	**$3,132.40**

The $15 an hour increases to $18.09 an hour, an additional $535.19 per month, or 20.6 percent of $2,598.00. (The CPP and EI costs quoted are 2002 rates—they will undoubtedly change each year.)

What happens at year-end?

After the final pay period for the year, employees' wage sheets are reconciled and a T4 tax receipt issued. A T4 summary is then completed, which reports all employee deductions and employer remittances that year to CCRA (see Appendix 2 for information on filling out these forms). If you have not remitted enough money, include the balance with the summary. A penalty is usually imposed for late remittances. Maintain meticulous payroll records and use this information when reviewing costings or financial figures.

What happens when an employee leaves?

When an employee leaves or is terminated, a record of employment form has to be submitted within five working days. The first two copies are given to the employee, one is sent to CCRA and one is kept for your records. CCRA or your local Human Resources Development Centre (HRDC) can answer any questions about these procedures.

$UCCE$$ $TRATEGY

GET IT IN WRITING: Wrongful dismissal cases and employee disputes with employers are common, so maintain a detailed file on each employee. Record details of conversations relating to job status, and if there are concerns with an employee, put them in writing to the employee so that should a legal problem arise, you have a detailed paper trail.

WORKERS' COMPENSATION BOARD

All businesses hiring employees or subcontractors who are not independently covered by WCB must register for Workers' Compensation. Rates are based on your industry's risk factor, claims record and your annual payroll, and adjusted annually.

The rate structure often confuses people. A crane operator may pay $6.50 for every $100 of wages paid, because of the high-risk factor. But the bookkeeper and management staff working in their office also pay the same amount based on the industry. There is no distinction between office workers, sales or operations. Include these costs in your cash flow and projections, as some industries' rates are expensive.

Once you are registered, you will receive an information package and notice of your registration. In most provinces, you must file a return and remittance every three months. At year-end, an annual summary must be completed, based on year-end payroll records and summaries of subcontractor and casual wages. If you are incorporated, shareholders' salaries are included in the calculation.

If you are a proprietorship with no employees, it is not necessary to register. However, if you use contractors, be sure they carry their own coverage; otherwise it is your responsibility to provide coverage. In some provinces, you can register yourself for optional personal coverage based on your net earnings.

OTHER LICENSING AGENCIES

Depending on your type of business, you may also have to register with one of the following agencies:

- Ministry for the Environment
- Ministry of Agriculture, Fisheries and Food
- Ministry of the Attorney General
- Ministry of Transport and Highways
- Ministry of Health.

Other areas where you may need to contact a licensing agency include dealing with:

- Weights and measures
- Packaging and labelling
- Hazardous products
- Precious metals
- Textiles
- Foods
- Patents, copyright, industrial designs and trademarks.

STEP-BY-STEP CHECKLIST

To ensure that you do not miss an important step, Figure 9.3 is a checklist to keep you on track.

Figure 9.3: LEGAL REQUIREMENTS CHECKLIST		
Check off and complete the issues that apply to you through the start-up stage.	**Apply**	**Done**
My business can be legally operated within my municipality.	❏	❏
I am aware of other municipal licensing requirements.	❏	❏
I have made appointments with these licensing agencies.	❏	❏
My home-based business conforms with the municipal bylaws.	❏	❏
I have chosen and submitted three preferred names for name registration.	❏	❏
I have registered my business name.	❏	❏
I have consulted a professional for incorporation advice.	❏	❏
The incorporation papers are completed.	❏	❏
I have applied for a municipal business licence.	❏	❏
I have opened a business chequing account.	❏	❏
I have applied for credit card facilities for clients.	❏	❏
I have opened a savings account for my GST.	❏	❏
I have registered with the province for collection of sales tax.	❏	❏
I have applied for a GST number.	❏	❏
I have applied to file GST quarterly.	❏	❏
I will be hiring employees or subcontractors.	❏	❏
I have applied to CCRA for a business number.	❏	❏
I have purchased a payroll book or software.	❏	❏
I have included all costs of hiring in my projections.	❏	❏
I will have employees and need Workers' Comp. coverage.	❏	❏
I have applied for Workers' Comp. registration.	❏	❏
I will need licensing through other federal/provincial agencies.	❏	❏
I have applied for all applicable licences.	❏	❏

IS BUSINESS AS SIMPLE AS ABC AND 123?

After all this mind-boggling information, it's time to have a little fun in the wonderful world of business, which should be a simple matter of earning a living—right? You sell a product or service, collect the money and make a whopping profit—right?

Wrong. Don't think it will be that easy. Big Brother is working hard to create as many headaches and stumbling blocks as possible to test your entrepreneurial determination, strength and patience.

Take for example that dense forest of acronyms. When you sell a product, you must collect the PST and remit it to the MOF, TIS, DOF or PTC, depending on your province. You must collect the GST/HST (which replaced the FST) and record your ITCs, paying CCRA the balance on a Form GST62. You pay your staff twice a month, deducting CPP, EI and tax, which is remitted monthly on a RC107 E(01). At year-end, you must prepare T4s and T4As for employees, so they can complete their T1 Specials or T1 Generals, including Schedules 1 through to 100. When employees leave your business, don't forget to fill out their ROE, so they can take it to HRDC and file for EI.

All businesses must register with the WCB and, if incorporated, your accountant will prepare your year-end and fill out a T2(E) corporate return, with relevant schedules beginning at T2S(1) through to T2S(30). If you are a sole proprietorship, you just need a simple four-page T2124A, including CCA schedules.

The only way to keep track of all this paperwork efficiently is to purchase a PC, of which the depreciation is deductible on a T2S(8). The choice is whether to purchase a 400MHz Pentium 4 with a 1.8GHz, 80GB 7200 RPM IDE UDMA hard drive and an ASUS P4B -266 C-WOA motherboard, 512MB of RAM plus CD-ROM and burner, firewall, scanner and colour printer, including a 20-inch LCD monitor, or a 40GB Pentium 4 with 256MB of RAM, a laser printer and ergonomic mouse—or should you purchase the whole zoo? Should you buy IBM or Mac? Which programs will you need? Perhaps Windows NT? XP Pro OEM? Office Suite—or furnish the whole house? Don't forget your Zip drive backup and 250MB disks, or your floppy MF 2HD backup disks. And as this is written, the above will no doubt be obsolete information anyway.

When you've made all that lovely money, you should invest it wisely. The choices are many—CSBs, GICs, mutual funds, RRSPs, BCSBs, RRIFs, or RESPs for the children. The decision seems easy, so don't waste too much time thinking about it. Right?

Now just think of your poor accountant when you bring in your year's paperwork. Before your GL, TB and statements are prepared, he or she will probably take a few ASAs or a large nip of CC before tackling your T2(E)s or T1s.

We live complex lives in a complex world, and even if you don't have a natural head for numbers or technical wizardry, you need to take time to learn the basics if you want to do better than just stay afloat.

WHAT IS THE NEXT STEP?

You have a great idea, it's well researched, your business plan is started and you know your approximate start-up costs. Things are looking good. But no business can succeed unless you understand how to market and plan a smart marketing campaign. It's the weak point for many businesses, so this next chapter will guide you through the basic steps to planning and implementing a winning marketing strategy.

CHAPTER 10

How do you market your business?

The idea is great, the plan is too.
Now how to tell the world about you?

WHAT IS A MARKETING PLAN?

Marketing terminology

No matter how wonderful your concept, without a sound and aggressive marketing strategy, you will be lucky to get past first base. Ineffective marketing is common amongst the newly self-employed, as marketing takes a combination of skills that do not come readily to most people. Some confuse marketing with advertising or selling, so let's define these terms:

* *Marketing:* To attract potential customers, you must inform them about your business and establish and maintain a customer base. Your "target" market is a defined group of people who may use your business.

* *Promotion:* To market a business, you must communicate your messages to the public. This is promotion. You tell or show people about your business by joining business associations and networking groups or participating in trade shows.

* *Advertising:* Advertising consists of an aired, rehearsed script on radio, television or the Internet; and printed descriptive text and/or pictures that convey your message in publications, mail- or fax-outs.

- *Sales:* Marketing brings potential customers through the doors but does not close a sale. Selling is the process of convincing customers that you can best fulfill their needs. A complete transaction involves the exchange of money in return for a service or a product.

The components of a marketing plan

Marketing is not placing an advertisement in the paper and waiting for the telephone to ring—you will have a long wait. A successful marketing strategy is an intrinsic combination of carefully planned components. The more you know about your industry, the better you can market your business. A well-researched marketing plan details your strategies, timing, costs and expected results.

$UCCE$$ $TRATEGY

BE CONSTANTLY CREATIVE: Your various techniques should always be changing, dependent on their success rates, the time of year and the economy. Be creative and make your marketing ideas stand out from the crowd. It takes time to learn what works for your business, and just as you think you have the answer, you may have to find new methods because the old ones stop working effectively. Never stop thinking of creative ways to market your business.

A marketing plan is a map of your ideas and timelines. Your plan should include the following components, discussed in this chapter:

- Clearly defining the product or service you are selling
- Knowing your target market and developing an "ideal customer" profile
- Knowing your competitive edge—your Unique Selling Proposition (USP)
- Setting pricing structures
- Knowing where your product is positioned in customers' minds
- Deciding how to distribute your product/service
- "Branding" your business and developing a corporate image

- Planning promotional strategies
- Preparing a marketing budget.

WHAT ARE THE FOUR Ps OF MARKETING?

Chapter 4 explains how to research the market to ensure that there is a place for your business and that it can withstand trends, time and the competition. By performing the SWOT analysis and doing a consumer market survey, you should now feel confident that there is a market for your business. Now to tell people about how great you are. Because there are many factors involved in marketing, let's break it down into "the Four Ps of Marketing."

Product **P**rice **P**lace **P**romotion

1. Product: what are you selling?

Now is the time to refine your product definition so you have a clear picture of what you are selling to whom. There are many types of accountants or lawyers, but most specialize in one area, such as corporate taxes or immigration law. New entrepreneurs often make the mistake of trying to cater to everyone and do not specialize in one area. To become known as "the expert" in your field—your ultimate goal—you must narrow down your product specifications. What is your product's position in relationship to the rest of the market? For a service business, you are the product, so you may need to further focus on your marketable expertise.

Who are your market and where are they?

Who will use your product? This is referred to as your *target market* and includes the people or businesses that you will market to. Most small businesses rely on their community for sales, so learn everything you can about the community or people who will use your business. You can then develop an *ideal customer profile.*

A woman selling mid-priced makeup may initially think her market is every woman. Yet upon narrowing down her market, she discovers that some women don't use makeup. Others prefer a particular brand, while some use either cheap or expensive makeup. Some have skin allergies and have to use medicated or hypoallergenic products. Don't waste money marketing to people who don't want or need your business. Define your potential consumers through research and by completing the questions in Figure 10.1. Depending on your type of business, you may have to modify the questions.

Figure 10.1: WHO ARE YOUR TARGET MARKET? (Retail example)

Find out...	Answer
1. Are most of them male or female?	_____
2. Are they an even mix of male and female?	_____
3. What is their average income bracket?	_____
4. Where do these consumers generally congregate?	_____
5. Do they live in apartments, houses or rural areas?	_____
6. Which radio stations would they most likely listen to?	_____
7. Which magazines are they most likely to read?	_____
8. Where would they most likely shop?	_____
9. What is their average age?	_____
10. What type of work do they do?	_____
11. What is the average family size?	_____
12. What are their interests?	_____
13. Do you know your business' geographic boundaries?	_____
14. Are you targeting retail, residential or commercial markets?	_____

Target your ideal customers

You can now build a profile of your ideal customer. The most successful businesses know exactly who their product or service appeals to. Once you know who you are targeting, you then research the best marketing methods to reach them. If your ideal customer reads gardening magazines, then advertise there. If they live mainly in apartments, don't advertise in rural areas. Match your geographic marketing to your ideal customers' lifestyles, and promote through the media they are most likely to read, hear or watch.

$UCCE$$ $TRATEGY

WATCH THE MARKET IN ACTION: Study consumers' purchasing habits. Visit busy malls, strip malls, out-of-the way locations, megastores and businesses similar to yours. Note when they are busy or quiet. Watch which products people buy that are similar to yours and what they are willing to pay. Note which weekdays are busy and which seasonal times of the year affect your industry either positively or negatively.

Develop your Unique Selling Proposition

An important part of marketing is knowing your position in relationship to other similar businesses. Many businesses offer the same services or products, so you must know what your competition offers and then decide how you can better position your business to attract customers. Analyze what you are selling. Will what you offer appeal to this market? What sets you apart from your competitors? It may be superior after-sales service, on-line ordering and delivery or in-home, after-hours consulting. This is called your *Unique Selling Proposition (USP)*. Once your USP is clearly defined, you use it as the basis for your marketing strategies.

CASE STUDY

UNDERSELLING HER USP

Marjory's Beauty Salon had operated for two years, offering hair-styling, manicures, make-overs, tanning and waxing. Although it was busy, the salon needed a more stable customer base. One Saturday, a relatively new customer was reading Marjory's brochure and saw in small print that the salon offered an in-home service and 24/7 appointments.

"You should have this splashed across the window and in large print everywhere to attract us busy professionals," commented the customer. "No one else in town offers this service." Marjory had a Unique Selling Proposition and didn't even realize it. She took her customer's advice, focussed her marketing strategy around promoting these services, and in a short few months, her business dramatically increased.

2. Price: how do you establish competitive pricing?

Establish a pricing policy in line with your industry that is competitive but not the cheapest in town—unless you are a discount store. There must be enough room to cover operational costs and to generate profits. If your research shows that you cannot compete or offer comparable quality, this business may not be a viable proposition. When your USP is well marketed, the perceived added value may allow you to marginally increase your prices over—or at least match—those of your competitors.

If prices are too low, consumers may think the quality is inferior. What are the deciding factors when you are price shopping? Do you choose the cheapest, mid-range or the most expensive? Knowing your ideal customer's profile and income level is important for product and price development. It's no use trying to sell expensive items to low-income earners or in an economically depressed region.

A bookkeeping service charging $15 an hour could be perceived by potential clients as "cheap—but what am I getting for that price?" Accounting clients expect to pay a certain amount for expertise. If the bookkeeping service is home-based, $20 to $25 an hour should be the minimum charge for quality work. However, if the service is located in an economically poor rural area, rates may have to be dropped accordingly, as competition is fierce when people are in survival mode. A bookkeeping service in a storefront setting has more overhead to absorb, so $35 an hour and upwards is acceptable as long as excellent service and expertise come with the package.

CASE STUDY

NOT SNAPPING UP THE SNAPS

A photographic studio chain tried pricing a glamour make-over—including makeup, hairstyling and one 8x10-inch colour print—for $25. The package was exceptionally hard to sell, even with extensive advertising. On expert advice, when the price was increased to $55, literally thousands of people booked appointments. At $25, the consumers' perception was that they wouldn't get good quality. At $55, the price was still quite cheap, but consumers were paying enough to put a perceived value on the quality of the package.

Compare prices

Because the economy, competitors and consumers are always changing, be sure to track price changes within your industry. It's not unusual to see price checkers strolling the supermarket aisles, because their sales are all about price—rarely service. Keep a close eye on your competitors and don't become complacent about your pricing. Closely monitor your customers. Do they only buy the advertised specials, or do they consistently purchase other products? A low-profit sale won't contribute much to the coffers. Your pricing should be reasonable and affordable to your target market.

3. Place: how will you distribute to your customers?

Setting distribution policies is key in marketing. You must understand where your business is placed or positioned in the market and how you can achieve a competitive edge. The way you provide your product or service to customers can give you that edge. Your ideal customer profile research should indicate how your product or service is purchased. Marjory's Beauty Salon provided a unique, in-home service to clients yet initially didn't promote this service in her marketing strategies.

If you are a service-oriented business, value-added customer service will set you apart from the competition. For example, will you offer:

* Normal trading hours only?

* After-hours appointments or servicing?

* In-home consulting or pickup and delivery?

* Same-day or emergency service?

Product-based businesses should know how they will get their goods to customers and ensure that this method is right for that clientele. Remembering that technology plays a large part in the way we now do business, your distribution methods need to be fast, efficient, cost-effective and technologically terrific. Manufacturing and distribution businesses may need warehousing facilities. Can customers buy direct from the warehouse? Will you deliver or use the Internet for ordering? When you establish your positioning in the market, be clear about what you are offering and promote your features and benefits.

$UCCE$$ $TRATEGY

OUT-SERVICE THE COMPETITION: Chapter 4 explored taking business to the customer, a wining strategy for today's busy people. While my husband and I were shopping for a vehicle recently, one Ford dealership salesperson paid strict attention to our needs. Because my husband works graveyard shifts, vehicle shopping is difficult. The salesperson offered to find only vehicles that perfectly suited our needs and deliver them to our door for a test drive. Can you beat that for service? Yes, we'll tell the world about it. Be creative and cater to the busy consumer.

4. Promotion: how will you promote your business?

Telling the world about your business is complex. There are so many ways to promote, so this subject will be covered in more depth later in this chapter. First, we'll define the three elements that give your business its distinct identity—branding, customer service and customer loyalty.

WHAT IS BRANDING?

1. Developing your corporate image or "branding"

Every facet of your operation needs branding with your distinct identity to let people know who you are and what you do. A combination of your name, logo, slogan, mission statement and corporate theme should be used extensively throughout your marketing. We all recognize large corporations' branding—such as Kodak or Sears—but even a small, one-person business can brand themselves and become well-known. Consult with a graphic designer to help you to project a professional image, as first impressions *are* important.

Let's briefly look at the components of branding:

- *Name:* Make your name work for you and tell people what you do. ABC Enterprises says nothing about you, whereas Professional Personnel Services does. It also projects a professional image.

- *Logo:* A logo graphically expresses who you are. Although not necessary for a small business, it adds a professional touch and helps people identify your business. We all recognize those golden arches.

- *Slogan:* A short slogan becomes an extension of your name, further describing what you do. Think of the many slogans you instantly associate with larger companies. Living in a rural area, I never forget our local septic tank company's slogan, "Your Business Is Our Business."

- *Mission statement:* A short statement of your beliefs and goals describes your commitment to customers and commits you in writing to strive for those goals. Customers like to see mission statements as they silently imply "We care about you." Splash your commitment onto all promotional materials, business cards and your Web site, then frame the words on the office wall.

◗ *Corporate colour theme:* To tie your branding together, choose a "corporate colour theme" that remains consistent and is used on all correspondence, marketing materials and signs. This cements your branding. Look around your community, in newspapers and at advertisements to study various branding techniques.

It takes time to develop your branding. For example, it took me many years to hone my SmallBizPro branding. See Figure 10.2 for the final results.

Figure 10.2: THE COMPONENTS OF SUCCESSFUL BRANDING

Name:
SmallBizPro.com Services

Slogan:
"Helping people and businesses realize and achieve their maximum potential."

Logo:
Signifies learning through the written and spoken word, represented by pages and sound waves.

Web site:
www.smallbizpro.com

Mission statement:
"To promote the message of how to succeed in both business and personal life through my consulting, speaking, training and writing. To help prevent business failure and to help people realize their dreams and maximum potential."

Corporate colours and theme:
Burgundy on parchment background, thin burgundy border on stationery, thicker border on promotional materials.

2. Providing exceptional customer service

Customers can be demanding and impatient in our "too busy" society. Some expect something for nothing and still complain, but mostly, people are easy to get on with if you take good care of them. For a small business, service is the one area where you *have* to excel to set yourself apart.

Clients expect both service and competitive prices. We all know how fast negative comments spread on the grapevine, so an unhappy client will spread negativity ten times faster than a positive referral. Your task is to perfect every aspect of your service, so review these important service components:

- *Guarantees:* Know what kind of guarantees you will offer and promote these in your marketing. Familiarize yourself with clients' needs and expectations, and if you can't meet them, tell customers before a sale rather than performing inadequately or selling them the wrong product.

- *Personal service:* Remember, customers are always right, even when they are wrong, so don't argue with them. Treat them as you expect to be treated. Remember names, faces and family details. This shows that you are attentive and care.

- *Telephone manners:* A sale can be lost or gained by that first call, so your communication skills must work overtime. Be polite, interested, friendly and positive, and be available by phone. If your advertisements are on the radio at 7 pm every evening or the talk show you just appeared on is at 8 pm, make sure your phone is being answered at these times.

$UCCE$$ $TRATEGY

THANK YOUR EMPLOYEES: Your employees are always marketing your business, and that is free advertising. Thank them at the end of the day and show them you appreciate their efforts. If you have to discipline an employee, do it privately without demeaning him or her in front of others. Everyone will respect you more and will usually work even harder to promote your business.

◗ *Employees:* Your receptionist or traffic controller—which may initially be you—is the direct link between you and your customers. Customers will either come to you or be diverted to the competition, dependent on how they are initially treated. Your employees must believe in you and your business and be willing to happily service customers. Train them well and treat them fairly—they are an important component of your business.

◗ *Physical appearance:* Your employees, premises or office, vehicles and you should always be clean and presentable.

CASE STUDY

CUTTING DOWN BUSINESS

A neighbour was having some trees cut down and removed. Another neighbour drove by and asked the worker if he would quote on trimming some overhanging branches. "You'll have to phone Bill, the boss," yelled the worker, without turning off the chipper. "The phone number's on the side of the truck." Had the employee stopped, turned off the machine and handed the neighbour a business card, it would have generated a sale. As it was, the neighbour had no pen and drove off feeling slighted, later using another company.

◗ *Follow-up:* Contact customers after a sale to ask whether they are satisfied or if there were any problems. Honour time and price commitments, even if you have made a mistake. If promised delivery dates cannot be met, call your customer immediately, apologize and reschedule.

3. Creating customer loyalty

Building a successful business means that you need repeat business. Unfortunately, for some, their loyalty lies with their bank accounts. You can't blame people for watching their shrinking dollars, so how are you going to keep customers? Use simple strategies, including excellent service. Offer incentives, such as additional discounts for regular business, a company coffee mug or chocolates at Christmas. Thank them for coming in and have a coffee pot and cookies available.

> ## $UCCE$$ $TRATEGY
>
> **SHOW THAT YOU CARE:** Be good to your customers and they will refer you. When this happens, send a thank-you card. If you meet on the street or at a dinner party, warmly acknowledge them. Even if you charge a little more than competitors, they'll become loyal to you. The fact that you took time out from your busy day to say thank you or to chat is not forgotten.

Think of simple ways to entice customers back. Our local bakery gives cookies to children. The deli gives a dozen buns free with orders over $9. The local independent supermarket always has free coffee available, along with draw and suggestion boxes. Cashiers willingly pack and wheel your groceries to the car. Senior citizens get a 10 percent discount on Sundays and a free weekly grocery delivery service. These small stores have successfully sustained a strong customer base for 20 years.

PUT YOUR PLAN TOGETHER

To review progress in your marketing strategies, take a few minutes to answer the questions in Figure 10.3. Use pencil as you may change some answers before your plan is finished.

Figure 10.3: COMPONENTS OF YOUR MARKETING PLAN

1. Clearly define the products or service that your business will focus on.

   _____

   _____

2. Describe your "ideal customer profile."

   _____

   _____

3. What is your Unique Selling Proposition?

   _____

   _____

4. How would you describe your pricing in relationship to your competitors?

   _____

   _____

5. How will you distribute your product/service to customers?

   _____

   _____

6. How would your customers perceive your business in relationship to others like yours?

   _____

   _____

7. What do you feel will be the most effective forms of promotion for your business?

_____

_____

8. Have you developed a slogan? If so, what is it?

_____

_____

9. What is your proposed mission statement or the message that it should carry?

_____

_____

10. What will you do to maintain and increase customer loyalty and repeat business?

_____

_____

HOW DO YOU PROMOTE A BUSINESS?

Develop strong communication skills

Everything we have discussed under the four Ps is a form of marketing, but which strategies will work for you? There are many effective methods that don't involve a lot of money but may require time. Developing excellent written and verbal communication skills and applying these skills to your marketing will bring you long-term and repeat business. Successful businesses use a combination of techniques, and without a doubt, networking—combined with consistent community or market exposure—is the best type of promotion. To start, let's look at techniques that involve the use of communication skills.

1. Networking—a powerful tool

Networking is meeting people and telling them who you are and what you do. It is referring people with a need to reliable people or businesses. A true networker unselfishly helps others while actively promoting and meeting potential clients. They always look for ways to help others as well as themselves, because if you network purely for selfish reasons, it shows, and the results are far less effective.

How and where do you network?

Your networking success will be enhanced if you enjoy people and have enough confidence to express yourself. Start by developing a strong 20-second "infomercial" about your business and yourself. When you meet a stranger, the first question is usually "What do you do?" Your mission is to have an informative answer ready. Start your introduction with "I am," not "My name is...," as in the following example:

> *"Hi Peter, I am David Johnson, and my business is* Community Living Magazine, *which is now two years old and enjoyed and respected by the community. Our circulation has grown from an initial 10,000 to 35,000. We focus on community issues, biographies, places and features of local interest. We have just started full-colour advertising at extremely competitive rates."*

David then presents his business card. In 20 seconds, he has introduced himself and his business, explained in detail about his magazine, its community acceptance and resultant growth. The listener hasn't had time to get bored, yet in a short time, knows much about David's business.

Build relationships

Part of networking is to first build a rapport and then a relationship. Give the other person a chance to tell you about themselves; show an interest in what they do. Ask for their business card "in case I know of someone needing your business." You are now a perfect audience and have made the first step toward building a relationship. If you're interested, call the next day, say how much you enjoyed meeting—how about coffee?

Network everywhere to build these important relationships—at meetings, trade shows and in a bank lineup. The opportunities are endless, although some tact and diplomacy should be practised. You can't be all about business, but you can be looking to help others, at the same time letting people know who you are and what you do.

Join one or two specific networking organizations, such as women's networks or leads referral groups. Ask your chamber of commerce for details; they are aware of well-established groups in your area. As relationships build, network members turn to each other when they require help.

2. Join the chamber of commerce

As a chamber of commerce member, you have the opportunity to utilize many benefits and discounts. Unfortunately, some people join and do nothing, so nothing happens. Attend dinners, seminars and special events, such as business-after-business networking. Offer your services to a committee, as chambers are mostly operated by volunteers. If you give time to your community, they in turn give back to you. You become known and referred, will expand your knowledge, meet business people, and feel satisfied with your community contribution. Join Rotary or similar groups for the same rewards.

3. Display at trade shows

Many people have the wrong expectations of exhibiting at trade shows, expecting people to flock to their table and place orders. Trade shows are excellent venues for meeting potential clients face to face and starting to build relationships. When your business is needed, you will probably be called. You also have the opportunity to glean creative ideas from other businesses and to see what the competition is doing.

$UCCE$$ $TRATEGY

EXHIBIT, INFORM AND EXCITE: When people visit your table, don't be aggressive. Be polite, excited about your business and informative; ask them what they do. Have a draw box on hand for business cards, and make sure they leave with a brochure, card or handout. Don't forget the candy! The key to success is following up with a polite phone call, conveying how much you enjoyed meeting and that you would be pleased to help, should the need arise.

4. Schedule personal appearances

As your confidence grows, build your reputation as "the expert" by utilizing your speaking skills. Apply to teach adult education classes, design workshops, or speak at chamber of commerce events, networking groups and anywhere you can get up in front of a group. Audiences consider you the expert and business will follow. Your name is networked not just within your own community, but further afield.

5. Attend conferences and seminars

New entrepreneurs often say they don't have the time or money to spend on education. Mistake. By attending these industry-specific and business-related events, you learn more about your field and changing business management techniques, meet new people and make new contacts, sometimes with the opportunity of setting up a display table.

6. Contact the media

You can't pay for the credibility that media interviews bring. Learn how to prepare a media kit and find creative ways to wangle interviews on either television or radio. Become known as the expert, the person that the media calls for input. These interviews build both confidence and business, and seal your "expert" reputation. Media experience looks good on your resumé too.

$UCCE$$ $TRATEGY

GET MORE *BIG IDEAS*: Great verbal and written communication skills are a tremendous boost to marketing your business. Also read my book *Big Ideas for Growing Your Small Business*, (McGraw-Hill Ryerson). Six chapters are devoted to marketing and sales, complete with many examples and with detailed information on how to build your communication skills.

7. Use evaluations and testimonials

A book is often judged by the back-cover testimonials. They are powerful, no-cost marketing essentials. Ask satisfied clients if they would mind writing testimonials and thank them with a gift. Testimonials are invaluable business references. Collect them, and put them into a "brag book." Use them on brochures and marketing materials (with written permission); frame them on the wall. I have seen whole walls of framed testimonials—most impressive. If you have a new product or service, find reputable clients who will test your product (you could offer it at cost price) in return for an evaluation or testimonial. Most people are happy to oblige.

8. Send out press releases

Newspapers are always looking for interesting items. Create a unique approach to your business and learn how to send out press releases (see *Big Ideas*). You may have a new environmentally friendly product or be holding a workshop of community interest. In one example, press releases promoting a one-day small business workshop were sent to newspapers, business networks, radio and the chamber of commerce. Of those registered, 59 percent read about it, nine percent heard through radio and 32 percent through networking.

9. Write articles

Submit well-written articles to business-related magazines, newspapers or e-zines. Once you are published, your credibility as "the expert" increases. You can use these articles to build your portfolio and media kit, as informational handouts for customers, and to post on your Web site.

Promote on a shoestring budget

It will take some trial and error to know which promotional methods work best for your business. You may be bombarded by advertisers vying for your business, so your task is to identify which methods are the least expensive and most effective to get your name quickly known. Consider the following methods as you plan your marketing budget. Some are "mass media" or "hit-and-miss marketing methods" because they rely on numbers and are not usually targeted at a particular market.

1. Newspaper advertising (non-targeted)

If your community is your primary market, the local newspaper's classifieds is a good place to start. For example, a three-line, ten-week advertisement costs $7 to $12 per insertion, and a one-inch display column $30 to $50. The longer you run the advertisement, the cheaper the cost. Some newspapers run special display pages, focussing on professional, home improvement or home-based businesses. A cheaper rate is usually offered if you advertise for 12 weeks or longer.

Large display advertisements are expensive, one-shot, hit-and-miss options that are not often read by the public. Some local newspapers are so loaded with junk mail and flyers that it's difficult to find the newspaper. Consumers are on media-overload and can't possibly read all this advertising. You may receive only one or two calls from your expensive display ad. In one example, a women's network routinely placed a $400, quarter-page, monthly advertisement in the local paper. After eight months, research indicated that only a few members even noticed it.

$UCCE$$ $TRATEGY

CREATE A SENSE OF URGENCY: Place a time limit on advertised specials and add a time-limited coupon to monitor results. This gives consumers a sense of urgency to call *now*. Note: if you use this technique in all your advertising, consumers eventually get smart.

2. Coupon books (non-targeted)

Although coupon books give your advertisement a longer shelf (or drawer) life than newspaper advertising, you are again targeting a mass market. Costs vary, but count on spending at least $500 to $600 for a 30,000 residential mail-out. The books are usually delivered with household mail or the local newspaper and can get lost in the junk mail. The response rate can be low (in one example, a run of 30,000 netted the advertiser five calls, or 0.02 percent), but the per book cost of 1.5 to two cents is cheap.

As with all mass mail-outs, you have to reach the right consumer at the right time, with the right product, when they can afford it and have time to shop. Ensure that you have enough product or the ability to service an influx of calls—you have to honour your advertisements. Coupon books are good for services such as dry cleaning, or for companies that have the staff to service the calls. Time limitations are important to monitor your response.

3. Flyers (non-targeted)

Your flyer is usually circulated amongst other junk mail, so plan when and to whom you will send them. Flyers are great marketing tools to use at targeted trade shows or focussed events. People do keep certain ones for reference, such as yard work or tree-topping, and will use your service when needed. Avoid summer for this type of advertising; in one example, a flyer circulation of 1,300 sent out during August had a response rate of three calls, a return of only 0.23 percent.

> ## $UCCE$$ $TRATEGY
>
> **TRY CONSISTENCY:** A local store that consistently puts out a weekly flyer will draw repeat business. In one example, a new produce store circulates weekly flyers always advertising excellent prices, and they have developed a large, regular clientele. Try delivering one or two hundred regularly around the neighbourhood and monitor the response.

Going door-to-door is best left to the professional salesperson who handles regular rejection well. For most, it's time-consuming and confidence-shattering. Local newspapers offer a flyer delivery service, with circulation broken down into specific areas. There is usually a minimum requirement of 2,000 flyers at an approximate cost of $45 per 1,000.

Canada Post offers a delivery service too, so call them for a quote or visit *www.canadapost.ca.* Flyers are delivered with the mail, and you can choose delivery days. Smart entrepreneurs choose a day when the local paper (and flyers) aren't delivered—preferably near the end of the week—when people have more time to read and can call (or e-mail) on the weekend or first thing Monday morning.

4. Brochures (targeted)

A professional business brochure will encapsulate its services. They are invaluable for networking events, trade shows, mail-outs, correspondence and promotions. Use a good graphic artist to design an appealing layout with lots of white space. Don't try to cram in too much information, as your brochure is a teaser. It should pique interest and generate a phone call. To be affordable, you need to order large quantities, which could become outdated. For smaller, customized runs, try a digital printer.

5. Handouts (targeted)

This is the information age, so prepare informational handouts for networking events, trade shows or seminars. Professional handouts help build that expert reputation. A garbage disposal business could prepare a handout on correct recycling, the benefits of composting or reducing harmful household bacteria. A vacuum store could prepare one on household allergens and moulds, and how to eliminate them. Include all your contact information on the handout; you'll be surprised how they get passed around. Post handouts on your Web site.

CASE STUDY

HEATING UP BUSINESS

Sherri-Lee started a home-based ozone steam sauna business, offering first-time clients a free sauna. We met at a chamber of commerce dinner, and Sherri-Lee thanked me for suggesting at a networking session that she write thank-you cards to new customers.

"It's a great idea," she said excitedly. "I write them while clients are in the sauna and mail them later. I include a coupon for a half-price visit and write on the card what the coupon is for. One client asked why I thanked her for a free visit. I explained that my clients are important to me. The client commented, 'It's amazing, nobody does that!'

"I get 50 percent of first-time clients returning for the half-price session and 50 percent of those returning for at least two or more full-priced sessions, or they purchase a package deal," says Sherri-Lee. "It's the best marketing investment for repeat business I ever made. I haven't spent a lot on advertising, and probably every regular client refers at least one person."

6. Target marketing (definitely targeted)

Service businesses such as those providing roofing, paving or tree-pruning can prepare low-cost customized flyers on their computer, preferably fitting two to a page. Photocopy the master onto brightly coloured paper and cut to size. Deliver 50 to 100 flyers to homes in the vicinity of where you will be working, inviting, "Drive by 34534 Willow Drive on Tuesday and see us at work." This is an effective method of promoting residential services, as humans want what their neighbours have—or better. It's called "keeping up with the Joneses." One landscape curbing company eventually concreted 11 gardens in one cul-de-sac by doing this. It's a cheap method of promotion, and you can customize addresses as required.

7. Simply say thank you (targeted)

A week shouldn't go by without finding a reason to thank someone. It could be a new client, someone who referred a client, a newspaper that printed a press release, or an associate who helped you find a reliable service provider. Perhaps someone gave you some good advice or helped you when you needed it. Send a thank-you card, for they are the support system that keeps your business in business.

8. Birthday, holiday and frequent user cards (targeted)

Birthday cards: The personal touch goes a long way and people don't forget you when you remember them. Retail stores can ask new customers to register for the birthday club and have a sign and forms at the cash register. Then send a discount coupon for use during your customer's birthday month, along with a card. People love these cards, and will often return to use their coupon—and to purchase other products.

Holiday cards: As an added touch that says, "We are thinking about you," send clients a handwritten seasonal greetings card. I look forward to cards each year from the local Cantonese restaurant and the family real estate agent. I tell everyone about the cards and refer the businesses to others.

Frequent user discounts: Most people's wallets (including mine) are crammed with frequent user cards, whether it's for coffee, pizza, books, restaurants, dry cleaning or photofinishing, to name a few. Consumers use them because they love to get something free. The standard "buy ten, get one free" works. With all these discounted promotions, ensure that you have built the discounts into your costing and are not losing money.

9. Follow-up and service programs (targeted)

The best way to get repeat business is to follow up and stay in touch with customers. Design a simple method of collecting new customer information—their address, phone number, birthday and e-mail address—and use a contact management system. Tell customers you like to stay in touch to notify them of specials or service dates. Follow up after a sale to ensure customer satisfaction.

$UCCE$$ $TRATEGY

FOLLOW UP FOR REPEAT BUSINESS: Touch base by telephone now and again to see if you can help your customers. Many appliances and products need servicing, but without a reminder, often nothing happens. Car dealerships are diligent about sending our service reminders—sometimes two. They are assured of repeat business and your vehicle stays well maintained. Whether you are a hairdresser, vet, accountant, farrier or computer servicing company, start a service/appointment reminder system. Not only are you assured of repeat business, you continue to build relationships. You would surprised at how *few* businesses use this simple, low-cost technique.

10. Ask for referrals (targeted)

You no doubt do your best to please your customers, so why not politely ask them to spread the good word? Give each a few business cards or brochures. As you sow, so you shall reap, just as Sherri-Lee did in the case study earlier. People are always looking for "a good hairdresser" or "a good mechanic." Many businesses have built a solid client base using the referral method, which is cheap and effective. Thank clients who refer you with a card and small gift.

11. Cross-promote (targeted)

Marketing is an expensive proposition, so why not share the cost? As you build relationships with other complementary businesses, discuss cross-promotion with them. You can then share advertising and promotion costs, hold joint events and have each other's brochures and business cards on display. For example, a computer servicing business could cross-promote with a Web page designer and an accountant. A hairdresser could cross-promote with a wedding shop, a photographer and a beauty salon.

12. Send e-mails and newsletters (targeted)

E-mail newsletters do solicit a positive response, and their cost is negligible. They shouldn't be fancy or too wordy—they are there to inform and to keep in touch. Let customers know about special events, sales, and industry and product information. Mary Trentadue of 32 Books Co. Inc. in B.C. says that *short* e-mails to her customers about special in-store events and new book releases is one of her best marketing techniques.

13. The Yellow Pages (targeted)

When people don't know who to turn to, they usually look in the Yellow Pages, so it pays to be listed. Before committing to an annual contract, study competitors' advertisements. If most are large displays, then obviously the Yellow Pages is working well for them. However, a smaller advertisement works just as well if you combine it with other marketing methods. People must be able to find you, but you don't need huge monthly advertising bills added to your phone account, so place an affordable advertisement and monitor the responses.

WHICH ADVERTISING MEDIA SHOULD YOU USE?

Advertising means spending money

Because you need to discover the advertising methods that work best for you, it is critical to monitor all responses in relationship to the dollars spent. Ask all customers, "Where did you hear about us?" and note their answers and the date—a simple way to monitor results.

When you start advertising, monitor every strategy. Sign up for ads in one magazine issue, one week of radio air time and two newspaper insertions, and compare the results. Successful businesses not only take advantage of the most obvious form of advertising, they *create* consumer demand for their products through effective marketing strategies. Traditional advertising includes a variety of methods including the following.

1. Point-of-purchase material

Point-of-purchase materials include posters, banners, table tents, brochures, displays, balloons and in-store coupons displayed next to your product to increase its visibility. Take advantage of the people who walk by your display by making it stand out. How many times have you impulsively grabbed something at the checkout because it caught your attention?

$UCCE$$ $TRATEGY

TELL THE NEIGHBOURS: If you perform a service that is visible to the public, get your customer's permission to place a sign telling the neighbourhood which quality company this customer chose. Similar in concept to point-of-purchase material, this method is geared more to service-oriented businesses. Your sign can even contain a brochure holder so passers-by can take one home.

---

2. Radio and television

Radio and television advertising is usually recommended for promoting highly consumable items or special events and to establish consumer awareness. If you don't have a large inventory, several outlets or fast-selling items such as hamburgers or computers, then use other forms of marketing. If you can afford radio or television air time, combine it with printed media. Used by itself, air time won't generate the expected business as it is short-lived. Getting the public to recognize your name takes repetition—and that is expensive. The cost is usually prohibitive for small businesses.

3. Transit advertising

For many larger businesses, transit advertising works well, but it is costly. The advertisements on the back or side of a bus are obviously visible. If you have sat behind a bus in traffic, you have probably read many. Smaller advertisements placed inside a train or bus are also effective—bored commuters often have nothing else to read. Large advertisements on the back of bus seats or inside shelters are effective, but be sure to advertise in the right geographic area.

4. The Internet

Marketing on the Internet is extensively discussed elsewhere, but suffice to say that competitive businesses keep up with technology and are accessible via e-mail and their Web sites. A site gives you a 24/7 presence and can be utilized in many ways.

Consumers are becoming more reliant on the Internet for paying bills, ordering from reputable companies—such as large office stationers—and for finding information. Even a business servicing a local market could benefit; for example, a local florist with an on-line catalogue and secure ordering provides a convenience for our "too busy" society.

$UCCE$$ $TRATEGY

INFORM, EDUCATE AND SELL: Surfers use the Internet to find specific information and to increase their knowledge. Sites offering free information get more visits, so include this component. For example, an accountant could prepare a series of articles such as "Ten Hot Tips for Saving on Your Taxes." By posting this information, a relationship of trust is already building with the user.

Those servicing a wider market—provincial, national or international—should consider a Web site. Hotels, resorts and bed and breakfasts gain regular international business this way. If you specialize in a product—for example, collector dolls—a Web site and secure ordering system is a great business booster.

People are still hesitant to buy over the Internet from unknown businesses, so be conservative about what you spend and monitor the results. Have a professional design the site and be prepared for a costly venture, depending on its size, bells and whistles. Consult first with other businesses and industry professionals. Splash your e-mail and Web site address on everything—business cards, stationery, brochures and all advertising, as consumers often visit a company's Web site first.

5. Specials

People love a deal and can't resist words like "sale," "special," "70 percent off" or "inventory clearance." Time-sensitive deals such as offering to pay the GST/HST for the first 20 customers create an urgency for people to call, particularly for higher-priced items. Specials will help clear out slow-moving inventory, stimulate cash flow and increase market awareness, but should not be unprofitable.

6. Mix and match

You may have been told that the more your advertise, the more effective the results, or that your first advertisements may not work for you. The truth is, every advertisement should work for you if it is correctly planned and priced. The more you advertise, the better the results. Response rate should gradually increase, so don't expect the telephone to ring off the hook after the third advertisement.

Two or three techniques combined in the same time period generate a better response. A new business can't afford to wait for customers to magically appear. You need to become known—quickly. For example, an "informational" advertisement in a magazine and radio advertising may not prompt people to call, but adding coupon books or flyers will. Your market is now surrounded with your information. They are informed of your business' benefits with one type of advertising, and you are encouraging them to come in with another.

Don't deplete your marketing budget to do this. For better air-time rates, either buy the same day, all day, every week, using the same time slot, or use the same time slot every day on the same days every week. Magazine, flyer and coupon advertising can be two-colour instead of full colour. Full colour isn't necessary, unless you are selling high-end products.

HOW DO YOU PLAN A MARKETING BUDGET?

How much can you supply?

Before you decide on how you are going to market, calculate how *much* you can sell. It's no use implementing a huge marketing campaign, only to discover that you can't keep up with the work or that you don't have the working capital to finance a larger inventory. Once you know your capabilities—both physically and financially—you can then better identify what may work best for you. Some calculations are necessary for all businesses to complete their business plan projections.

Service businesses

A sole proprietor wears 60 hats, so you can't work religiously eight hours a day generating income. The accepted calculation is a maximum of four billable hours a day. If you deduct time for weekends, statutory holidays, vacations, administrative and education or conference days, you'll find you have about 185 working days available. If you bill $65 an hour for those 185 four-hour days, your maximum annual income—without extra help—is $48,000. Use this figure to calculate what percentage of income you are going to use for marketing. A new business should be prepared to spend between ten and 20 percent of sales in the first year. What will you spend? At 15 percent, that is $7,200 a year, or $600 a month.

Product-based businesses

The calculation for sales projections for product-based businesses will be more complex. You must take into account the following factors to establish monthly sales projections and then calculate your marketing budget from there. Answer these questions:

- How much product can you physically house?
- How much product can you physically sell?
- How much product can you afford to purchase?
- Do you know your seasonal peaks and ebbs?

Try a simple marketing budget calculation using Figure 10.4.

Figure 10.4: CALCULATING A MARKETING BUDGET

a) Annual working days: _____   b) x daily hours worked   _____
                                                (service businesses):

c) x hourly rate or   _____
    daily sales:

Estimated annual income: $ _____   Marketing % (10-20%):   _____

Total budget: $ _____   Monthly budget: $ _____

Plot your sales and marketing curve

For budgeting purposes, plot a month-by-month graph showing projected sales, join the dots and create a sales curve. Ascertain when and how you should be promoting your business to capitalize on seasonal times of the year, for example, Easter, Mother's Day and back-to-school. If your product sells well on Valentine's Day, your marketing push should start a month before. Department stores start advertising Christmas as early as September, because advertising in December is too late. Magazines often have a two- to three-month copy deadline, while newspapers are weekly. Mall and trade show space must be booked and paid for months in advance. Timing and budgeting are crucial.

Although you need to capitalize on seasonal sales peaks, your first year's budget should make allowances for a stronger push when the business opens and during the first few months. It should also reflect periods when marketing for many businesses can be a waste of time, such as summer. Next, plot how much you can spend each month, based on the sales curve, and in which months you need to spend it.

Few businesses achieve their first year's projected sales as many are overly optimistic. Success is based on achieving close to these figures. Perhaps you will be one of the few who meet—or even surpass—your projections. Make sure you have the right product available at the right time and promote it the right way.

$UCCE$$ $TRATEGY

PLAN EACH YEAR: Reduce your second year's marketing budget to seven to ten percent of sales. By now, you will know more about your business, how it relates to the consumer and which strategies work for you. Your third year's budget should be more accurate, based on the second year. By your fourth or fifth year, you should be able to reduce your budget to as low as four or five percent of sales, but don't spend less than this.

Plan how you will spend

The last step is to look at each month's budget, combined with the seasonal projections, and decide how you will spend your marketing dollars. Some monthly expenses will be consistent, such as chamber of commerce dinners, monthly networking meetings and a Yellow Pages advertisement. Your start-up marketing costs will be high, as they include expenses such as brochures, grand opening events and advertising. Talk to others in similar businesses to see what works for them. Review and digest the low-cost, targeted options in this chapter before deciding how to spend your money. More detailed information can be found in *Big Ideas for Growing Your Small Business.*

WHAT IS THE NEXT STEP?

It's a subject that most people don't want to discuss and a chore they don't want to do—accounting. Yet you are in business to make money, and the only way you can ascertain whether you are or why you are not is to count the beans and be organized. The shoe-box system doesn't work for most businesses, and flying by the seat of your pants only creates a giant hole. So get out the coffee pot again and perk up the brain to digest the basics about accounting.

CHAPTER 11

How do you organize your accounting, time and paperwork?

She filed bills under B and letters under L.
Where the rest of it went, who can really tell?

HOW DO YOU ORGANIZE YOUR FILES?

No doubt about it, you have to be organized to keep on top of the paperwork. As soon as you start a business, you are inundated with a mountain of correspondence from various government agencies and an assortment of advertising. If you organize efficiently from the start, the paperwork won't bog you down. Too many people let papers pile up, leaving mail unopened for days and even weeks. They then hurriedly scan it without paying attention. This sloppy practice leads to mistakes. Organization is an essential ingredient for a successful business.

Start with a 20-second filing cabinet

The more crowded your files, the less organized you are. Buy a four-drawer filing cabinet, suspension frames and different coloured legal-sized hanging files and file folders for easy identification. Use tabs for visibility and follow Figure 11.1, which suggests the files you will need and which drawer to use. You will no doubt add to the list over time. This efficient filing system allows you to find any paper in 20 seconds or less.

File paperwork as follows:

1. **Numerically:** File sales invoices both numerically and chronologically, with the latest number in front. Do this after they are posted (entered) to your books.

2. **Alphabetically:** For each accounts payable supplier, put the last paid invoice in front. The most recent purchases are now at your fingertips in chronological order.

3. **Chronologically:** All other files, including correspondence, are filed chronologically, the latest in front.

4. **Year-end:** After financial statements and taxes are completed, store the last 12 months' accounting in a storage box, and reuse the file folders. Keep your accounting records for seven years. Keep important information accessible, such as incorporation papers or asset purchases. Revisit all files and discard unnecessary papers.

Figure 11.1: YOUR 20-SECOND FILING CABINET STRATEGY

Top drawer:

- GST/HST: one file for remittances and one for information pamphlets
- CCRA payroll: one file for schedules, one for employee records
- Provincial sales tax remittances and information
- Workers' Compensation
- Accounts to be paid, organized alphabetically
- Cheque and deposit books, spare cheques
- Posting file for accounting ready to be entered to books
- Quotations for work pending
- Quotations for purchases you make
- Monthly accounting papers and year-end documents
- Current Visa receipts and invoices.

Second drawer:

- Incorporation papers and related correspondence
- Other licensing agencies

- Telephone, cell, Yellow Pages contracts
- Bank account and Visa merchant documents
- Asset register and invoices for purchases over $200
- Business vehicle information and bills
- Expense reports, completed and spare sheets
- Completed job costings
- Client correspondence
- Business start-up information
- Insurance policies—a file per policy
- Contacts and leads information.

Third drawer:

- Paid accounts, a file for each main supplier, two for miscellaneous
- Reconciled bank statements and cancelled cheques
- Posted cash expenses for costs you personally paid
- Posted petty cash receipts
- Posted sales invoices or invoice books (use a three-ring binder for large quantities)
- Advertising information and rates.

Fourth drawer:

- One previous year's accounting
- Spare Visa credit card slips and information
- You'll find a use for the rest.

HOW DO YOU ORGANIZE YOUR TIME AND PAPERWORK?

Learn to work to routines

Keep on top of paperwork by dispensing with it as soon as possible. Keeping a daily and weekly routine helps achieve this goal.

Each day...

When mail arrives, sort it into accounts to be paid, cheques to be deposited, government correspondence, items requiring immediate attention and the rest. Tackle one pile at a time. Check supplier accounts for correct pricing and note in your day planner or calendar the due date. Then file them alphabetically.

Match cheques to be deposited with an invoice number, ensuring the full amount has been paid. Note any discounts taken, short payments and the invoice number. Put the cheques into your deposit book, ready to write up the deposit. Read all government correspondence, such as payroll, GST/HST or provincial tax remittances; note when payment is due and then file. Scan your advertising mail and either file or recycle it. Attend to the important things at once or you will probably forget.

$UCCE$$ $TRATEGY

ITEMIZE CHEQUE STUBS: When you write cheques, record the GST on the stubs, then subtract the GST from the total paid to get the net expense. Write this amount on the cheque stub with a short description of the expense (e.g., office supplies). This saves you or your bookkeeper time, as the expense will be allocated to the right account, and it will save you accounting dollars.

Each week...

Regularly review and pay your bills. When you pay an account, take it out of the accounts-to-be-paid file, write the cheque, then record the cheque number, date and amount paid on the invoice. This is a cross-reference in case there is a dispute over payment. File the paid account. Review accounts receivable and make some collection calls. Service businesses should bill clients weekly. Put a copy of the mailed invoice into the posting file for entry to your books.

Empty your wallet weekly of those cash receipts for gas, lunches, stamps and miscellaneous items. Put them into your posting file, clipped together. Separate petty cash items and balance the float. Staple the receipts together with a piece of paper detailing the amount, the cheque number and date. If receipts are illegible, write on them what they are for. File in the posting file. Keep credit card receipts and invoices in a separate file so they can later be matched to the statement.

Each month...

After month-end, sort through the posting file, putting the papers into the following order for entry to your books. If you use an accounting software system, either you or your bookkeeper should code each piece of paper using the correct chart of accounts number (shown later in Figure 11.3).

Deal with each of the following categories:

1. **Sales invoices:** Batch sales invoices numerically, starting with the oldest. Locate missing invoice numbers. Attach a tape totalling the completed monthly invoices. They are now ready to enter to the books and you know how much you billed.

2. **Cheque stubs:** Remove the month's cheque stubs from your binder, carrying the balance forward to the next cheque. Clip the stubs together, filling in any missing information.

3. **Cash expenses:** Sort receipts into the various expense categories, staple together each expense type with a tape total, and indicate the type of expense.

4. **Bank deposits:** If possible, order a triplicate copy bank deposit book. Then remove a copy of each deposit, staple them together in date order and attach a tape of the monthly total. If you use the deposit book for posting, tape-list the deposits and staple the tape to the last deposit for the month.

5. **Miscellaneous:** Note or include anything else of relevance for the book-keeper or your accountant.

6. **Credit card statements:** If you use credit cards for personal and business expenses, go through each statement when it arrives and highlight the business expenses. Take the credit card receipts and corresponding invoices and attach them to the statement in the order the charges appear.

$UCCE$$ $TRATEGY

BE THOROUGH WITH CREDIT CARD RECORDS:
Detailed information is required of each credit card transaction, and for audit purposes, each charge must have an accompanying invoice. A common mistake is to include only the credit card slips with accounting records. No one can work from a credit card statement or the yellow slips, and accountants charge big bucks at year-end if all the necessary documents aren't presented.

Start a priority list

With so much to do, prioritizing is essential. Sometimes, work is overwhelming and you feel out of control. If organization is not your strength, use the weekly priority list system.

Using an eight-column pad, set up columns across the top titled Things to Do, Deadline, A+, A, B and C priorities as shown in Figure 11.2. List all the things to do, decide on a deadline for each task—even if that task's deadline is weeks away—and then indicate the priority for each job. Work first on the A+ priorities, starting at the earliest deadline, crossing them off the list with a highlighter as completed.

Figure 11.2: WEEKLY PRIORITY LIST

THINGS TO DO: WEEK ENDING JUNE 15, XXXX

THINGS TO DO	DEADLINE	A+	A	B	C
Bill clients	June 9	✔			
Pay monthly accounts	June 9	✔			
Order business cards	June 12			✔	
Write thank-you cards	June 10		✔		
Clean filing cabinet	June 15				✔
Follow-up phone calls	June 11	✔			
Quotation for Mrs. Baxter	June 10		✔		

Review the list daily and add new priorities. You will be surprised at how many C priorities can eventually be crossed off without taking any action. Move outstanding chores to your new weekly list as necessary. There is a certain satisfaction at seeing work crossed off the list, which is also a constant reminder not to forget anything important. This simple system works efficiently—if you use it.

CASE STUDY

NO ACCOUNTING FOR TASTE

In my public practice, I am often presented with shoe-boxes crammed with papers one week before the April tax deadline. These business owners don't have a clue where their businesses stand financially. Accounting has also arrived in fruit boxes, zip-lock and grocery bags (both paper and plastic). The most repulsive scenario was a well-used, gravy-stained, family-sized cardboard fried chicken tub, complete with dried coleslaw on the bottom. Then there was the plastic bag, full of unopened mail, obviously swept off the kitchen table along with some sandwich crusts. Such filing systems say a lot about the business owners, who are also charged "dirt" time.

Unorganized people usually create cash flow problems for themselves. An unexpected tax bill for thousands of dollars, coupled with late GST/HST payments, soon puts such businesses in deep financial waters. Some people get so far over their head that bankruptcy is the only alternative. Not surprisingly, neither the chicken tub nor the sandwich crust business owners are in business now.

HOW DO YOU SET UP YOUR ACCOUNTING?

Shoe-box or systemized?

Each business has different accounting requirements, depending on its size and the volume of transactions, but the principles are the same for everyone. A small, one-person business may need only one journal to record all the monthly accounting. Once a business starts generating more paperwork, an accounting software program is a good idea. It's smart to start with a manual system so that the basic accounting concepts are understood before becoming technologically terrific.

Always get your accountant's help to set up and monitor your progress. Some people have a mental block about using their accountant for advice—and about paying their bills on time. Respect your accountant; he or she has your best interests at heart. Learning how to understand your accounting system and keep it up-to-date—the future of your business relies heavily on you being informed.

What accounting records do you need?

Many pieces make your accounting puzzle fit together. If you keep "source documents"—that is, every piece of paper—well organized, it's much easier to record your accounting information. Both a manual system and accounting software record the same transactions. Your accounting books should consist of the following:

1. **Sales journal:** records sales and taxes

2. **Cash receipts journal:** records all money coming into the business

3. **Synoptic or cash disbursements journal:** records cheques written, the expense and bank charges

4. **Cash expenses journal:** records out-of-pocket and petty cash expenses

5. **Accounts payable journal:** records unpaid trade and supplier accounts

6. **General journal:** records adjustments made to your books, usually made by your accountant

7. **General ledger:** combines the above books, ready for the preparation of the financial statement

8. **Trial balance:** a listing of your financial accounts to show that the books balance

9. **Financial statements:** A compilation of all of the above which reflects the financial situation of the business.

If you opt for a manual system, you use the first seven journals. For small businesses, the first five can be combined into one simple book. An accounting software program combines all the above functions with a one-time entry, eliminating the need for columns and cross-additions and posting the first six journals to the general ledger, which then has each page totalled and the whole book cross-balanced. (I can see some accounting software proponents after that statement.)

$UCCE$$ $TRATEGY

LEARN THE PROGRAM FIRST: Unless you have a thorough understanding of bookkeeping, don't even attempt to do your own accounting using a software program until you have formally learned how to use it with your accountant's guidance. If you enter a wrong account number or code an account incorrectly, your financial information will be wrong, and often, the mistakes are never picked up.

Data entry takes meticulous manual preparation. Information is posted in batches, which at month-end are balanced to an accounting control. Accounting means that every figure has to be entered to the books twice, thus the term double-entry bookkeeping. One entry acts as a control—either to the bank account, accounts receivable or payable records—the other is descriptive and tells you what the amount is for.

What is a chart of accounts?

A chart of accounts is a directory of your accounting information, called accounts. Each one is usually allocated a three- or four-digit number, and the chart is listed in the order of a financial statement. Each business needs a slightly different chart of accounts. Figure 11.3 shows a simple chart of accounts for Jason's Garden Service. The following pages show examples of his accounting journals, with explanations to help you organize your system.

Figure 11.3: CHART OF ACCOUNTS: JASON'S GARDEN SERVICE

Current assets:

1000 Bank account

1020 Accounts receivable

1030 Inventory

1040 Prepaid expenses

Current liabilities:

2000 Accounts payable

2010 Provincial tax payable

2020 GST/HST collected

2030 GST/HST paid

2040 Bank loan payable

2050 Wages payable

2100 Loan payable–R. Davies

Fixed assets:

1200 Automotive equipment

1220 Office equipment

1230 Office furniture

Equity:

3000 Owner's capital

3010 Owner's draws

3030 Retained earnings (profit)

Income:

4000 Sales–supplies

4010 Sales–delivery

4020 Other income

Cost of sales:

4500 Material purchases

4510 Truck fuel

4520 Truck repairs

4530 Truck insurance

4540 Driver's wages

Expenses:

5000 Accounting fees

5010 Advertising

5020 Bank charges

5030 Discounts

5040 Fees, licences & dues

5050 Insurance

5060 Loan interest

5080 Office supplies & printing

5090 Promotion–meals

5100 Rent & property taxes

5120 Telephones & Internet

5130 Travel & accommodation

5140 Utilities

5150 Workers' Compensation

1. The sales journal (monthly sales invoices)

A sales journal records each invoice billed or daily cash sales, and is used to compile your accounts receivable records. Jason divided his sales into categories such as bark mulch, gravel, topsoil, sand and delivery charges. Each month, his sales journal gives him the dollar value of goods sold (see Figure 11.4). This information helps when he reorders supplies and indicates seasonal trends. Provincial taxes and the GST are also recorded.

Figure 11.4: SALES JOURNAL: JASON'S GARDEN SERVICE

Sales Journal: September XXXX

DATE	NAME	INV. #	TOTAL Dr +	SAND Cr –	MULCH Cr –	SOIL Cr –	GRAVEL Cr –	DELIVERY Cr –	PST Cr –	GST Cr –
09/01	J. Stein	2346	171.00	35.00	35.00	50.00		30.00	10.50	10.50
09/03	B. Jones	2347	969.00	150.00	200.00	200.00	200.00	100.00	59.50	59.50
09/15	I. Chow	2348	513.00				400.00	50.00	31.50	31.50
09/27	S. Bull	2349	214.00			165.00		35.00	7.00	7.00
TOTAL			$1,867.00	$185.00	$235.00	$415.00	$600.00	$215.00	$108.50	$108.50
			=	+	+	+	+	+	+	+

Sales journal analysis

Jason can now review his monthly sales to see which products sold well. He can now complete his sales tax return and pay it on time. He files GST quarterly and has the three months' sales figures ready for when the return is due.

The *Dr +* and *Cr –* signs under the headings denote debit and credit entries. When the columns are added across the page, the total debits should equal credits. If you calculate the totals on an adding machine tape, the balance should be zero. The plus (+) and minus (–) signs are there to help those challenged by bookkeeping. The accounting rule is: *add all debits and subtract all credits to balance your books.*

Jason can now convert sales figures into percentages to help with costing and budgets. For example, gravel is 36.4 percent of his total sales, before tax. Percentages are easily obtained using this formula:

Gravel sales	$\underline{\$\ 600.00}$ x 100.0% = **36.4%**
Total sales	$1,650.00

2. The cash receipts journal (daily bank deposits)

This journal records everything deposited to your bank account and keeps a record of the money's origin, as not all funds are from sales. If you have more than one bank account, enter each one separately, either on another page or underneath the first completed one. If you enter two bank accounts together, your books will be a nightmare to correct!

Keeping an accurate cash receipts journal is simply a matter of clearly itemizing everything. To correctly record a bank deposit, follow these steps:

1. Match each cheque to the paid invoice numbers, noting discounts or short payments. (You made these notes when sorting the mail.)

2. Put the cheques into alphabetical order and enter them into the deposit book. Next to the cheque or on the opposite page, note the invoice numbers being paid—the same applies to cash being deposited.

3. If other funds are deposited—such as capital, loans or rebates on expenses—note in your deposit book whom the money came from and what it is for.

4. Now enter each daily deposit into the cash receipts journal using the correct columns (see Figure 11.5):

   a) Date:　　　　The date of the bank deposit.

   b) Invoice #:　　The invoice number(s) being paid with each cheque.

   c) Total Bank:　The total of the daily deposit, which should equal the total of each cheque listed in "bank in" column.

   d) Bank In:　　A line-by-line breakdown of each cheque, which equals the "total bank" column.

   e) Discount:　　The amount of discount taken.

f) Accounts Receivable: The total of the paid invoice including discounts. The total of the cheque plus discount equals the total accounts receivable.

g) Account #:   The chart of accounts number which identifies any deposits other than accounts receivable.

h) Amount: The amount of the above deposit.

i) Description: Note what this money is for.

Figure 11.5: CASH RECEIPTS JOURNAL: JASON'S GARDEN SERVICE

Cash Receipts Journal: September XXXX

a)		b)	c)	d)	e)	f)	g)	h)	i)
DATE	NAME	INV. #	TOTAL BANK	BANK IN Dr +	DISC- Dr +	A/REC. Cr −	A/C #	AMOUNT Cr −	DESCR.
09/07	J. Stein	2346		167.58	3.42	171.00			
09/07	B. Jones	2347		949.62	19.38	969.00			
09/07	S. Swan	2333	1,667.20	550.00		550.00			
09/10	J. Darjeeling		1,000.00	1,000.00			(3000)	1,000.00	Capital
09/15	I. Chow	2348		513.00		513.00			
09/15	R. Davies		2,513.00	2,000.00			(2100)	2,000.00	Loan
09/27	S. Bull	2349		209.72	4.28	214.00			
09/27	J. Toms	2327	539.72	330.00		330.00			
	TOTALS:		$5,719.92	$5,719.92	$27.08	$2,747.00		$3,000.00	
			=	=	+	−		−	

The cash receipts journal should not be closed off at month-end until the bank statements are received. Then each deposit in the "total bank" column is checked against those on the bank statements as it is easy to make mistakes. The bank may issue a credit memo, or the account earn interest, which must be entered into the journal, ready for the bank reconciliation.

3. The cash disbursements journal (cheques written)

The cash disbursements journal records the details of every cheque you write and monthly automatic payments from the bank account, such as loans, car insurance and bank charges. If you miss one item, your books won't agree with the bank statement.

Accounting software

Your cheque stubs are, of course, well detailed. If you use accounting software, total all cheques on a tape at month-end, highlight other deductions from the bank statement and add these on to the tape. When the bank account is reconciled, then enter the cheques. Ensure that each cheque stub is coded with the correct account number. When everything is entered, the bank account month-end total in your records must agree with the manual reconciliation.

$UCCE$$ $TRATEGY

CODE AS YOU GO: To avoid errors made while hurriedly coding a pile of cheques at month-end, keep a copy of your chart of accounts in the plastic wallet of your cheque binder. When you write a cheque, code it immediately while you have the relevant information—such as the paid invoice—in front of you.

Manual systems

Cheques and automatic bank deductions are manually entered into the cash disbursements journal, and the bank reconciliation completed after month-end. A 20-column journal is ample. Set out the columns according to the expenses you incur the most. Those you incur infrequently are entered into the miscellaneous column, along with a short description. Jason's main expenses are materials, GST, truck costs and wages. Figure 11.6 shows Jason's journal.

Figure 11.6: CASH DISBURSEMENTS JOURNAL: JASON'S GARDEN SERVICE

Cash Disbursements Journal: September XXXX

DATE	NAME	CH. NO.	BANK OUT Cr −	GST Dr +	MATERIAL Dr +	WAGES Dr +	TRUCK Dr +	DRAW Dr +	MISC. Dr +
09/01	Leasit Co.	024 ✔	749.00	49.00					700.00 Rent
09/01	FuelUp	025 ✔	995.10	65.10			930.00		
09/03	Office Co.	026 ✔	69.55	4.55					65.00 Office
09/03	Gravelpit	027 ✔	856.00	56.00	800.00				
09/08	Sandpile	028 ✔	428.00	28.00	400.00				
09/15	S. Jones	029 ✔	525.00			525.00			
09/15	D. Spence	030 ✔	650.00			650.00			
09/15	CCRA	031 ✔	730.00			730.00			
09/15	Min. Finance	032 ✔	350.00						350.00 Sales Tax
09/27	Supply Co.	033o/s	1,125.00	73.60	1,051.40				
09/30	J. Davies	034 ✔	500.00					500.00	
09/30	S. Jones	035o/s	525.00			525.00			
09/30	D. Spence	036o/s	600.00			600.00			
09/30	Loan	--- ✔	450.00						450.00 Bank loan
09/30	Charges	--- ✔	35.00						35.00 S/charges
TOTALS:			**$8,587.65**	**$276.25**	**$2,251.40**	**$3,030.00**	**$930.00**	**$500.00**	**$1,600.00**
			=	+	+	+	+	+	+

4. Bank reconciliation (balancing the monthly bank account)

Reconciling your bank account monthly is a priority, as it's the main book-keeping control. It's easy to miss entries, transpose figures or forget an automatic bank deduction. A reconciliation assures you that what you have written in both your cash receipts and disbursement journals balances to your bank statement. It doesn't mean you have allocated the expenses to the right account, but at least every cent is accounted for. Here's how to do it in five simple steps:

a) Check your accounting

When the bank statements arrive for the previous month, close off by performing the following checks:

- All cheques should be written in numerical order
- Voided cheques should have the number recorded and marked "Void"
- Ensure each expense is correctly coded or entered to the journal
- Don't close off either journal until the bank is reconciled
- Ensure all deposits are entered.

b) Compare bank deposits

Check each deposit in the cash receipts journal against the bank statement; check it off either with a highlighter or checkmark. Correct wrong or missed deposits and credit memos. Your deposits total should now agree with the bank statement.

c) Compare cheques

Sort the cancelled cheques from your bank statement into numerical order. Using the cash disbursements journal, check off each cheque under your bank statement's "debit" column against your records. Highlight entries on the bank statement not in your journal—such as service charges or NSF cheques—and enter them. The cheques in your journal not yet shown on the statement are marked with "o/s"(outstanding). Now total the "bank out" column. When the bank account is reconciled, you can total, cross-add and balance both journals.

d) Prepare your manual reconciliation

See how it's done for Jason's reconciliation, Figure 11.7.

Figure 11.7: BANK RECONCILIATION: JASON'S GARDEN SERVICE

Bank Reconciliation: September 30, XXXX

Balance end of August:	$ 4,296.53
September deposits from cash receipts journal:	5,719.92
	10,016.45
September cheques from disbursements journal:	(8,587.65)
Balance September 30 (Jason's books):	**$ 1,428.80**
Bank statement balance September 30:	3,678.80
Less outstanding cheques: 033	($1,125.00)
035	(525.00)
036	(600.00)
Balance as per bank statement:	**$ 1,428.80**

e) Complete the reconciliation

Correct your cheque book balance if it differs from the reconciliation. If one of the outstanding cheques is not listed on the bank statement the following month, carry it forward on your next reconciliation as outstanding and phone the recipient. If the cheque has not been received, put a stop payment on it and issue another one. Reverse the old cheque out of your books by entering it in parentheses ($600.00) across the page, then deduct this amount from that month's totals.

5. Petty cash and out-of-pocket expenses

One journal—set up similar to cash disbursements—can record both petty cash and your out-of-pocket expenses. Figure 11.8 shows you how. Set up the expense columns to suit your business. Jason kept a petty cash float and spent some of his own money on business expenses.

Figure 11.8: PETTY CASH JOURNAL: JASON'S GARDEN SERVICE

Petty Cash Journal: September 30, XXXX

DATE	PAID TO	PETTY CASH Cr −	CAPITAL IN Cr −	GST PAID Dr +	OFFICE Dr +	MATERIAL Dr +	GAS Dr +	OTHER Dr +
09/02	Gas-up	53.50		3.50			50.00	
09/04	Office World		48.15	3.15	45.00			
09/07	Harry's Place		26.75	1.75				25.00 Bus. Lunch
09/09	Haul-it	32.10		2.10				30.00 Delivery
09/11	Rockpit	64.20		4.20		60.00		
09/15	Drugmart	46.01		3.01	43.00			
09/18	Gas-up		21.40	1.40			20.00	
09/22	Spark 'N' Shine	16.05		1.05				15.00 Windows
09/27	Telemart	37.45		2.45				35.00 Phone
TOTALS		$249.31	$96.30	$22.61	$88.00	$60.00	$70.00	$105.00
		=	=	+	+	+	+	+

6. Other journals

If you maintain these four journals above and reconcile your bank account monthly, most of your accounting information will be in excellent shape. If you need a quick financial statement, your accountant can easily prepare one. Many small businesses manage quite efficiently using just one journal, the combined journal, which is explained below. Other accounting journal requirements are:

Accounts payable journal

Most small businesses do not need an accounts payable journal; this system is used more by larger companies, although most accounting programs come with one built in. Whenever you need a financial statement, outstanding accounts payable should be recorded in this journal.

General journal

Because this journal records transactions not usually recorded in other journals, these entries are normally prepared by your accountant at year-end or when a financial statement is required. These transactions include depreciation, adjusting prepaid expenses, the business portion of home office and vehicle expenses, corporate taxes due and inventory changes. Leave these to your accountant—that's why you pay them. However, keep a file detailing unusual transactions, such as trades, and explain them to your accountant.

General ledger

Monthly totals from all the above journals are entered to the general ledger, which is maintained in order of your chart of accounts and is used to prepare your financial statement. Accounting software enables accountants to take manually prepared journals, enter the monthly totals and other details into their own program, and prepare your general ledger. This is more efficient than spending hours—or even days—manually preparing the information.

Combined journal

This method suits many small businesses with minimum paperwork. Your accountant can easily set one up and show you how it works. The combined journal is so called because sales, cash receipts, cash disbursements and cash expenses are combined into one book. If you need a more detailed breakdown of sales or expenses, one journal may not work. Some businesses record more detailed sales information in the back of the combined journal, as journals with more than 20 columns are awkward to use.

What does your accountant require?

Your books are closed off to prepare a financial statement at year-end or if you need one during the year. Because a financial statement is a snapshot of your business taken at a particular date, there can be no loose ends. Figure 11.9 is a checklist of "things to do" for your accountant.

Figure 11.9: YEAR-END "THINGS TO DO" ACCOUNTING CHECKLIST	
Task	**Complete**
1. Record all sales invoices and taxes collected.	☐
2. Record all bank deposits and correctly allocate.	☐
3. List outstanding accounts receivable, balanced to your books.	☐
4. Record all cheques and correctly allocate.	☐
5. Reconcile bank accounts for the year.	☐
6. List accounts payable, amounts and what they are for.	☐
7. Complete petty cash and proprietor's cash expense journal.	☐
8. Obtain annual loans statements from lenders and banks.	☐
9. Reconcile outstanding payroll and other tax accounts.	☐
10. List any prepaid expenses (your accountant will check this).	☐
11. Take an accurate physical inventory figure and cost.	☐
12. Prepare information for general journal entries.	☐
13. Total and cross-balance all manual journals.	☐
14. Prepare accountant's copy of computer-generated reports.	☐
15. List all home-office expenses and vehicle mileage.	☐

Your accountant will outline all the required information before a statement is prepared. However, your statements could still be inaccurate in areas that your accountant has no control over. They are your responsibility. Here's why:

- Inventory could be incorrectly costed

- Sales invoices may not have been entered

- Supplier accounts in the mail are not recorded

- Expenses are entered to the wrong account.

Mistakes every bookkeeper makes

Countless errors happen with bookkeeping, and I've made them all—repeatedly. After all, we're only human, no one is perfect, we get tired, the phone rings, it's boring and we lose concentration. These are my excuses—you will undoubtedly create your own as you stumble through this exciting learning experience. Attending evening bookkeeping classes will turn on some light bulbs and convert this foreign language into something less formidable.

When your books don't balance, use a slow, methodical process of elimination to find the errors. Here are some common mistakes—and their remedies:

- Simple addition and subtraction errors occur as a sales invoice, cheque or bank deposit is broken down. Check extensions across the page, line-by-line, to ensure each line cross-balances.

- Figures are transposed. *Here's a hot tip:* If the amount you are out is divisible by 9, check your figures until you find the transposed one. For instance, if $325 is written as $352, the difference is 27, which is divisible by 9. Try this with any figure; it always works.

- You may have incorrectly added a column. Re-add.

- You added a credit balance or subtracted a debit balance. (This reverse psychology confuses those new to accounting as bank statements reflect the opposite principle. Ask your accountant or bookkeeper to explain it to you.)

- You incorrectly carried forward totals to the next page. Re-add the totals across the top of the page to ensure they balance.

HOW DO YOU COST INVENTORY?

Counting and costing inventory are not enjoyable tasks, yet if you make errors, your financial figures will be way out. Inventory is just like having cash in the bank, only it is represented by material items. Although your business software may maintain a theoretical inventory, once a year, this dastardly chore still has to be done, because theoretical figures are often wrong.

CASE STUDY

NOT COUNTING THE LOSSES

One retail company I knew carried a large inventory of small items with a valuation of approximately $150,000. They used an industry-specific software program that also recorded a theoretical inventory value. Because counting inventory meant closing the store for a few days, it had not been physically counted for many years. Yet something was wrong with the financial information... When inventory was finally counted, the theoretical figure was $30,000 higher than the physical count. The business immediately lost $30,000 in profit.

Here is the correct way to prepare your inventory:

1. Prepare inventory sheets ready to list each item, quantity, price and the extension total.

2. Have two people count each item together.

3. Record each item purchased for resale or used for manufacturing. Don't include fixed assets or stationery.

4. If you have partially completed manufactured or assembled goods, estimate their current value, including labour. These goods are called "work in progress."

5. List damaged, obsolete or slow-moving items that should be devalued. Try selling them on clearance or dispose of them. Give your accountant a value and list of these goods.

6. Price items at your cost, not retail price.

7. Extend all calculations and have a second person check them. Ensure that handwritten calculations are legible.

What is a "landed cost"?

A landed cost is the total cost of purchasing, assembling or manufacturing a product. You need this information to determine selling prices and to monitor gross profits and production. For example, if you import shafts and hardware to build garden umbrellas and have a stock of completed shafts, your costings would be calculated as in Figure 11.10.

Figure 11.10: COSTING PRODUCT - GARDEN UMBRELLA SHAFTS	
Umbrella shafts, 2 feet long	.90 each
Umbrella shafts, 3 feet long	1.30 each
Metal tapers	.50 each
Hinges	.40 each
	3.10 each
Duty on shafts	.35 each
Duty on hinges & tapers	.25 each
Freight on components	.45 each
Landed cost:	**4.15 each**
Assembly	1.30 each
Completed cost of shaft:	**$5.45 each**

WHICH BUSINESS EXPENSES ARE TAX DEDUCTIBLE?

Common expenses

Most expenses incurred to start and operate a business are deductible, although there are limits to some, and others are *not* allowable. CCRA prefers that you start a business with the intention of making a profit and that you keep expenses within reason. A business making sales of $20,000 a year, incurring $4,000 in promotional meals and claiming a loss of $10,000 will eventually attract their attention. Here are the most common tax-deductible business costs:

1. ***Research:*** Literature, vehicle expenses, training, start-up kits, travel and other expenses related to out-of-town conferences and seminars, consultations with professionals, educational courses.

2. ***Start-up:*** Building repairs, fees and licences, legal, accounting, business plan, loan application, appraisal and financing fees, leases, telephone lines, printing and stationery, marketing, advertising, samples, promotions.

$UCCE$$ $TRATEGY

LEAVE THE CASH UNDER THE TABLE: Don't fall for the trap of hiring people who ask to be paid "cash under the table." Every time you pay cash without getting a receipt, you are not only losing out on your tax deduction, you are understating business expenses and encouraging cheaters to abuse the system. Leave the tax liability to the subcontractor—it's their choice to be honest or not.

3. ***Operational:*** Costs related to manufacturing or purchasing products for resale. These include raw materials, freight, customs, duty, brokerage fees, inventory, equipment repairs and maintenance, wages, wastage and damaged inventory.

4. ***Direct:*** Costs related directly to selling, including sales wages, commissions, referral fees, displays, samples, delivery, discounts, rebates and coupons.

5. ***Overhead:*** Expenses incurred to sustain the day-to-day operation of the business. See Figure 11.11 for a detailed list. Limited expenses include:

- Business insurance is fully deductible, but personal insurance and disability policies are not, unless your business is incorporated and the business is the benefactor of the policies.

- Business meals are 50 percent deductible. Meals eaten alone are not deductible, unless you are travelling out of town. As there are limits to claims for certain types of entertainment, talk to your accountant.

- Conferences are limited to two a year, including travel costs.

- Clothing and dry cleaning are not usually deductible, but uniforms or "promotional corporate clothing" bearing your business logo are.

- Subcontract and casual labour are deductible if you have a receipt from the contractor.

- If you incur theft of cash or products, you can claim the portion not compensated by your insurance company.

- Passenger vehicle lease, loan interest and depreciation—ask your accountant for the annual limits.

WHAT IS A BREAK-EVEN POINT?

Your break-even point is the amount of sales net of taxes that you must generate to cover all operating costs, excluding profits. Calculate a break-even point for your business plan projections, and once you are operating, recalculate it again based on actual costs. Revisit it regularly; calculating a simple break-even point every few months can ensure that your costs are not getting out of hand.

Once you know your break-even point, divide this figure by 4.33 to arrive at a weekly sales figure, or you can even break it down to a daily sales figure. Knowing your daily sales figure target should be motivational—because if you don't know where you are, there is no motivation to reach a goal. If sales are slow, it should motivate you to do something (panic excluded). It helps you to plan your cash flow, motivates you to collect outstanding accounts receivable and encourages you to strive for better profits.

How do you calculate a break-even point?

If your business is product-based, you must know your approximate gross profit margin. For example, if you operate on a 35 percent gross profit margin—as does the retail furniture store example in Figure 11.11—you need to generate enough profit after purchases to cover all overhead costs. This 35 percent gross profit margin contributes $35 gross profit for each $100 in sales, which in turn pays for the overhead expenses. First list your estimated monthly overhead expenses.

For a service business, simply list the monthly operating costs plus a desired wage and you have your break-even point right there. Calculate your break-even point using Figure 11.11 as your guide.

Figure 11.11: CALCULATING A SIMPLE MONTHLY BREAK-EVEN POINT

Direct overhead costs:

Wages to salesperson	$1,750.00
Delivery	300.00
Damaged goods	150.00
Freight in	75.00
Discounts	220.00
Total direct costs:	**$2,495.00**

Overhead costs:

Accounting fees	100.00
Advertising	650.00
Bad debts	50.00
Bank charges	60.00
CPP & EI expense	260.00
Fees, licences & dues	30.00
Insurance	75.00
Loan interest	250.00
Promotion	75.00
Promotion–meals	75.00
Office supplies	150.00
Office salaries	1,500.00
Rent & taxes	850.00
Repairs–store	50.00
Repairs–equipment	30.00
Sign rental & security	65.00
Telephone, fax & cellular	260.00
Utilities	350.00
Vehicle–gas	110.00
Vehicle–repairs, insurance	200.00
Workers' Compensation	35.00
Total overhead costs:	**5,225.00**
Combined overhead costs:	**$7,720.00**

The combined monthly overhead costs are $7,720. This calculation does not include the cost of purchasing furniture, which is taken into the 35 percent gross profit calculation. Now make the following calculation:

$7,720.00 overhead divided by 35 and multiplied by 100 =

$22,057.14 (monthly gross sales)

Gross sales needed for month:	$22,057.00
Furniture cost (65% of retail price):	14,337.00
Gross profit (35%):	7,720.00
Overhead costs:	7,720.00
Break-even point:	**$22,057.00**

The store has to generate $22,057 in sales to cover all costs. If the profit margins decrease or expenses increase, a loss will occur. These calculations don't take into account the owner's wages. You must decide how much you need from the business monthly to cover your personal needs. If you need $2,500, calculate as follows:

Total overhead costs:	$7,720.00
Owner's wages:	2,500.00
Total new overhead:	10,220.00

$10,220 divided by 35 and multiplied by 100 =	**$29,200.00**

To pay a $2,500 owner's salary, the store has to generate an additional $7,143.00 in sales.

7,143.00 x 35% gross profit =	$2,500.00

HOW DO YOU RECORD VEHICLE EXPENSES?

Vehicle expenses are an accountant's nightmare because most people are alarmingly sloppy in this area. Because most proprietors use their personal vehicle for both business and personal use, the business portion of the expense must be calculated. The way this is done depends on the status of the vehicle and the business, including whether:

1. Your business is a proprietorship (or partnership) and you own the vehicle

2. Your business is incorporated and the business owns the vehicle

3. Your business is incorporated but you own the vehicle.

1. A proprietorship, you own the vehicle

You operate your vehicle for both business and personal use. How do you track expenses? Purchase an auto mileage log from the stationery store and keep it in your vehicle. Note the starting reading on your odometer (for example, 120,000 km).

Each time you use the vehicle for a business-related trip, note the date, your destination and the mileage. At year-end, note the final kilometres travelled, and total the business kilometres. Keep all operating costs receipts, as you can claim a portion of the following:

- Gasoline

- Repairs and maintenance

- Insurance

- Loan interest (restricted)

- Leasing costs (restricted)

- Depreciation (restricted).

At year-end, your accountant will prepare the following cost calculations:

Gas	$1,350
Repairs and maintenance	850
Insurance	1,220
Loan interest	730
Depreciation ($18,000 value)	5,400
Total costs:	**$9,550**

Ending kilometres:	140,225
Starting kilometres:	120,000
Total kilometres for year:	20,225
Business usage from log:	14,375 = 71.07%
Allowable claim:	**$ 9,550 x 71.07% = $6,787.18**

If you lose a receipt, you will pay more tax. A $20 lost gas receipt could increase your taxes by $5 to $8. The same applies for business miles not logged. CCRA demands that a log be kept for audit purposes or your vehicle claim could be denied. Keep it religiously up-to-date and log every business-related trip, including research, start-up travel, banking or the garage for repairs. It mounts up surprisingly quickly.

2. Your incorporated company owns the vehicle

If your incorporated company owns the vehicle, expenses are paid by the corporation. The same vehicle value limitations apply, so talk to your accountant, who will also tell you about the tax implications of the personal usage portion. CCRA does not like people driving Mercedes and writing off all the costs against their businesses, so make the most of the depreciation allowance but be sensible in your vehicle selection.

3. An incorporated company, you own the vehicle

If you use your own vehicle for business in an incorporated company, a mileage allowance is paid to you. The per kilometre rate changes, so ask your accountant for the amount. This allowance should cover all vehicle running costs, including depreciation. Keep a log and submit regular vehicle expense claims to the company. Another option is to calculate this amount biannually or annually and add the monies owed to your shareholder's loan.

Whew! Are you still there?

If you are still reading, congratulations on sticking with it. You have probably decided by now that the only way to avoid this tedious, time-consuming, brain-draining paper-shuffling and chicken-scratching is to hire a book-keeper. That's not a bad idea—make it a short-term goal to build your business to be able to do just that. Then you can focus on growing your business. Until then, learn to do it yourself. A good manager understands the financial workings of the business and never completely relinquishes financial control to someone else.

Here is a lighter story from the other side—an accountant's perspective. Think about these poor people as you industriously prepare your year-end accounting, and do the very best job possible.

BE NICE TO YOUR ACCOUNTANT

Accountants are mostly very nice people. It's not their fault they sometimes appear a little stoic or dry. Think about it—if you spent seven years or more studying this profession, you'd probably be a little staid yourself. It's a lot for the brain to digest, and accountants have a huge responsibility to their clients. Their life consists of number-crunching and shoe-box sorting, one hand attached permanently to the adding machine, the other on the keyboard or telephone. Accountants have to be serious. Would you appreciate your accountant cracking a joke as he informs you that you are bankrupt?

As January approaches, accountants prepare themselves for the four-month onslaught of paperwork that must be assembled, perfectly processed and submitted by April 30th. Do you, the taxpayer, ever stop to think about the trauma these poor people go through? As the deadline approaches, latecomers line up in droves, clutching piles of triplicate T3s, T4s, T5s and miscellaneous mountains of official paraphernalia.

When all is said and done, accountants are only human, although they are expected to create godlike miracles with your tax returns, wondrously creating refunds from thin air. If taxes are due, of course it is the accountant's fault—don't you agree? There is also a serious misconception that accountants survive on no sleep for four months, work eight days a week, 30 hours a day and do not make mistakes—all for a modest fee.

You may notice that as the tax deadline approaches, you are greeted by smiles forced through gritted teeth, accompanied by monosyllabic conversations and outsized sighs of despair. If you have acute hearing, you will catch under-the-breath, rambling mutterings as you leave the office. Other signs of ATTSS (Accountant's Tax-Time Stress Syndrome) are receivers slamming in clients' ears after their 10 pm late-filing phone calls. Don't confuse this with office doors slamming after tardy clients leave, or greetings on the accountant's voice-mail informing clients who call at 11 pm Sunday evening that they are in Tahiti.

Trembling hands, black, baggy eyes, nicotine-stained fingers, coffee dribbles on clothes and nervous twitches are all identifying signs of accountants who suffer this annual affliction. Most symptoms are a direct result of clients leaving their year-end until the last minute, then presenting the whole shooting match in the proverbial grocery bag—unsorted, of course—and demanding a refund.

Accountants survive on a different diet than do Ordinary People. A Real Accountant needs five to six pots of coffee daily; half a bottle of Stress Tabs and assorted vitamins; two cartons of cigarettes; a two-for-one pizza order; and at least half a bottle of premium Scotch, followed by Valium chasers. If these important daily dietary requirements are not met, your accountant will not survive this crucial time of year. There is no time allocated in the agenda for sleep—this process is time-consuming and the stand-down pay is lousy.

You can easily identify an accountant on May 1st. Visit the airport and study the departure areas for flights to Alaska, Iceland, Tahiti, Barbados, the Caribbean, Tibet or Australia. You will notice a long lineup of hunched and ragged robotic types, stumbling to the check-in counter.

Fifty-five percent of all passengers will be accountants. Then check the bookings for the most desolate and isolated interior fishing or health resorts. Fifteen percent of accountants will be heading for a bush hideaway. Twenty percent fly to Las Vegas with fiendish gleams in their eyes to gamble away your accounting fees. Sadly, if you check the admissions to private and mental health institutions, five percent of accountants will be newly registered. Last but not least, the obituary column will reveal the whereabouts of the final five percent of this loyal, devoted breed.

But you—yes, you—can help change these sad statistics! Visit your friendly accountant in early January with all your paperwork in neat, organized and legible order. Stop our dollars from being heavily invested into other countries on accountants' recuperative vacations. Reduce mental health costs, and stop the unnecessary trauma of accountants' funerals and family grief. Make your New Year's resolution now—always be nice to your accountant, get your taxes in early and don't gripe about your bill.

WHAT IS THE NEXT STEP?

Well, this chapter probably put you off wanting a large business, in fact, not everyone wants a big business and the big headaches that can accompany it. Many opt for starting and staying at home—an idyllic place to have a small office and generate a nice little income in the comfort of one's pyjamas. Or is it idyllic? Read on and see for yourself.

CHAPTER 12

Your home office—
heaven or hell?

Home is where the heart (i.e., computer, fax, photocopier,
answering machine, telephone and dirty laundry) is.

IS A HOME OFFICE FOR YOU?

The heaven

As technology embraces the world and makes doing business from a bed-room an achievable goal, countless entrepreneurs of all ages opt for starting a home-based business. Having worked in a storefront office for many years before moving my business home in 1986, I couldn't entertain the thought of working anywhere else. There is no substitute for living on a small acreage on a quiet and friendly street, surrounded by birds, horses, wildlife, trees, peace and quiet. This serene atmosphere allows one the luxury of uninterrupted work without uninvited guests.

Did I say quiet and uninterrupted? Who am I fooling? This long-term SOHO (sole operator home office) stint has allowed me to experience just about every conceivable situation, both good and bad. Evaluate for yourself whether a home-based office will suit your needs, because working from home is not everyone's cup of mocha. Most people think it will be wonderful, until reality sets in and they experience the isolation and other inherent home-office problems. Read on to decide whether you are cut out for this lifestyle.

The dreamers

Starry-eyed entrepreneurs-to-be imagine an idyllic scenario—shuffling into the office in pyjamas and slippers, sipping coffee and ready to start work at 9:30 am, or putting on the voice-mail to slide off for a round of golf. Although there is nothing stopping you from doing this, to survive a home-office environment, you need military-style discipline and planning. You may start your day with good intentions, but "things" always happen that are beyond your control. Four stray cows on the front lawn will destroy your well-planned day. Mothers in particular find working from a home office a complex, frustrating, hectic, job-juggling experience requiring phenomenal patience and split-second time management.

What's heaven about a home office?

As times and people's lives change, a home office can be the solution to a multitude of problems and have the following advantages.

1. Low overhead

A home office eliminates many overhead expenses that even a small leased office incurs. Leases, phone lines, fancy office furniture, utilities, signs and reception costs are expensive. First impressions are important when clients enter a business, and cheap furnishings don't make a good first impression. You have to generate high sales just to cover overhead costs. What a waste of profits. Wouldn't you prefer they go in your pocket rather than to the landlord?

The office should be staffed from nine to five. Nothing irritates a customer more than a sign reading "Closed for lunch—back in half an hour." A walk-in customer may not come back. Haven't you experienced this same frustration? A home-based office means you don't have to staff the office at lunchtime or eat a brown-bag lunch.

2. Home-office tax deductions

Just like any business, your home incurs operating costs. With a home-based office, a portion of these costs are claimed on your tax return (discussed later). CCRA only allows you to claim home-based office expenses if it is the business' head office, not if you lease premises as well.

3. Flexibility in planning

Family: The flexibility of operating a home office is attractive to parents, particularly mothers. You can take children to school and after-school activities, and if the school phones to say your daughter is ill, you can pick her up and nurse her at home instead. My daughter was ill for two weeks, and although her demanding presence was trying, working from home was a blessing.

Hours: If you are ill, you can use voice-mail or take the cordless phone to bed. If you lose time during the day, can't meet a deadline or the computer crashes, you can burn the midnight oil in pyjamas and slippers. Client appointments can be organized around your schedule. If you are a late riser or a night owl, you can often book appointments at a time convenient to you. Portable phones make life easier: you can be in the garden (or the washroom) without using voice-mail.

$UCCE$$ $TRATEGY

BREAK THE ICE: If you think new clients may feel uncomfortable visiting a home-based office, make them feel at ease. When making the first appointment, ask whether they prefer tea or coffee and let them know a muffin is waiting. This strategy usually breaks the ice.

If you don't have a consulting room, keep one room comfortable and spotless, and meet there. My clients like to sit in the bright and cheery family room, where they can watch (and sometimes visit) the horses and see an attractive garden. A comfortable setting usually relaxes first-time clients.

Lunch: You can use up leftovers for lunch instead of buying a calorie-laden lunch and read newspapers or open mail. You can walk around the garden or the block to get some energizing exercise and stress relief. My horse always neighs for his lunch at noon, so there is no option but to stop work, break out the hay for both of us, and then go for a brisk walk to refresh the brain.

Dress: When you are not expecting clients, you can dress casually instead of donning business attire, saving on your clothing costs. Dress neatly however—

someone will eventually catch you if you work in your dressing gown until eleven in the morning. You won't work productively in your robe and without a shower.

4. Security and disaster control

Working at home brings a strong sense of security, as you know there won't be a burglary, which often happens when people are away at work. If something goes wrong, you can immediately deal with it. I have dealt with disasters ranging from freezing and flooding to snowbound famine, malfunctioning appliances, toilets and garage doors; burst pipes, overflowing gutters, sick animals and children, lost puppies, stray cows and injured family members. As inconvenient as it is, it's good to be there when disaster strikes, although when your spouse arrives home asking, "Did you have a nice day dear?" the answer is not always "Yes."

5. Safety in inclement weather

Driving during freezing rain, black ice, whiteouts, blizzards, flooding, wind, ice storms and heavy snowfalls is potentially life-threatening. With a home office, you can continue working in these conditions without taking one step outside into the danger zone. Feel deep sympathy for those brave entrepreneurs who must open their doors on these treacherous mornings.

6. Parents can be parented

An increasing number of baby boomers have the added responsibility of caring for their ageing parents in their home. A home-based office caters to this need. Although ageing parents can be demanding and time-consuming, it is peace of mind to know that they are close should an emergency arise. My dear mother—aged 93, bless her heart—is now an important part of our family.

Why is a home office hell?

So far it's all sounding heavenly, so what is hellish about a home office? A majority of home-based businesses don't fly because of lack of structure, discipline and self-motivation. It's not easy being stuck alone in a small bedroom office—particularly if you have come from a corporate environment. You might notice that this list of potential problems is longer than the "heavenly" one.

1. Business is not taken seriously

Only you can set your goals and decide whether you are going to get serious about your business. Many people putter along at home without goals, business plans or structure. Because you work alone, you must design a structured working environment. If you don't take your business seriously, how can you expect your family, clients and friends to?

Learn to practise the three Rs:

- **Routine:** set a daily routine and follow it
- **Rules:** instigate work rules for your family
- **Reinforce:** both of the above regularly.

Hold a family meeting to stress to your spouse and children that your work at home is important to you. Ask them to respect the ground rules—and be patient. It may take everyone time to adjust to the new situation. Once you set the rules, don't bend them or you will lose the family's respect.

Part-time operators should allocate two or three set days for work and others for family. Inform family that on your "at-home" days, you are completely available for them and their interests. On workdays, always make quality time for your children afterwards. You will accomplish more by structuring your time and won't feel guilty of ignoring the children.

$UCCE$$ $TRATEGY

UTILIZE A FULL DAY: If you have young children, plan to work beyond school hours by organizing a babysitter or after-school care. Otherwise, you will lose valuable work time through your days being constantly broken into pieces. During those work-days, make every hour productive or you will never feel any sense of accomplishment.

---

2. Families may not be "trained"

Before you start a home-based office, sit down with your spouse and discuss the business, as you will need his or her complete support. Then talk about it with your children. Working from home can affect family routines and lifestyles, and their support is necessary. It can be difficult to ignore their demands. You have to train them to respect the fact that you are working, and this is no easy task.

Younger children often find your working at home a difficult concept to grasp. Mothers will need more help with household chores to prevent burnout, so allocate chores to both spouse and children, even if you have to increase allowances to get this help. Instill the entrepreneurial spirit into your children at a young age.

$UCCE$$ $TRATEGY

GET PHONE SMART: Teach children telephone etiquette and use a "smart ring"phone system, where one ring denotes a business call and the other a personal call. Don't give friends your "business" number. You then have the choice of whether to answer the home line while you are working. Instruct your children not to pick up the telephone when it rings during business hours, as it sounds unprofessional to the caller.

Circumstances will arise when children do answer the telephone, so for these occasions, teach them to answer politely with the business name. With so many choices in modern communication and technology, there are inexpensive options to help solve the home/office telephone problems.

3. Neighbours can be a nuisance

If your neighbours are a friendly bunch, you will have to train them too. The hardest ones to train are those who don't work, as they can't relate to a structured home-office environment. They have a habit of dropping by for a quick cup of coffee and staying forever.

When the doorbell rings and it's a neighbour, answer wearing glasses, holding a pen, a pile of papers and the portable phone. Answer the door with, "Oh, hi Julie, can't talk, I have a strict deadline to meet. My how I envy you not having to work!"

When neighbours phone to chat, tell them, "I'm up to my ears in paperwork, can I call you after supper?" or "I have a deadline to meet, I work Fridays, you know." After much practice you will get these lines down pat and the message will eventually get through. Learn to be tough.

4. Home chores tempt the weak

It's difficult to ignore all the chores beckoning you. You may be tempted to load the laundry while you are working—but don't do it! You don't need any distractions. Abandon all thoughts of housework. If you can't complete chores before nine in the morning, leave them until after five. Just ensure the house or office is presentable if clients are expected. The rest can—and must—wait. If you don't keep to a regular schedule, working at home will become a stressful nightmare.

5. You are easily isolated

Isolation is a common and difficult problem to overcome, and it takes a real effort to become visible to both clients and your business community. Marketing is difficult enough for any business, but it's even harder from a home-based office. To stay in touch with the business world and to find and network with potential clients, you have to "come out of the closet."

$UCCE$$ $TRATEGY

GET OUT OF THE 10 x 12: The phone won't ring unless you create action. A reminder: join associations, networks, the chamber of commerce or Rotary and become visible. Find one organization that really interests you, so you can also enjoy a social life. Initially, it's easier to network among friends and acquaintances than in a room full of strangers.

6. Lack of motivation

You are now the boss, the only person who decides the future of your business. Motivation is synonymous with goal setting, passion, organization, confidence and communication. No one else cares whether your business is working or not—this is your job. An organized, structured routine, a sound and workable business plan and a love for your work are all motivational factors that should inspire you to move forward.

Here are some words to delete from your vocabulary: later, lethargy, apathy, I can't, tomorrow, I'm scared, no time, and it can wait. Keeping a positive attitude is so necessary. Instead, add these words to your daily vocabulary: drive, positive, organized, incentive, inspirational, initiative, ambitious, priorities, I can, and now.

7. Good weather means playtime

As silly as it sounds, fine weather makes working at home difficult. If your office or work space becomes stuffy, concentration levels drop and thoughts of going outside become urgent. If the temptation is too great, plan to work to a certain time and take a couple of hours off to enjoy the sun. You will achieve more by motivating yourself to finish in time, you'll not feel cheated of some playtime and you will probably work twice as hard.

The alternative is to start work earlier, take a sun break, or work in the evenings. During the summer I sometimes ride my horse in the cool of the morning. I achieve more by not depriving myself of this ultimate pleasure. If you can successfully combine work and play, do it. You will feel motivated, exercised, relaxed and ready to toil again.

8. Difficult to keep to routines

A home office requires strict self-discipline. Businesses remain mediocre without a disciplined mind; working at home compounds the problem. Start at the same time each morning, take regular mini-breaks and a lunch break, and don't finish until 5 pm. Something will always interrupt your work, so deal with unscheduled dilemmas as they occur. Ensure you put in at least six productive hours a day.

CASE STUDY

THE CORPORATE COMMUTE

A corporate executive of many decades was downsized and decided to consult from home. No matter how hard he tried, he couldn't adjust to walking from the bedroom to the corporate home office. He couldn't focus, concentrate or get motivated. In desperation, he dressed for the old office each morning, made coffee and got into his car, drove a few miles in traffic and "arrived" at the corporate home office, ready to start work. The "commute" enabled him to get his mind into gear as he had done for so many years sitting in traffic. Do whatever works for you.

9. You eat, sleep and breathe work

You may close your office door, but switching off the brain is not as easy. Clients forget that you have another life besides work and will call at all hours unless you train them. Most new entrepreneurs make the mistake of allowing after-hours calls rather than offending new clients—we have all been guilty of that.

$UCCE$$ $TRATEGY

GET PHYSICAL: Plan some daily physical activity—do a little gardening, take a short walk or go swimming. Pursue some home interests that are strictly yours, such as painting, reading, carpentry or working out in your home gym. Find at least one personal interest that gets you out of the house to refresh and relax your racing brain cells.

Don't accept business calls after hours, excluding emergencies. Inform new clients of your working hours and tell them that quality family time is a priority. Most people respect this. If clients call on evenings or weekends, tell them you are busy and will return their call in the morning. If you have to work at night, stop by 9 pm and relax for an hour or two before bedtime. Otherwise your brain will work all night and you'll awaken feeling exhausted, listless and unmotivated. Remember: *We work to live, not live to work.*

10. Business outgrows the home

Growth can become a big headache if your business suddenly needs more space and there is nowhere in the home to expand to. You may not be large enough to move out of your "incubator" and into larger, leased premises. Your work becomes hampered by a disorganized work space.

When reaching this stage, some people impulsively rent commercial space without being financially or mentally ready for this huge step. This is why planning your future goals and cash flow projections is crucial. In the planning stages, estimate the maximum space needed to reach your projected sales working from home. Determine by the projected sales figures when you will need larger premises or employees—or both, and research and know this information before start-up. You will then know if those sales can support the extra overhead. If they can't, think how you could reorganize your home space, or research other alternatives.

WHAT HOME-OFFICE TAX DEDUCTIONS ARE AVAILABLE?

Because your home office replaces leased or purchased space, most costs related to that space are tax deductible. Deductions are calculated proportionately, based on the number of square feet your home business occupies. This includes storage sheds or outbuildings used for business purposes. First measure the home's total square footage including outbuildings to be used. Then, calculate the square footage of the business portion. Figure 12.1 demonstrates how this calculation is done.

Figure 12.1: CALCULATING HOME-OFFICE USAGE

Your office is 12' x 14', and you use a 15' x 12' garage as work space, so the business portion of your home is 348 square feet. The house is 1,750 square feet in total, so the business portion is calculated as a percentage of the whole home, in this case 19.89 percent. Deductible expenses are:

1.	Mortgage interest (or rent)	$ 5,700
2.	Property taxes	2,120
3.	Heating, electricity	2,310
4.	Garbage disposal, water	470
5.	Repairs and maintenance	1,630
6.	House insurance	770
	Total annual costs:	**$13,000**

Business portion: $13,000 x 348 sq. ft.   = $2,585.14
**   1,750 sq. ft.   or 19.89%**

If you do specific renovations, alterations or repairs to your work space, separate these costs, as most are 100 percent deductible. Major repairs, such as replacing a roof, will be amortized by your accountant over a number of years as the full cost cannot be written off in a one-year period. The same rule applies to major renovations specifically for housing the business, such as an extension to your office.

Maintain good records

Keep all home-related expenses in a file for year-end so your accountant can include them in both your accounting records and your business tax return. As home-maintenance costs mount up quickly, keep good records of all costs. Small items such as vacuum bags, garden maintenance costs, cleaners, and coffee for clients constitute part of your home-office expenses.

If you don't have a business telephone line, you can't claim the full monthly residential line rental. When the telephone bill arrives, separate out the business portion, pay that portion of the bill with a business cheque and pay the personal portion with a personal cheque. At year-end, prepare these costs for your accountant as per Figure 12.1, including the square footage. This saves your accountant time and you money.

Home usage exceptions

There are some exceptions to home-based business usage and its space calculations. One example is a child care business, which is calculated on a different formula:

$$\frac{1{,}350 \text{ sq. ft.}}{1{,}800 \text{ sq. ft.}} \times \frac{12 \text{ hours}}{24 \text{ hours}} \times \frac{5 \text{ days}}{7 \text{ days}} \times \frac{50 \text{ weeks}}{52 \text{ weeks}} \times \$7{,}000 = \$1{,}802.88$$

This formula takes into account the number of rooms used for child care, over the total square footage, multiplied by the number of hours in a day the home is used for business, multiplied by the number of days a week the business is open, multiplied by the number of weeks in a year it is operated, multiplied by the total home expenses! Your accountant will figure it out.

$UCCE$$ $TRATEGY

FIFTY IS NOT NIFTY: If you use over 50 percent of your primary residence for a business—as with some daycare operations—when you sell the home, the business portion will be subject to capital gains tax. When you plan your business, keep the business usage under 50 percent to avoid paying this tax.

Unused home-office deductions

For a proprietorship filing a T2124 self-employment Statement of Income and Expenses, home-office expenses are deducted at the end of the return. The deductions can be used to bring your profit to zero but cannot be used to create a loss situation. If your business makes a loss before these deductions, or the deductions exceed your profit, the remaining home-office deductions are carried forward to a year when they can be utilized. Some businesses—such as bed and breakfasts that use a lot of home space but make little income in comparison to expenses—often have thousands of dollars in unusable deductions because their profit never exceeds their operating expenses.

CAN YOU HANDLE THE HOME-OFFICE CHALLENGES?

Working from home suits many people, but for others, it's a disaster. Running a successful SOHO takes practice. Think carefully and complete the checklist in Figure 12.2 before making a decision. Revisit it after you have been operating for a few months and compare answers. Will your home-based office be heaven—or hell?

Figure 12.2: CAN I HANDLE THE HOME-OFFICE CHALLENGES?		
Can you answer yes to at least 15 questions?	**Yes**	**No**
1. I have discussed having a home-based business with my family.	❏	❏
2. My spouse/partner is in full support of my business.	❏	❏
3. I have focussed goals and timelines.	❏	❏
4. I have, and will use, my business plan.	❏	❏
5. I intend to take this business seriously.	❏	❏
6. I have given my children chores and responsibilities.	❏	❏
7. I have organized a professional phone answering system.	❏	❏
8. My family understand the telephone rules.	❏	❏
9. I have informed neighbours and friends of my working hours.	❏	❏
10. I have structured set working hours and days.	❏	❏
11. I have organized after-school care on those days.	❏	❏
12. I will not do home chores during working hours.	❏	❏
13. I have joined business/networking associations.	❏	❏
14. I have joined a club/organization of personal interest.	❏	❏
15. I will ensure that I get enough physical activity.	❏	❏
16. I will plan quality family time daily.	❏	❏
17. I will maintain a positive attitude.	❏	❏
18. I will close the office door at least two hours before bed.	❏	❏
19. I will inform new clients of my working hours.	❏	❏
20. I have organized support services for my ageing parents.	❏	❏
21. I have enough space to operate the business for two years.	❏	❏
22. I have calculated when the business will outgrow this space.	❏	❏
23. I have additional residential space I can use as I grow.	❏	❏
24. I checked local bylaws to see if I can hire employees at home.	❏	❏
25. I know the sales point and cost of moving to larger premises.	❏	❏

WHAT IS THE NEXT STEP?

Well, you are nearly there—on the way to becoming a successful entrepreneur. This book is your companion and guide to help ensure that each step you take is a step in the right direction. Consider setbacks as challenges you can conquer, turn adversity into an advantage, keep positive and keep learning. We don't stop learning until we start pushing up daisies. The next chapter highlights some successful entrepreneurs who each have experienced all the pitfalls and pleasures of self-employment. Be inspired by their stories. The next step is up to you.

CHAPTER 13

What will your story be?

---

*Now make your dream a reality, because you
know where you are going and what you are doing.*

TRAVELLING THE ENTREPRENEURIAL ROAD

There's a lot of information in this book that will take time to digest. You'll probably want to read some sections a few times to absorb the messages. If you follow the advice closely, and if your business choice is sound, you are on your way to success and a new, exciting way of life. Don't expect it to be easy because it takes hard work and commitment. You will grow as you learn and be enriched with new knowledge and skills.

To further inspire you, here are some entrepreneurial stories that run the gamut, from a retired couple living in a remote area of Nova Scotia to inspired teenage entrepreneurs. Read of their battles, victories and success secrets as they travelled along the entrepreneurial road. None are large businesses, but each person had a vision and the desire to succeed.

A PASSION FOR PARENTING: NEW PARENT RESOURCE GUIDE

Motherhood doesn't come with an instruction manual, and Jennifer McCallum felt lost after the birth of her first daughter. Where to go for information? The more she looked for help, the more she realized that there wasn't any good local source to help her through this life-altering experience. The idea for her new parent resource guide was born.

Jennifer talked to a broad cross-section of parents from all walks of life—fathers and mothers, from teenagers to people in their 40s. The vision was now cementing as the response to her idea became overwhelming. She approached sponsors to advertise in the proposed guide, and with nothing to show but her passion, vision and research, she soon had $10,000 in advertising funds.

"I remember the first cheque," says Jennifer. "It was a diaper company. They mailed a cheque, sent the artwork and asked if they could write an article. I felt like I won the lottery."

Jennifer approached the Small Business Centre in London, Ontario to enrol in their self-employment program. There she learned how to formally put the business plan together, and that business plans can—and should—be changed as a business takes shape.

For a stay-at-home-mom who just wanted a little business on the side, this vision has a bright future ahead. She has now published two annual resource directories, the second edition consisting of 130 pages of valuable parenting information. The 5,000 copies are distributed free of charge to parents through local London hospitals, midwives and adoption agencies.

Jennifer attends trade shows, baby events and prenatal health fairs. She writes a quarterly newsletter and has a dynamic Web site loaded with resources. She prints posters and stickers and puts them everywhere. Media coverage includes six months of sponsorship by a local television station, which runs five to six commercials a week, and stories in local newspapers and on radio stations.

Enquiries arrive from across Canada daily through her site. Yes, the business is making profit and quickly growing. Jennifer's vision is to franchise the guide and expand to providing parent resources for school-age children. She has a larger, secret vision, and knowing her passion and commitment, it too will become reality.

"I couldn't have done this without the support of my husband, Peter," says Jennifer. "It's really important to have a strong support system. I think my greatest strengths are having a vision and the determination to expand into other cities."

There is no doubt that Jennifer will achieve just that.

Jennifer McCallum can be contacted at 519-645-7342,
e-mail info@parentguide.ca, Web site: www.parentguide.ca.

TAKE A PAGE FROM THIS BOOK: SANDHILL BOOK MARKETING LTD.

Nancy Wise didn't know that she was destined to be self-employed. Working various jobs through college and university—including freelance copywriting and editing—she eventually ended up in sales-oriented jobs and discovered she loved selling. After work in the clothing and electronics industries, she later took over her mother's office plant care business. Self-employment seemed a good solution to increasing her income.

Helping a college instructor edit and sell his guidebook was the first step in establishing her book distribution business, Sandhill Book Marketing. Nancy soon realized that if she had more than one book to sell, it would maximize time spent travelling to bookstores. Word spread and Nancy was soon distributing a number of books by B.C. authors, the only interior business providing this service. Determined to specialize, she created a niche. Her company is now known nationally for its success in distributing single and small press titles to Canadian bookstores.

Cementing her name as a self-publishing expert, Nancy co-authored *How to Self Publish and Make Money: Writing, Publishing and Selling Your Book in Canada* with Marion Crook. Now in its second edition, it's considered the bible of Canadian self-publishing and is used in colleges and university publishing courses across Canada. (I used it religiously when I first wrote this book.)

Nancy firmly believes in asking questions of knowledgeable people, analyzing responses, reading copiously and always learning. A passion for selling books is her motivator. "I have a drive to sell with the goal of always achieving higher numbers," she says. "I am very conservative in terms of spending. I believe you should spend less than you make, and I am almost fanatical about paying bills."

Nancy admits that she didn't start with a business plan, unless it could be summed up in one word: Sell! Her goals are more focussed on achieving short-term projects.

"My biggest challenge is time," admits Nancy. "It takes an enormous amount of time and energy to generate and maintain sales. Managing employees, coping with new systems to accommodate industry changes and dealing with huge amounts of paperwork requires patience and tenacity." She manages this by prioritizing and delegating, but handles certain sensitive issues herself.

Nancy considers follow-up critical to success, encompassing sales leads, contacts, orders and promises to customers. Often working 12 hours a day, she has the wonderful support of her husband, who works in the business and thus understands her challenges. "If initially I'd known how complicated the book business really is, I wonder if I would have continued," Nancy reflects. "Sometimes, 'blindsight' is a blessing!"

Nancy's passion for books and selling, along with her determination, drive and customer commitment, has built a business selling one title in 1984 into a successful national distribution company. She is a true entrepreneur who deserves to enjoy her success.

For more information about Sandhill Book Marketing Ltd., visit the Web site at www.sandhillbooks.com.

WIRED FOR SUCCESS: WINKEYS WIRELESS "WATCHDOG"

When Gerry Lelievre's wife—who suffers from Alzheimer's disease—wandered off without his knowledge and was brought back by a neighbour, he knew that he had to find a way to monitor her movements. Yet there appeared to be little help available. On searching for a solution, all he found was other people suffering the same dilemma—how do you cope with people with Alzheimer's or other forms of dementia who exhibit uncontrollable tendencies to wander?

Gerry quickly devised a hard-wired prototype device that could monitor his wife's movements. He then met his partner, Johan Jordaan, while working together at the same company. Johan joined Gerry as the research and development manager, and the partners spent nearly three years developing a wireless, portable unit. In May 2001, when both were laid off, they made the decision to start a full-time business and approached the Small Business Centre in London, Ontario to enrol in the Self Employment Benefit Program.

The partnership has some fine ingredients. Gerry's strengths are in design, manufacturing, marketing, time and business management, and understanding the market. Johan's strengths lie in design, people management and broadcasting experience. The small business program enabled them to develop a practical business plan and understand bookkeeping and the financial aspects of operating a business, as well as marketing, communication, community involvement and pricing.

"If it hadn't been for the program, we would have underpriced ourselves and approached our marketing from the wrong direction," says Gerry. "We would have floundered without Gord Evans, our mentor, who has been an unselfish gold mine of information."

With the unofficial support of both the Alzheimer's Society and Alzheimer's Outreach Services, word of the "Watchdog" monitor is spreading fast. Through newsletters, referrals and the Web site, global enquiries are being received. The partners plan to set up an autonomous site with on-line ordering, utilize search engines for high placement, and later use a global distributor so they can spend time in developing more product lines.

"We visit our business plan monthly," says Gerry, "as our goal is to keep the cost as low as possible, so we watch the financials closely. We are not starving nor are we millionaires. Our market is huge and I foresee us being extremely busy over the next few years trying to keep things from growing out of control."

From seeing a need to finding an obvious niche, Gerry's desire to help both himself and others has given birth to a successful product that can help people globally. It's an obvious winner.

To contact Gerry Lelievre and Johan Jordaan, call 519-871-2820, e-mail glelievre@winkeyswireless.com, Web site: www.winkeyswireless.com.

WORKING TOGETHER IN HARMONY: KEMPT LAKE GALLERY

With retirement age approaching, job stress and health problems, Lauren and Winston Seaton explored moving back to Nova Scotia from British Columbia. They had previously spent many years living in N.S., where Winston, an artist, painted with a group of friends called the Harmony Lake Group of Painters. Lauren had dabbled in soap-making for a couple of years.

In the summer of 1999, while visiting the family cottage at Harmony Lake, they saw a property for sale in Kempt with a store, a house on "lakefront" (a marsh with a resident beaver) and four acres. The idea of starting an art gallery and gift shop materialized.

Research indicated that there was a large artist population in nearby Bear River and Annapolis Royal, and that ferry passengers travelling between

St. John and Digby and from Bar Harbour, Maine, to Yarmouth, Nova Scotia, often used Route 8, where the gallery is situated. Kempt is a remote area of Nova Scotia surrounded by small villages with an aggregate population of 1,500. The nearest town, Annapolis Royal, is 36 kilometres away. Most business comes from tourists passing through the area on their way to the South Shore, and campers from nearby Kejimkujik National Park.

With their second season completed, the 900 square foot gallery and gift shop opens from May 24th until Thanksgiving, but they are looking to extend the operation with reduced hours. The business includes the gallery, featuring the Harmony Lake Group of Painters, Lauren's Harmony Natural soap and body care products, consignment crafts, sculptures, tapestries and art prints.

"It's quite an eclectic mix," says Lauren. "We chose a very remote area to plant our gallery business so it's important to understand your goals and where you want the business to take you. We had to face different realities than most."

The husband and wife team ran businesses for most of their lives. Lauren is the bookkeeper, Winston a good money manager and graphic designer. He designed an appealing interior, marketing materials and signage. They share financial responsibilities. Various forms of local marketing ensure that their gallery is visible to tourists. A Web site is on its way.

Even with the huge challenge of this remote location, the gallery is covering all costs, including some for expansion. Future plans include a year-round operation and for Winston to teach art classes. What an ideal way to ensure that Lauren and Winston's future years are interesting, income-generating and shared in a happy, healthier environment.

Lauren and Winston Seaton can be reached at 902-682-2369 or by e-mail at wseaton@sympatico.ns.ca.

RAKING IN THE BUSINESS: BUSYKIDS LAWN AND YARD CARE

Fifteen-year-old Vanessa Butcher lives in Legal, a small rural town of 1,500 outside Edmonton, Alberta. Five years ago, there were few job opportunities for a ten-year-old girl, so Vanessa made her own. Starting by cutting her neighbour's lawn, she had the idea of creating a family business with her ten-year-old brother, Blair, and father, Gord. They initially promoted it with flyers on community bulletin boards, and when the local press wrote a story, the business gained real community credibility.

From one lawn mower originally, the garage is now crammed with an assortment of machinery. Two years ago, they decided to promote spring cleanup and lawn care, working after school and work and on weekends to keep up with the response.

The first year of spring cleanup brought a few jobs, but the second year got quite busy. Vanessa would sometimes work five hours a day, study for two and then fall exhausted into bed. Now the business has a clientele of 60 for spring cleanup work, plus regular customers for lawn and garden care.

In August 2001, I met Vanessa while speaking to a group of 13- to 15-year-old young entrepreneurs who were attending a week-long Alberta Youth Entrepreneurship Camp. The camp is organized by Entré-Corp Business Development Centre Ltd., in partnership with 13 Community Futures Development Corporations of southern Alberta.

I was impressed by her serious business attitude and her eagerness to learn. These 56 young people truly inspired me. At the camp, the teenagers learned all aspects of owning a business, from concept, business plan preparation, purchasing and marketing, teamwork, increasing confidence and self-esteem to presenting the plan to a bank loans officer. Vanessa learned many valuable tools that she now applies to the family business, including how to work under pressure, how and where to market, keeping proper accounting records and professional business presentation.

Her father, Gord, increased business by joining the local chamber of commerce and attending events. The business is licensed and advertises in the local newspaper, where they get "lots of response."

"We even hired a new kid," says Vanessa, "and we pay proper hourly wages and are more organized." Vanessa hopes to work in a trade, and one day, perhaps own another business.

Contact Vanessa, Gord and Blair Butcher at BusyKids at 780-961-4167.

A DESIRE TO DESIGN: NUTOK INTERACTIVE

After Luke Cyca successfully designed a Web site for his first client while still in Grade 8, he realized that he had marketable skills. Along with some friends, Luke started a small Web design company. When his friends lost interest, Luke continued on his own, licensing the business and working from the basement of his parents' home. NuTok Interactive was born.

After a year and a half, Luke moved his office to the Swift Current Entrepreneurial Centre, hiring a part-time employee. Of course, the office needed furniture and all the trappings. Luke now had a full-fledged business. He worked after high school, in the evenings and on weekends, steadily growing his business.

At 15, Luke's biggest challenge was having clients take him seriously, but as his portfolio of quality sites grew, this obstacle became less of an issue. In three years, he has been recognized in the *Saskatchewan Business Magazine* and other publications, nominated for the Swift Current Business Excellence awards and featured in a credit union micro-series commercial.

"By definition, an entrepreneur is motivated by profit," says Luke. "But in the case of NuTok Interactive, I have been motivated not only by profit but by the challenge of running a successful business at a young age. There's a certain satisfaction in competing on a playing field with people who are much older and more experienced than you. It's exciting to know that there are companies who rely on your work. It's a big responsibility, but it's exciting."

Luke has a real entrepreneurial spirit, and now aged 18, he is studying computer sciences at Simon Fraser University in British Columbia. He maintains his clients' Web sites and hosting, but is "putting the business on the back burner" so that he can focus on improving his skill set and knowledge. His future goal is to own his own full-time business. Armed with his entrepreneurial spirit, the knowledge that he can do it, his technical expertise and business experience, Luke's road to success as a young entrepreneur is already well-paved.

Luke Cyca can be contacted at inquiries@nutok.com,
Web site: www.nutok.com.

IN CLOSING

Vanessa and Luke have both inspired me, as I realize that these teenagers are full of creativity, new ideas, energy and enthusiasm. Their thoughts are not jaded and their minds are open. Adults owe it to our younger generation to take the time to mentor, encourage and help them, because *they* are our country's future.

I wish you all good luck, and don't be afraid of commitment and hard work. Follow the step-by-step start-up information in this book, take your time in choosing the right business, do your research and homework thoroughly, prepare and use a business plan, work on developing excellent communication skills, and keep focussed. Set those goals, give them a defined time, and don't let the sky be your limit—you can achieve anything you believe in.

Follow those dreams down the entrepreneurial road and make them happen. May your path be smooth yet exciting, paved with learning, not potholes, and may each corner you turn bring you a step closer to inner happiness and success.

I wonder what your story will be?

APPENDIX 1

Telephone and Internet directory for small businesses

Where do I go, who do I call?
I hope this directory will have it all.

This directory contains telephone and fax numbers and Web site addresses for several agencies you will need to contact for your business. For provinces with multiple branches, contact the main branch as listed, and they can give you the number you need. With ever-changing government structures, all information may be subject to change. CCRA has consolidated many of its offices into central taxation centres, so call the numbers listed for all payroll, forms and GST/HST information. Telephone numbers are listed alphabetically by province.

Both Canadian and American Web sites contain valuable information for starting a business, including interactive business planners, statistical information, start-up and business management tips and other useful resources.

GOVERNMENT OFFICES

CANADA: *www.gc.ca*

Canada Customs and Revenue Agency: *www.ccra-adrc.gc.ca*

Business Enquiries	1 800 959-5525
Child Tax Benefit	1 800 387-1193
Customs	1 800 461-9999
Forms & Publications	1 800 959-2221
GST & HST	1 800 959-1953
Income Tax Refund	1 800 959-1956
Individual Income Tax	1 800 959-8281
T.I.P.S. Automated Service	1 800 267-6999
TTY Enquiry Service	1 800 665-0354

ALBERTA: *www.gov.ab.ca*	**Telephone**	**Fax**
Canada Business Service Centre		
The Business Link,		
Business Service Centre	(780) 422-7722	(780) 422-0055
www.cbsc.org/alberta		
Business registration and incorporation		
Alberta Registries, Corporate Registry	(780) 427-7013	(780) 422-1091
www.gov.ab.ca/gs		
Provincial sales tax office		
Edmonton	(780) 427-3044	(780) 427-0348
www.revenue.gov.ab.ca		
Workers' Compensation Board		
Edmonton	(780) 498-4000	(780) 498-7999
www.wcb.ab.ca		

	Telephone	Fax
BRITISH COLUMBIA: *www.gov.bc.ca*		
Canada/B.C. Business Service Centre	(604) 775-5525	(604) 775-5520
One Stop Business Registration		
www.smallbusinessbc.ca		
Business registration and incorporation		
Ministry of Finance and		
Corporate Relations	(250) 356-2893	
Name registration, partnerships	(604) 775-1044	(250) 356-1428
Incorporations	(604) 775-1045	(250) 356-8923
www.fin.gov.bc.ca/registries		
Provincial sales tax office		
Vancouver	(604) 660-4524	(604) 660-4784
www.rev.gov.bc.ca/ctb	1 887 388-4440	
Workers' Compensation Board		
Richmond	(604) 273-2266	(604) 244-6490
www.worksafebc.com	1 888 922-2768	1 888 992-6622
MANITOBA: *www.gov.mb.ca*		
Canada Business Service Centre		
Winnipeg	(204) 984-2272	(204) 983-3852
www.cbsc.org/manitoba		
Business registration and incorporation		
Manitoba Consumer and		
Corporate Affairs	(204) 945-2500	(204) 945-1459
www.gov.mb.ca/cca/comp_off/index.html		
Provincial sales tax office		
Taxation Division, Department of Finance	(204) 945-6444	(204) 948-2087
www.gov.mb.ca/finance/taxation		
Workers Compensation Board		
Winnipeg	(204) 954-4321	(204) 954-4999
www.wcb.mb.ca		

	Telephone	Fax

NEW BRUNSWICK: *www.gnb.ca*

Canada Business Service Centre
Fredericton — (506) 444-6140 — (506) 444-6172
www.cbsc.org/nb

Business registration and incorporation
Ministry of Corporate Affairs — (506) 453-2703 — (506) 453-2613
www.snb.ca

Provincial sales tax office
Education and Inquiries Revenue Division — (506) 453-2404 — (506) 453-3044
www.gnb.ca

Workplace Health, Safety and Compensation Commission
Saint John — 1 800 222-9775
www.whscc.nb.ca — (506) 632-2200 — (506) 632-2819

NEWFOUNDLAND AND LABRADOR: *www.gov.nf.ca*

Canada Business Service Centre
St. John's — (709) 772-6022 — (709) 772-6090
www.csbc.org/nl

Business registration and incorporation
Department of Government
Services and Lands — (709) 729-3317 — (709) 729-0232
www.gov.nf.ca/gsl

Provincial sales tax office
Tax Administration Branch — (709) 729-3831 — (709) 729-2856
www.gov.nf.ca

Workplace Health, Safety and Compensation Commission
Nfld. users: — 1 800 563-9000
www.whscc.nf.ca — (709) 778-1000 — (709) 738-1714

NORTHWEST TERRITORIES: *www.gov.nt.ca*

Canada Business Service Centre
Yellowknife — (867) 873-7958 — (867) 873-0573
www.cbsc.org/nwt

	Telephone	Fax
Business registration and incorporation		
Registrar of Companies,		
Department of Justice	(867) 873-7492	(867) 873-0243
Territorial sales tax office		
Ministry of Finance	1 800-661-0820	
N.W.T.	(867) 920-3470	(867) 873-0325
Workers' Compensation Board		
Yellowknife	(867) 920-3888	(867) 873-4596
www.wcb.nt.ca		

NOVA SCOTIA: *www.gov.ns.ca*

	Telephone	Fax
Canada Business Service Centre		
Halifax	(902) 426-8604	(902) 426-6530
www.csbc.org.ns		
Business registration and incorporation		
Registry of Joint Stock Companies	(902) 424-7770	(902) 424-4633
www.gov.ns.ca/snsmr		
Provincial sales tax office		
Retail sales: Tax Information Section	(902) 424-6300	(902) 424-0660
www.gov.ns.ca		
Workers' Compensation Board		
Halifax	(902) 491-8999	(902) 491-8326
www.wcb.ns.ca		

NUNAVUT: *www.gov.nu.ca*

	Telephone	Fax
Canada—Nunavut Business Service Centre		
Iqaluit	(867) 979-6813	(867) 979-6823
www.cbsc.org/nunavut	1 877 499-5199	1 877 488-5299
Workers' Compensation Board		
Iqaluit	(867) 979-8500	(867) 979-8501
www.wcb.nt.ca/home.htm	1 877 404-4407	

	Telephone	Fax

ONTARIO: *www.gov.on.ca*

Canada Business Service Centre

| Toronto only | 1 800 567-2345 | |
| *www.csbc.org/on* | (416) 775-3456 | (416) 954-8597 |

Business registration and incorporation*
*Call the CBSC for all other local listings:

| Toronto | 1 800 361-3223 | |
| *www.cbc.gov.on.ca* | (416) 314-8880 | (416) 314-0102 |

Provincial sales tax office:
Fuel and tobacco

Taxpayer Services Branch	(905) 433-6393	(905) 436-4511
Retail sales:		
Retail Sales Taxpayer Services	(905) 432-3332	(905) 436-4474
www.trd.fin.gov.on.ca		

Workplace Safety & Ensurance Board

| Toronto only | 1 800 387-0080 | |
| *www.wsib.on.ca* | (416) 344-1007 | (416) 344-2707 |

PRINCE EDWARD ISLAND: *www.gov.pe.ca*

Canada Business Service Centre

| Charlottetown | (902) 368-0771 | (902) 566-7377 |
| *www.cbsc.org/pe* | | |

Business Registration and Incorporation

| Dept. of Provincial Affairs, Attorney General | (902) 368-4550 | (902) 368-5283 |
| *www.gov.pe.ca* | | |

Provincial Sales Tax Office

| Taxation & Property Records Division | (902) 368-4171 | (902) 368-6164 |
| *www.gov.pe.ca* | | |

Workers Compensation Board

| Charlottetown | (902) 368-5680 | (902) 368-5705 |
| *www.wcb.pe.ca* | | |

	Telephone	Fax

QUEBEC: *www.gouv.qc.ca*

Canada Business Service
Montreal · (514) 496-4636 · (514) 496-5934
www.infoentrepreneurs.org

Business Registration and Incorporation
Inspecteur general des institutions financiers · (418) 643-3625 · (418) 643-3336
www.igif.gouv.qc.ca

Provincial Sales Tax Office
Revenue Quebec, Quebec only · 1 800 567-4692
www.revenu.gouv.qc.ca · (514) 873-4692

Workers' Compensation Board
Quebec · (418) 266-4850 · (418) 266-4669
www.csst.qc.ca

SASKATCHEWAN: *www.gov.sk.ca*

Canada Business Service Centre
Saskatoon · 1 800 667-4374
www.cbsc.org/sask · (306) 956-2323 · (306) 956-2328

Business registration and incorporation
Saskatchewan Justice Corporations Branch · (306) 787-2962 · (306) 787-8999
www.saskjustice.gov.sk.ca/corporations/default.htm

Provincial sales tax office
Taxpayer Services, Revenue Div. · 1 800 667-6102 · (306) 787-9644
www.gov.sk.ca/finance/revenue/default.htm

Workers' Compensation Board
Saskatoon users: · 1 800-667-7580
www.wcbsask.com · (306) 787-4370 · (306) 787-4205

	Telephone	Fax

YUKON: *www.gov.yk.ca*

Canada Business Service Centre

	Telephone	Fax
Whitehorse	1 800 661-0543	
www.csbc.org/yukon	(867) 633-6257	(867) 667-2001

Business registration and incorporation

	Telephone	Fax
Department of Justice, Corporate Affairs	(867) 667-5442	(867) 393-6251
www.justice.gov.yk.ca		

Commodity tax office

	Telephone	Fax
Revenue Services, Department of Finance	(867) 667-5345	(867) 393-6217
www.gov.yk.ca/depts/finance		

Workers' Compensation Board

	Telephone	Fax
Whitehorse	1 800 661-0443	
www.wcb.yk.ca	(867) 667-5645	(867) 393-6279

SMALL BUSINESS WEB SITES

Canada

Canada Business Service Centres: *www.cbsc.org*
Everything you need to know to start a small business can be found on this multi-lingual Government of Canada site—on-line workshops, resources, business start-up information and registration.

CBSC's On-line Interactive Business Planner: *www.cbsc.org/ibp/*
Part of CBSC's site is an on-line business planner with sample plans, tips, projections and cash flow sheets, walking you step-by-step through preparing your business plan.

CCRA tax information:
www.ccra-adrc.gc.ca/tax/business/smallbusiness/index-e.html
All you need to know about GST, payroll taxes, forms, on-line payroll deduction tables, a small business guide, customs, employer information and small biz info-fairs.

Canada One: *www.canadaone.com*
An excellent, resource-loaded, free small business e-magazine featuring over 700 resources, on-line workshops, toolkits, articles, discussion group and book reviews. A must to visit.

Canadian Federation of Independent Business: *www.cfib.ca*
With over 100,000 members, the CFIB is the national spokesperson for our small businesses. The site is full of media resources and links, small business information, links and up-to-date news, including tax information. Join it and stay in touch.

Community Futures Development Corporation: *www.communityfutures.ca*
With over 300 offices across Canada, CFDCs are responsible for the economic development of their communities and train entrepreneurs to start a successful business. Click on your province for more information.

Industry Canada: *http://strategis.ic.gc.ca*
Everything you need to know about starting a business in Canada, e-commerce, exporting, and managing people.

InnoVisions Canada and the Canadian Teleworker's Association: *www.ivc.ca*
This top Canadian teleworking site is hailed as a mine of information on the subject. Loaded with articles, resources, books, news and tips, it's a valuable resource for anyone considering working from home.

Small Business Information Canada: *www.sbinfocanada.about.com*
An A to Z resource guide for small businesses, everything from starting a business to selling one to women in business, with links to all the resources and publications.

SmallBizPro.com Services: *www.smallbizpro.com*
The author's site contains many helpful articles on starting and growing a business. Take the entrepreneurial test and read excerpts from my books.

Statistics Canada: *www.statcan.ca*
If you need Canadian statistics on population, business, the economy or health, this is the site to visit.

Western Economic Diversification: *www.wd.gc.ca*
Committed to helping Western Canadian small and medium businesses grow, a resource-loaded Government of Canada site. Try the in-depth entrepreneurial quiz.

United States

Biz Office: *www.bizoffice.com*
Apart from a huge resource library, forms and letters, Web marketing opportunities and government grant information, this site has dozens of links to other small business sites and resources.

Business Plans.com: *www.bplans.com*
Information on all areas of small business, including a business plan and financing wizard. You can view sample plans for 60 different types of businesses and glean ideas as you prepare your own plan.

Entrepreneur Magazine: *www.entrepreneurmag.com*
New articles each month on everything a small business owner needs to know, from marketing, money and management to e-business and business opportunities, plus an archive of past issues.

Inc. Com: *www.inc.com*
An on-line magazine with tons of resources and articles for start-up and business growth. Many other tools and services provide a wealth of small business information.

The Small Business Advisor: *www.isquare.com*
An on-line newsletter containing book reviews, links, glossary, U.S. government business, tax advice, resource books, tips, trade show information and articles.

U.S. Business Advisor: *www.business.gov*
Find the right answers to those questions about laws and regulations, financing, taxes, workplace issues, international trade and more.

U.S. Chamber of Commerce: *www.uschamber.com*
Find the nearest chamber of commerce on this site, review the various business resources and see how joining a chamber of commerce can help your business grow.

U.S. Small Business Administration: *www.sbaonline.sba.gov/*
With offices across the United States, this site offers detailed information on a multitude of small business programs and many necessary resources such as laws and regulations, plus on-line classrooms and counselling. A definite must surf for new entrepreneurs.

Working From Home: *www.homeworks.com*
Popular small business authors Paul and Sarah Edwards have designed a site loaded with help for the home-based business. It includes radio show clips, many tips and information on how to successfully operate a home-based business.

APPENDIX 2

How do you
fill out those forms?

All these boxes and lines I must complete.
Some help would be a welcome treat.

This appendix includes information, instructions and some examples showing how to fill out the following forms:

QUARTERLY GST/HST REPORT

Filing options

Small businesses have the option of filing either a quarterly GST/HST return or paying accurate quarterly installments. Filing a quarterly return keeps your accounting and cash flow better organized. If you pay by installments, the year-end report is due and any balance payable by June 30th of the following year. Keep the top portion of your return as a working copy and complete the corresponding remittance on page 295.

Instructions

Line 101:   Total sales net of all taxes for the three-month reporting period.

Line 103:   Total the GST/HST collected on the above sales. If you charge GST on all sales then the amount on Line 103 should equal seven percent of Line 101.

Line 104:   Add in GST/HST collected that belongs to a prior period and not previously reported.

Line 105:   Total all GST/HST collected for the period.

Line 106:   Enter the total GST you paid on purchases for the reporting period and unclaimed ITCs (input tax credits) from any previous periods.

Line 107:   Enter any further GST adjustments not yet reported.

Line 108:   Total all GST paid as reported.

Line 109:   Net tax: deduct the GST paid (Line 108) from the GST/HST collected (Line 105).

Line 110:   Deduct any annual installments paid.

Line 111:   Deduct any further applicable rebates.

Line 112:   Total Lines 110 and 111.

Line 113A: Enter the new balance payable or balance due.

Line 113B: Enter any other debits due (see detailed instructions on form).

Line 113C: Enter the balance. If a refund is due, enter a minus sign in the box before the balance.

Line 114/115:   Enter a refund due to Line 114, a balance payable to Line 115.

Web site

Detailed instructions can be found on the CCRA Web site at:
www.ccra-adrc.gc.ca/tax/business/gsthst/menue-e.html.

QUARTERLY GST/HST REPORT

Figure A1: EXAMPLE OF CCRA QUARTERLY GST/HST REPORT (GST62-2)

Canada Customs and Revenue Agency / Agence des douanes et du revenu du Canada

GOODS AND SERVICES TAX / HARMONIZED SALES TAX (GST/HST) RETURN (NON-PERSONALIZED)

Business Number: 11139 1264 RT0001   Name: Fine Foods Inc.   **Part 1**

Reporting period From: 2003-07-01 To: 2003-09-30   Due date: 2003-10-31   **Working copy / Disponible en français**

▸ Copy the amounts from the **highlighted** line numbers in **Part 1** of this return to the corresponding boxes in **Part 2**. Keep the top portion (**Part 1**) of this return for your records.

Privacy Act Personal Information Bank number RCC/P-PU-080.

Enter your total **sales and other revenue**. Do not include provincial sales tax, GST, or HST. (If you are using the quick method of accounting, include the GST or HST.)   **101** 16490 00

NET TAX CALCULATION

Enter the total of all **GST and HST** amounts that you collected or that became collectible by you in the reporting period.   **103** 804 30

Enter the total amount of **adjustments** to be added to the net tax for the reporting period (e.g., the GST/HST obtained from the recovery of a bad debt).   **104** 0

Total GST/HST and adjustments for period (add lines 103 and 104). ▸ **105** 804 30

Enter the GST/HST you paid or owe on qualifying expenses (**input tax credits - ITCs**) for the current period and any eligible unclaimed ITCs from a previous period.   **106** 317 05

Enter the total amount of **adjustments** to be deducted when determining the net tax for the reporting period (e.g., the GST/HST included in a bad debt).   **107** 0

Total ITCs and adjustments (add lines 106 and 107). ▸ **108** 317 05

109 487 25

NET TAX (subtract line 108 from line 105). If the result is negative, enter a minus sign in the separate box next to the line number.

OTHER CREDITS IF APPLICABLE

Note: Do not complete line 111 until you have read the instructions in the box on the reverse side of this return.

Enter any **instalment** and other annual filer payments you made for the reporting period. If your due date is June 15, see instructions on the back.   **110** 0

Enter the total amount of the GST/HST **rebate** you are applying for on forms GST284, GST66, or GST189, if you are filing the form with this return.   **111** 0

Total other credits (add lines 110 and 111). ▸ **112** 0

BALANCE (subtract line 112 from line 109). If the result is negative, enter a minus sign in the separate box next to the line number.   **113 A** 487 25

OTHER DEBITS IF APPLICABLE

Note: Do not complete line 205 or line 405 until you have read the instructions in the box on the reverse side of this return.

Enter the total amount of the GST/HST **due** on the acquisition of taxable real property.   **205** 0

Enter the total amount of **other** GST/HST to be self-assessed.   **405** 0

Total other debits (add lines 205 and 405). ▸ **113 B** 0

BALANCE (add lines 113 A and 113 B). If the result is negative, enter a minus sign in the separate box next to the line number.   **113 C** 487 25

Line 114 and line 115: If the result entered on line 113 C is a negative amount, enter the amount of the refund you are claiming on line 114. If the result entered on line 113 C is a positive amount, enter the amount of your payment on line 115.

REFUND CLAIMED — **114**

PAYMENT ENCLOSED — **115** 487 25

GST62-2 E (00/04)

▼ Detach and Return Lower Portion (Part 2) ▼

Canada Customs and Revenue Agency / Agence des douanes et du revenu du Canada   **GST/HST RETURN (NON-PERSONALIZED)**   001800   **Part 2**

GST62-2 E (00/04)

YOU MUST COMPLETE THIS AREA.   Reporting Period

Business Number: 11139 1264 RT0001   From: Year 2003 Month 07 Day 01   To: Year 2003 Month 09 Day 30

Sales and other revenue **101** 1 1 4 9 0 0 0

Instalments and other annual filer payments **110** 0

Rebates **111** 0

GST/HST due on acquisition of taxable real property **205** 0

Other GST/HST to be self-assessed **405** 0

Total GST/HST and adjustments for period **105** 8 0 4 3 0

Total ITCs and adjustments **108** 3 1 7 0 5

Net tax **109** 4 8 7 2 5

Refund claimed **114** 0

Payment enclosed **115** 4 8 7 2 5

I certify that the information given on this return and in any attached documents is, to the best of my knowledge, true, correct, and complete in every respect, and that I am the person required to file this return, or that I am authorized to sign on behalf of the person. It is a serious offence to make a false return.

Betty McDonald   2003 / 10 / 15
Authorized signature   Date

This form was reproduced and adapted from Canada Customs and Revenue Agency's current form, GST62-2, and reproduced with the permission of the Minister of Public Works and Government Services, 2002.

CCRA PAYROLL REMITTANCE

Payroll records

Deductions made at source from employees' payroll cheques must be remitted to CCRA by the 15th of the following month. You will receive a monthly RC107 E(01) remittance form in the mail. The upper portion reflects your calculations and is kept for your records; the lower portion is the remittance which accompanies the payment.

Maintaining detailed payroll records involves ensuring that individual payroll records are reconciled monthly, totalled on a cumulative basis (ready for your T4s at year-end), a monthly reconciliation prepared and your CCRA remittance paid on time, as interest charges and penalties are hefty.

Your payroll records should agree with the general ledger payroll accounts. If you are not sure how to do this, ask your accountant to show you.

Step-by-step instructions

To prepare monthly manual payroll records for the remittance, follow these steps:

1. Each month, total the gross wages, CPP, EI, tax and other deduction columns for each employee, ensuring that the columns balance across to the net amount of the payroll cheques issued.

2. As in Figure A2 on page 297, list each employee's monthly totals on a payroll reconciliation sheet, calculate the balances and then use these amounts to calculate your CCRA remittance using the equation shown.

3. Transfer these amounts to the front of the payroll remittance for your records and then complete the remittance information (see example in Figure A3) on page 298 and attach your cheque for payment. Keep all remittance copies for year-end reconciliation purposes.

Figure A2: MONTHLY PAYROLL RECONCILIATION

Name	Gross Wages	CPP	EI	Tax	Net Wages
John Kenny	2,500.00	105.04	55.02	389.80	1,950.14
Cynthia McDonald	1,800.00	71.94	40.44	254.50	1,433.12
Phillipe LeFrenier	1,800.00	71.94	40.44	254.50	1,433.12
TOTALS:	**$6,100.00**	**$248.92**	**$135.90**	**$898.80**	**$4,816.38**

CPP deducted for month:	248.92}	
Employer's contribution:	248.92}	= $497.84
EI deducted for month:	135.90}	
* Employer's contribution x 1.4 =	190.26}	= $326.16
Tax deducted:	898.80	
Remittance due:	**$1,722.80**	

* Note: Employer's contribution is calculated at 1.4 times the employee's contribution.

Web site

Detailed instructions can be found on the CCRA Web site at:
www.ccra-adrc.gc.ca/tax/business/payroll/menu-e.html.

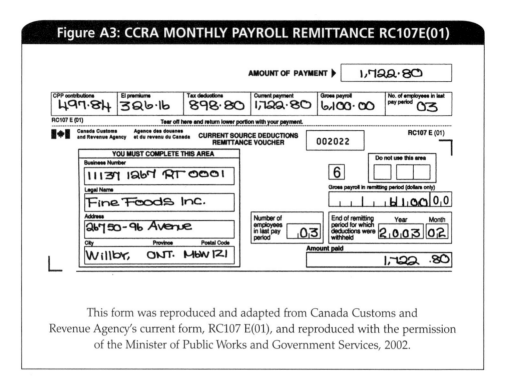

Figure A3: CCRA MONTHLY PAYROLL REMITTANCE RC107E(01)

This form was reproduced and adapted from Canada Customs and Revenue Agency's current form, RC107 E(01), and reproduced with the permission of the Minister of Public Works and Government Services, 2002.

YEAR-END T4 PREPARATION

Instructions

If you balance your payroll monthly and keep cumulative totals, the T4 year-end preparation work is minimal. After the last payroll for the year, follow these steps:

1. Total each employee's payroll sheet for the year, including gross wages, CPP, EI, tax deductions, other deductions and net wages. The total net wages plus all deduction columns should equal the total gross wages.

2. Refer to your payroll guide from CCRA to find the minimum insurable earnings for each pay period for each employee. If you did not previously enter these amounts, do it now.

3. Check that each gross wage paid qualifies for insurable earnings. If the wages for the period don't, subtract them from the annual gross wages to arrive at your annual insurable earnings amount.

4. Now transfer the annual payroll totals to a reconciliation spreadsheet, adding columns for addresses, social insurance numbers and insurable earnings, plus other deductions such as registered pension plan contributions, pension adjustments, union dues and donations. You should now have all employees' information on a master sheet.

5. Enter each employee's details on the spreadsheet, total each column down, then check the final balances to ensure that cross-additions agree.

6. Check the final wage totals with your general ledger to make sure accounting records and payroll agree.

7. Enter each employee's details onto a T4. The following boxes should be completed:

Box 54: Business number, found on payroll remittance.

Box 10: Province of employment.

Box 12: Employee social insurance number.

Box 28: Check box only for employees under 18 and over 65 who are exempt from CPP.

Box 29: Check box if shareholders are exempt from EI (if they own more than 40 percent of a business). If you don't check these two boxes, CCRA sends a request for payment of the unpaid CPP or EI.

Box 14: Gross income before deductions including all taxable allowances and benefits.

Box 16: Employee's CPP contributions deducted from payroll.

Box 17: Employee's QPP contributions deducted from payroll.

Box 18: Employee's EI premiums deducted from payroll.

Box 20: Employee's registered pension plan contributions deducted from payroll.

Box 22: Income tax deducted for the year.

Box 24: Annual EI insurable earnings up to the yearly limit found in the payroll guide.

Box 26: Annual CPP pensionable earnings up to the yearly limit.

Box 44: Total annual union dues deducted from payroll.

Box 46: Total charitable donations deducted from payroll.

Box 50: Pension plan or DPSP registration number.

Blank boxes: Enter other amounts, such as commissioned income or taxable benefits, which should also be included in the gross earnings in Box 14 (refer to the payroll guide for more information).

8. When all T4s are completed, total all boxes to ensure they equal the master sheet figures. Start with gross wages, followed by CPP, EI, tax and any other deductions. If the records don't agree, check off the amounts on your tape against the master record to find your errors. If a T4 cannot be corrected neatly, void it and prepare another one.

9. When all records agree, separate the T4s: the top copy goes to CCRA with the T4 summary, the second and third copies go to the employees, and the fourth copy is kept by the employer.

Web site

Detailed instructions can be found on the CCRA Web site at: *www.ccra-adrc.gc.ca/EmenuHSI.html.*

YEAR-END T4 SUMMARY

Instructions

Once your T4s are completed, the last job is to fill in the T4 summary. In Box 88, enter the number of T4s being filed. Then continue to complete the employer information. To calculate whether you have paid enough in annual deductions to CCRA, complete the following calculation:

Total CPP deducted for year:	$1,250.00
Total employer's portion of CPP:	1,250.00
Total EI deducted for year:	675.00
Employer's portion x 1.4	945.00
Total tax deducted for year:	4,465.00
ANNUAL REMITTANCE:	**$8,585.00**

Compare this total to the amount shown on your last CCRA remittance, which you receive in January. The two figures should agree. If you have underpaid, you must remit the balance (subject to penalties and interest) with the T4 summary. If you have overpaid, CCRA will credit your next year's account, or you can request a refund.

Now it is time to fill in all those little boxes with the information from your master sheet.

Box 14:   Enter the gross payroll for the year.

Box 20:   Enter the total registered pension plan contributions from employees.

Box 52:   Enter the total pension adjustment amount.

Box 16:   Enter the total employees' CPP deductions.

Box 27:   Enter the employee's CPP contributions, which equals Box 16.

Box 18:   Enter the employees' EI deductions.

Box 19:   Enter the employer's EI contributions, which should total 1.4 times the employees' deductions in Box 18.

Box 22:   Enter the total income tax deducted.

Box 80:   Total all deductions reported in Boxes 16, 27, 18, 19 and 22.

Box 82:   Enter the amount of your CCRA remittances for the year from your statement received in January, and subtract the difference from Box 80.

Box 84/86: If you have underpaid, enter the amount in Box 84. If you have overpaid, enter the amount in Box 86.

Fill in the required information in Boxes 74 through 78, sign, date and certify your return. Attach the top copy of the T4s to the top copy of the summary. Keep the last copy for your payroll records, attaching your T4 copies, and file by February 28th.

Web site

Detailed instructions can be found on the CCRA Web site at:
www.ccra-adrc.gc.ca/EmenuHSI.html.

WORKERS' COMPENSATION

General information

Workers' compensation is payable in all provinces by employers as a form of accident insurance on behalf of their employees. Industry rates, coverage, methods of calculation and wages subject to compensation vary provincially. Coverage paid by the employer is based on provincial industry rates as determined by each Workers' Compensation Board.

In some provinces, insuring shareholders' salaries is optional; in other provinces, such as B.C., shareholders' salaries must be insured. Some require shareholders to contribute based on a minimum coverage whether they actually draw wages or not. There is usually an annual limit per employee for wage insurance. If subcontractors or casual labourers do not carry their own coverage, you must take their earnings into consideration when calculating your premiums.

Some provinces offer a personal optional insurance plan for self-employed proprietors or partners, which is based on their annual taxable earnings. Workers' Compensation is usually calculated on a cumulative basis for each quarterly period. At year-end, an annual summary is sent, and all over-payments and adjustments are made on this form. Payments made during the year are then deducted from the annual total owing, and the balance is payable. Don't be late with payments, as penalties and interest mount up quickly.

Index

About the Author

Frances McGuckin is an award-winning, best-selling author, business management consultant, small business expert, professional speaker and columnist. She travels across North America delivering passionate, powerful, information-packed and motivational messages to small business owners.

Recognized for her contributions to women in business and Canadian small businesses, Frances is a 2004 YWCA Women of Distinction nominee. She received the 2003 Volunteer of the Year Award from the Canadian Association of Professional Speakers (Vancouver), the Surrey International Writers' Conference's 2003 Special Achievement Award, one of Vancouver's 2002 five Most Influential Women in Business awards and Langley's 1999 Business Person of the Year Award.

As an active participant in the Prime Minister's Task Force on Women Entrepreneurs in 2003, Frances had some of her recommendations for women entrepreneurs federally adopted in the final report.

Business for Beginners, Frances' first book, has sold over 125,000 copies in its three editions. It is used to teach entrepreneurship in many Canadian self-employment programs, high schools and colleges. A Russian edition was published in January 2004. Intuit Canada purchased the electronic rights for four business and tax programs. U.S. editions of *Business for Beginners* and *Big Ideas for Growing Your Small Business* will be available in 2005.

Her home-based businesses, SmallBizPro.com Services and Eastleigh Publications, are in their 20th year. She has been actively teaching entrepreneurship for 18 years, teaching the first accredited Equine Entrepreneurship course at Kwantlen University College in Langley, British Columbia. She founded a Toastmasters group and was a founding member and coordinator of the Langley chapter of the Valley Women's Network, which has since sponsored seven other chapters.

A popular media guest across Canada and recognized as a small business expert in the U.S., Frances has been interviewed for many American publications, including *Home Business Journal, Black Enterprise Magazine, The Chicago Tribune* and *Entrepreneur Magazine.* She writes for various business publications, including *Business in Vancouver,* and contributes a monthly column for the Vacuum and Sewing Dealers Trade Association of Iowa.

Married to Michael for 22 years, Frances cares for her 95-year-old mother, has a teenage daughter, Katrina, is a grandmother of two and has a 34-year-old son, Richard. Her menagerie includes a horse, pony, chinchilla, two cats, a dog, fish and a hamster. In her spare time, she practises fitness daily and makes quality time for her rather large family of people and pets. Bubble baths are not in her Daytimer. For more information, visit her Web site at *www.smallbizpro.com.*

PRAISE FOR *BIG IDEAS*

Whether you've been in business two weeks or ten years, this exciting new "big book of BIG IDEAS" helps you to **take it to the next level**. If you want bigger, better, more profits or more time, this indispensable **companion book** to the **best-selling** *Business for Beginners* is loaded with **BIG IDEAS**. It offers practical, affordable, "do-it-now" solutions to common growth problems:

- Being "too busy" to get organized and efficient
- Finding, motivating and keeping good employees
- Increasing customers; marketing and selling effectively
- Coping with growth and operational crises
- Improving verbal, written and communication skills
- Finding time for family, fun and fitness
- Keeping control of the financial reins...and loads more.

Download free sample chapters, testimonials and content information at **www.smallbizpro.com**. Both **SMALLBIZ DREAM TEAM** books have a user-friendly lay-flat binding and come loaded with checklists, questionnaires, case studies, tips, strategies, Web references and examples to help small business owners better understand and navigate the complexities of starting and growing their businesses.

Starting a business is a challenge.
Survival, growth and success are even bigger challenges.
The **SMALL BIZ DREAM TEAM** turns dreams into reality.

Speaking of Business…

DOES YOUR ASSOCIATION OR COMPANY RELY ON THE SUCCESS OF ITS SMALL BUSINESS MEMBERS OR DEALERS? FRANCES MCGUCKIN, THE SMALLBIZPRO, WILL DYNAMICALLY DELIVER THE RIGHT MESSAGES TO YOUR CONFERENCE ATTENDEES.

"…An absolutely wonderful keynote during our international trade show in Toronto. Our dealers found her speech entertaining, inspiring and motivating. She suggested highly innovative ideas that the dealers can take home and put into play right away to be more successful…"

JUDY PATTERSON, PRESIDENT
VACUUM AND SEWING DEALERS TRADE ASSOCIATION, IOWA

Customizing keynotes and workshops specifically to her clients' needs, Frances' presentations are full of creative ideas, humour and energy. Your audience will leave with tools they can immediately utilize to grow both their businesses – and themselves.

Topics Include:
- Business growth
- Low-cost marketing
- Change management
- Goal setting and balance
- Presentation skills … and more

Contact: SmallBizPro.com Services
Frances McGuckin: **1-888-771-2771**
E-MAIL: contact@smallbizpro.com   WEB: www.smallbizpro.com

A Member of: